The Northwest
Ordinance

The Northwest Ordinance

Constitutional Politics and the Theft of Native Land

ROBERT ALEXANDER

Foreword by STAUGHTON LYND

McFarland & Company, Inc., Publishers

Jefferson, North Carolina

Illustration Credits: *The Northwest Territory.* Map by Ellen R. White. *Fort Stanwix Treaty Line.* Map by Ellen R. White. *Jefferson-Hartley Map.* Courtesy of the William L. Clements Library, University of Michigan. *Draft of the Northwest Ordinance.* Papers of the Continental Congress (National Archives); digital image courtesy of Fold3. *The Ohio Country, 1787.* Map by Ellen R. White.

LIBRARY OF CONGRESS CATALOGUING-IN-PUBLICATION DATA

Names: Alexander, Robert, 1949– author.
Title: The Northwest Ordinance : constitutional politics and the theft of native land / Robert Alexander ; foreword by Staughton Lynd.
Description: Jefferson, North Carolina : McFarland & Company, Inc., Publishers, 2017. | Includes bibliographical references and index.
Identifiers: LCCN 2017002543 | ISBN 9781476665191 (softcover : acid free paper) ♾
Subjects: LCSH: United States. Ordinance of 1787. | Northwest, Old— History—1775–1865.
Classification: LCC E309 .A44 2017 | DDC 977/.02—dc23
LC record available at https://lccn.loc.gov/2017002543

BRITISH LIBRARY CATALOGUING DATA ARE AVAILABLE

ISBN (print) 978-1-4766-6519-1
ISBN (ebook) 978-1-4766-2761-8

On the cover: Fort Harmar, from Bensing J. Lossing, *The Pictorial History Book of the War of 1812* (New York, 1868), p. 39

Printed in the United States of America

McFarland & Company, Inc., Publishers
 Box 611, Jefferson, North Carolina 28640
  www.mcfarlandpub.com

For Katie

The Northwest Territory

Table of Contents

Foreword
by Staughton Lynd

The Northwest Ordinance, writes James Oakes, "occupied an almost sacred place in the constitutional politics of the antislavery movement." It was "the statutory link between the abolitionists and the Founders, its very language eventually reproduced in the Thirteenth Amendment that would abolish slavery forever."[1] Even today, the Northwest Ordinance serves to keep alive the notion that the Founders wished to put an end to slavery as soon as possible, and in the Northwest Ordinance took the longest step toward its abolition possible at the time.

In this book Robert Alexander suggests that, notwithstanding a revealing comment by President James Madison to his secretary Edward Coles,[2] historians have failed to confront overwhelming evidence that the Northwest Ordinance provides "an intimate link between the two original sins of the nation: the enslavement of millions of African men, women and children—and the theft of millions of acres of Native land."

How shall we evaluate the head-on conflict between these contrasting images of the Northwest Ordinance? An obvious place to begin is the text of the Ordinance. The Ordinance (reproduced as Appendix D) begins with elaborate, detailed instructions for the future government of the area between the Allegheny Mountains on the East, the Great Lakes on the North, the Mississippi River on the West, and the Ohio River on the South. This huge tract of land became a "territory," that is, a possession but not yet a state, of the United States in the treaty with Great Britain ending the war for independence.

With respect to the Native Americans who inhabited the Northwest and claimed it as their own, the Northwest Ordinance declares:

The utmost good faith shall always be observed towards the Indians, their lands and property shall never be taken from them without their consent; and in their property,

1

rights and liberty, they shall never be invaded or disturbed, unless in just and lawful wars authorised by Congress; but laws founded in justice and humanity shall from time to time be made, for preventing wrongs being done to them, and for preserving peace and friendship with them.

These words stand in self-evident contradiction to the full paraphernalia of settler colonialism set forth in previous paragraphs of the Ordinance: provisions for the inheritance of property, for a governor, a secretary and a Court, for the promulgation of laws, for a legislature, for a commander in chief of the militia, for lesser public officials, for the extinction of Indian titles, for the election of representatives, and for the admission of this preliminary government to the federal government as a state "on an equal footing with the original States."

As to slavery, the very last article of the Ordinance deals with both the prohibition of slavery in the Northwest and with its assumed continuance elsewhere, as follows:

There shall be neither Slavery nor involuntary Servitude in the said territory otherwise than in the punishment of crimes, whereof the party shall have been duly convicted; provided always that any person escaping into the same, from whom labor or service is lawfully claimed in any one of the original States, such fugitive may be lawfully reclaimed and conveyed to the person claiming his or her labor or service as aforesaid.

The critical point about these words is not the prohibition of slavery north of the Ohio River, where climate made it unlikely to begin with. Rather it is the fact that slavery was expected to continue in another part of the United States from which slaves might try to flee to the Northwest. That other part of the new nation was, of course, the states of Virginia, North Carolina, South Carolina, and Georgia, where, as George Mason put it during the Constitutional Convention, plantation owners were already "calling out" for slaves whose labor they could exploit in the Southwest.

Until July 1787, every draft for the temporary government and ultimate admission to the Union of states formed from the western territories of the United States had, as a matter of course, applied to *all* the western territories.[3] This was evident in the proceedings of the Continental Congress as late as May 1787. The ordinance adopted by Congress in July 1787 was, for the first time, a *Northwest* Ordinance applying only to territories north of the Ohio River. This change in the scope and jurisdiction of Congressional action, by failing to prohibit slavery in new states formed from territories in the Southwest, opened the door for the expansion of plantation slavery into the future states of Kentucky, Tennessee, Alabama, Mississippi, and Louisiana, and beyond.

A homely example illustrates the importance of remembering what the Northwest Ordinance did not do, as well as what it did. In Arthur Conan

Doyle's story "Silver Blaze," Sherlock Holmes is asked to investigate the crippling of a racehorse just before a major race. As Dr. Watson and the great detective leave the barn where Silver Blaze was housed, Watson asks Holmes what he thinks. Holmes remarks on the "curious incident" of the dog kept in the barn. But, Watson protests, the dog did nothing in the nighttime. That, Holmes responds, was the curious incident. The dog did nothing because the man who hamstrung Silver Blaze was the horse's trainer, with whom the dog was familiar.

So here, the fact that Congress did not legislate for the Southwest when it passed the famous Ordinance silently permitted Southern plantation owners to move westward with their peculiar institution unregulated and intact.

In Sophocles' drama *Oedipus Rex*, Oedipus met a stranger at a location where three roads came together, and unknowingly killed his own father. The special virtue of Dr. Alexander's narrative is that he chronicles in great detail three chains of fact as they came together in New York and Philadelphia during the second week of July 1787 to create a tragic outcome, the Northwest Ordinance.

The first such factual "road" was the struggle in the Continental Congress of the new nation to agree on the precise process whereby western territories would become states. Madison's conversation with Coles emphasized the fact that a number of men were delegates to both the Continental Congress meeting in New York and the Constitutional Convention assembled in Philadelphia. When the Convention convened, several such men left New York to assume their roles in Philadelphia, thus depriving the Congress of a quorum. Early in July a number of Southern delegates to both bodies[4] traveled from Philadelphia to New York so that the Congress might regain a quorum. Between Monday, July 9, and Friday, July 13, a Southern majority of states created a new committee of the Continental Congress with a Southern chairman; this committee produced a new ordinance governing the admission to the Union of territories north of the Ohio River, and shepherded it through three readings to final passage.

A second chain of facts includes the remarkable circumstance that Convention delegate Gouverneur Morris on Wednesday, July 11 passionately condemned any mention of slaves in the new constitution, and the Convention rejected the formula for representation in the lower house of the new federal legislature that would add three-fifths of all other persons, understood to be slaves, to the number of free inhabitants in calculating the number of representatives for each state in the new Congress; but on the morning of the next day Morris supported the three-fifths clause, describing it as a "bridge" between North and South, and it passed. Adopted for representation of existing states on July 12, the three-fifths clause was also explicitly adopted on the next day, July 13, for states to be formed in the future.

Finally, a third strand of narrative—and Dr. Alexander's most original contribution to the story as a whole—concerns the prospect that federal acquisition and sale of land in Ohio still possessed by Native Americans would serve both to reduce the massive national debt and to richly reward speculators, many of whom were the very delegates to Congress and Convention considering the future of the Northwest. To make the stew of cause and effect still thicker, these delegate-speculators had to contend not only with Native Americans who claimed to own the land in perpetuity but also with waves of white squatters who sought to move into southern Ohio and farm there.

The convergence of these three stories was indeed a meeting of three converging roads, worthy of comparison to the tragedy of Oedipus.

Dr. Alexander and I are in solid agreement that all these facts are connected, but we have somewhat different views on how they all fit together. Over a number of years we have learned from each other in attempting to construct a coherent narrative. I describe my own hypothesis here, not with a desire to be proved correct, but as an incentive to Dr. Alexander and other younger scholars to probe these matters further.

To begin with, I now think Dr. Alexander is right that Manasseh Cutler's efforts on behalf of the Ohio Company are best understood as part of the third story, concerning speculation in western lands, and were probably not essential to the decisions of the Convention about representation. I think he is also right that the initiative for the "Compromise of 1787" probably came from southern delegates at the Convention. Here is how I now think events may have unfolded:

1. Southern delegates to the Constitutional Convention feared that if a new federal government were given more power, that power might be used to dismantle slavery in the existing Southern states or to prevent its expansion into the Southwest.

2. As New England delegates to the Congress discovered to their surprise, Southerners in New York and Philadelphia were not particularly concerned that slavery might be prohibited north of the Ohio River. The Southern delegates readily agreed to language in the Ordinance prohibiting slavery in states to be made from territories in the Northwest. What was important to them was that Congress should not prohibit slavery in the territories of the Southwest.

3. Several Southern delegates at the Convention who were also members of the Congress, together with Richard Henry Lee, who was a delegate only to the Congress but spent a week at the Convention en route to New York, traveled to New York with the shared intention of passing an ordinance for government of the western territories that left the territories south of the Ohio River unregulated.

4. A new committee of the Congress, with a Southern majority and a Southern chairman, was appointed on the day that Congress regained a quorum, Monday, July 9, for the purpose of drafting a new ordinance for the government of the western territories and their admission to the Union.

5. On Tuesday, July 10, the new draft of the ordinance was shown to Manasseh Cutler. He suggested some changes and left for Philadelphia that same day. After a stopover with George Morgan, a gentleman who, like himself, was interested in speculation in western lands, Cutler arrived in Philadelphia on Thursday, July 12.

6. On the evening of July 12, Cutler met with a number of delegates to the Convention at the Indian Queen Tavern in Philadelphia. Those present included several Convention delegates from the South, and Alexander Hamilton, whom Cutler described as "Mr. Hamilton of New York."

7. George Washington had written to Hamilton that the Convention was in crisis and he wished Hamilton were present. Hamilton had responded that he would return from New York "if I have reason to believe that my attendance at Philadelphia will not be mere waste of time."

8. If Hamilton left New York during the day on Tuesday, July 10, knowing as did Cutler the general outlines of the new Northwest Ordinance, he could have reached Philadelphia by the evening of July 11. That would have given him an opportunity to exchange information with his close friend Gouverneur Morris. We can imagine Hamilton stressing to his friend the need to create a stronger national government with power to lay an effective national tariff and to pay off the national debt with proceeds from the sale of western lands. He might also have emphasized that the geographical limits of the new Ordinance could give the Southern states the assurance they sought about the safety of their property in slaves.

Thus Hamilton's report that the Northwest Ordinance would be limited to territories north of the Ohio River could have prompted Morris's promotion on July 12 of the three-fifths ratio he had denounced the day before.[5]

9. News that the federal ordinance concerning the western territories would be limited to land north of the Ohio River would have been doubly welcome to Southern delegates to the Convention because it meant that slaves in the Southwest would increase Southern representation in the electoral college and in Congress and, hence, increase Southern influence over the new national government.

10. In sum, the Northwest Ordinance served not only as a marker along the path to abolition but also as a concession to the slave South that in fact resulted in Southern control over the federal government for the next seventy-five years.

Supposing for the moment that the general drift of Dr. Alexander's book (and of this foreword) were to win acceptance, a question would arise as to how, if at all, this new way of looking at the Northwest Ordinance might affect our overall assessment of the American Revolution.

Thomas Paine thought the Revolution gave humanity a chance to start over again. And indeed, alone of the Founders he consistently tried to end the practice of slavery in the new United States. Prior to the war for independence, two essays condemning slavery appeared in Philadelphia, attributed to Paine by Benjamin Rush. Paine served as clerk to the Pennsylvania legislature during the war for independence at the time that body passed a law for gradual emancipation, and may have written the law's preamble. Together with Benjamin Franklin he attended a Philadelphia committee seeking the welfare of African Americans. In revolutionary France, Paine hobnobbed with members of the "Friends of the Blacks" and developed a supportive attitude toward the Haitian revolution. Perhaps most memorably, after the Louisiana Purchase, when Paine was ostracized for his religious views and living alone in New Rochelle, he wrote a long letter to President Jefferson as to how freehold farming rather than slavery might be encouraged in the Louisiana Purchase, commenting that he wished for the city of Liverpool (center of the British slave trade) the fate of Sodom and Gomorrah.

Paine's opposition to slavery in the Louisiana Purchase contrasts with the attitude of President Jefferson, who, Dr. Alexander observes, made no attempt to restrict the growth of slavery west of the Mississippi River. As the United States Senate began debate on the purchase, "President Jefferson sent a secret note to his floor manager, instructing the senator to insert a clause in the bill for establishing a government in Louisiana: 'Slaves shall be admitted into the territory.'"[6]

In recent years historians, sensitized by new discoveries about Jefferson and about slavery, have begun to feel equally conscience-stricken about the hypocrisy and bullying routinely employed by the new Federal government in its dealings with Native Americans. Native Americans considered that the land north of the Ohio River belonged to them and, unless they agreed otherwise, was destined to be their hunting ground forever. A great strength of Dr. Alexander's narrative is that at so many points he brings us the words of Native American spokespersons as they patiently tried to explain to their white counterparts the current status of the territory and the intentions of the Great Spirit for its future.

Staughton Lynd is a scholar and an activist. His work on the period of the Northwest Ordinance includes books on Class Conflict, Slavery, and the United States Constitution *and* Intellectual Origins of American Radicalism, *both recently republished by Cambridge University Press.*

Preface

The half-dozen years between the Treaty of Peace (1783) and the seating of the first Congress under the Constitution (1789) form an interregnum of sorts—the United States being no longer a colonial domain and not yet a true republic. The policies undertaken during these years set the stage for much that happened during the next century, including a civil war that killed nearly a million citizens and a conflict between the Federal government and the indigenous peoples of the continent that, some would say, continues still. In July 1787, while the Constitutional Convention met in Philadelphia, the so-called Old Congress, meeting in New York, passed the Northwest Ordinance, defined in the United States Code as one of the four organic laws of the nation.[1] Setting out a future vision of territorial expansion, the Ordinance would prove crucial as the geographical center of the country moved slowly westward.

The Constitution itself has been dissected by politicians, political scientists, and historians since the day in September 1787 when it was first sent to the states for ratification. Yet the relationship between it and the Northwest Ordinance has received little comment, despite the fact that James Madison himself referred to relevant "conferences and inter-communications" that took place between the members of both Congress and Convention.[2] This study examines in detail one aspect of that relationship, suggesting an intimate link between the two original sins of the nation: the enslavement of millions of African-American men, women, and children—and the theft of millions of acres of Native land.

Brothers—
You landed here in this Island, and you begged the favor of my Nephew to let you remain only one night on shore, he replied to you that he was not Master, that there was a great man where he came from who was his Uncle, that he could not give him a positive answer until he sent back to him.

Brothers—
I permitted you to remain one night as you had requested of me, and after this you begged of me to let you have a little ground to make your fires upon, as you said you would visit me very often, and the quantity of land you requested of me was as much as one cowhide could cover.

Brothers—
My nephew then agreed with you for as much land as one cowhide could cover, and you gave him a little of your tempting liquor which left him a little giddy & foolish, and in the meantime you cut this cowhide into a string that covers a considerable quantity of ground, and that is the way you first took me in for a piece of land in this country.

Brothers—
After my nephew came to his sense & saw what you had done to him, he said to you, you have cheated me for once, is this the way you are going to treat me always, while you remain in this country? You replied then, No Brother, far from it. I do not mean to treat you in that manner, but still you had another request to make of him, that was an addition of more land to that you had already got, as you would go no distance out to hunt, but only round the fences—not only this, but you had a great many people to take care of, and that place was too small.

Brothers—
My nephew complied with your request for a quantity of land as far as a man could go in a day and back again, and you had one of the swiftest runners out of Europe who did this business for you to our surprise. When we came to measure we could scarcely get to where he turned in a day, and that was the way you got the second quantity. These are the dreams that I have dreamt … but here are pieces of parchment with some writing upon them. It seems very dirty at present.

—Chief Shendeta of the Wyandots[3]

Introduction

This systematic occupation of the heart of the Great Republic, originating with its conquerors, the army, and carried forward step by step under most enlightened direction, marks as distinctively the landing at Marietta on the seventh of April, 1788, of the founders of the central empire as the landing at Plymouth or Jamestown set the historical landmarks of civilization on the Atlantic seaboard.

— William Parker Cutler[1]

Today, as I write, it's Friday, July 13, the 225th anniversary—even to the day of the week—of the law which became known as the Northwest Ordinance. Meeting in 1787 at Federal Hall in New York City, the Old Congress, organized under the Articles of Confederation, passed the Ordinance as one of its last important pieces of legislation. This document, 3,225 words in length, set out the form of government by means of which the territory north of the Ohio River was to achieve statehood. One of its most famous provisions was the sixth article, which forever outlawed slavery in the region.[2]

In my opinion, the signing of the Ordinance formally initiated the United States' policy toward the First Nations east of the Mississippi—"Indian Removal"—which reached its apotheosis under President Andrew Jackson, unless we conceive of it beginning when the first Englishman walked ashore at Jamestown, or when the first European sailor, high up in his crow's nest, spotted a vague shape on the horizon which foreshadowed the American continent. After the Civil War, the Northwest Ordinance was celebrated north of the Mason-Dixon line as the "ordinance of freedom," because of its sixth article—and was honored along with the Declaration of Independence and the Constitution as one of the "sacred" texts of American government. For the indigenous population of Turtle Island, however, it was anything but liberating. Despite the fact that this territory had once been guaranteed by the British Crown, at least temporarily, to the First Nations who lived there, the Ordinance presumed that they would willingly part with their homeland—

9

a presumption that was underlined by warfare lasting until the defeat of the United Indian Nations at the Battle of Fallen Timbers in 1794.[3] Comprising nearly half a million square miles, the Northwest Territory was divided, in succeeding years, into the states of Ohio (1803), Indiana (1816), Illinois (1818), Michigan (1837), Wisconsin (1848)—and a slight sliver of Minnesota (1858).

On July 13, 1787, while the Constitutional Convention was meeting in Philadelphia, the "United States in Congress Assembled"—as the government under the Articles of Confederation formally referred to itself—voted unanimously by states to pass the Northwest Ordinance. What makes this particularly significant was that of the eight delegations present that day, five were from Southern states that would, seventy-some years later, secede from the Union—and only one representative, a Northerner, opposed the measure. This marked the only time that antebellum Southerners in Congress agreed *unanimously* to limit the expansion of their so-called peculiar institution. Moreover, just a few years after passage of the Ordinance, controversy began over the expansion of slavery into the remaining Federal territories—territories which soon expanded beyond the Mississippi River. This conflict grew in ferocity until, in the 1850s, it broke out into open warfare in Kansas.[4] During the Civil War itself, the five free states created out of the Northwest Territory supplied the Union armies with a million men, who turned the tide of battle between North and South.

All of which prompts the question: why did the Southern states agree in 1787 to limit the spread of slavery? The traditional explanation is that the Southerners were acting altruistically, in the best interests of the young Republic—that a "tranquil spirit of disinterested statesmanship ... took possession of every southern man in the assembly."[5] However, debates at the Constitutional Convention, that same hot summer of 1787, make it clear that Southern politicians were no more willing at that time to give the Federal government any power over their "peculiar institution" than Southern soldiers would be in 1865, when Federal armies finally removed the question from the table. As Pierce Butler of South Carolina phrased it in Philadelphia, "The security the Southern States want is that their Negroes may not be taken from them, which some gentlemen ... have a very good mind to do." In fact, Southerners at the Constitutional Convention threatened disunion if their "peculiar species of property" was challenged under the new law of the land. In the words of John Rutledge, another delegate from South Carolina, "The true question at present is whether the Southern states shall or shall not be parties to the union."[6]

Curiously, on July 12, 1787, one day previous to passage of the Northwest Ordinance in New York, the members of the Constitutional Convention—meeting ninety miles away—approved the so-called three-fifths compromise, according to which slaves would be included in the apportionment of

Congressional seats and Electoral College votes (counting the free population "and three-fifths of all other persons"). This extra political clout would have incalculable consequences in the antebellum period, helping to ensure that Southerners dominated the Federal government until, in 1861, they walked out of Congress following the election of Abraham Lincoln. Starting with Thomas Jefferson's defeat of John Adams in 1800, these extra votes would influence the course of Presidential elections as well as the outcome of key votes in Congress. For example, one of the most important Congressional decisions during that era—the annexation of Texas—was made possible by votes in the House of Representatives provided by these so-called Negro delegates. According to the Constitution, annexation should have been enabled by a treaty, ratified by a vote of at least two-thirds of the Senate—but because many Northern Senators opposed the addition of so much new slave territory, there weren't enough supporting votes to form the necessary supermajority, and therefore, at President John Tyler's urging, the annexation was carried out by a bill passed by simple majorities in both houses of Congress. This outcome would without question have been different if the South had lacked the votes in the House of Representatives provided by the three-fifths compromise.[7]

In 1966, Staughton Lynd published an essay, "The Compromise of 1787," in which he discussed these two key decisions of the Constitutional summer:

> On July 12, 1787, the Constitutional Convention, meeting in Philadelphia, adopted the three-fifths compromise regarding apportionment of the House of Representatives. On July 13 the Continental Congress, meeting in New York City, adopted the Northwest Ordinance ... [which] was in Ulrich Phillip's words "the first and last anti-slavery achievement by the central government in the period."[8]

Lynd goes on to say, "I think one can justifiably present the hypothesis that there occurred in July 1787 a sectional compromise involving Congress and Convention" [207]. Building upon Lynd's work, I've concluded that there was an agreement made between delegates to the Constitutional Convention and the Confederation Congress, which tied together the anti-slavery clause of the Northwest Ordinance and the three-fifths compromise in the Constitution. Unlike the Missouri Compromise (1820) and the Compromise of 1850, both of which were argued out in public debates that can be read about in the pages of the *Annals of Congress* and the *Congressional Globe*, this earlier rapprochement occurred in secret—so that to this day it hasn't been accepted by many historians as having, in fact, taken place.[9] Furthermore, those two later events took place when a Congressional cohort from the North attempted to limit the expansion of slavery in the face of great opposition from the South. In 1787, on the other hand, it was the Southerners who actually initiated the insertion of a clause restricting the spread of slavery, and the one dissenting vote came from a Congressman from New York, Abraham Yates. As Nathan Dane, the delegate from Massachusetts who drafted the Ordinance, wrote to his colleague Rufus King at the Constitutional Convention, he was surprised to find that Southerners were amenable to the clause—and that he wouldn't otherwise have submitted it to a vote.[10] Had the Southerners not spoken up at this point, there would have been no anti-slavery clause in the Ordinance, and slavery would have been free to spread to future states in both the Southwest *and* the Northwest.

Historians such as Paul Finkelman have argued that the timing of the two crucial votes—in two different cities, ninety miles and twenty-four hours apart—makes a political deal unlikely; that given the slow communication of the day, it would have been impossible for the Congressional delegates in New York City to become aware on July 13 of what their colleagues in the Constitutional Convention had decided a day earlier.[11] It's clear from existing evidence, however, that such quick communication was indeed possible between the two cities. While assistant postmaster of the colonies, Benjamin Franklin had overhauled the mail system to include express riders who carried lanterns so that they could travel in the darkest hours, and a message, even as early as 1764, could easily pass overnight from one city to the other.[12] Moreover, there is proof of this taking place in 1787; when Congress in September passed the resolution sending the Constitution out to the states for approval, news reached the Pennsylvania legislature the next day by means of an overnight rider dispatched by William Bingham.[13]

So why did Southerners in Congress, that week in July 1787, tell Nathan Dane that it was a propitious time for him to include an anti-slavery clause in the Northwest Ordinance—and why did they vote unanimously in its favor? In a letter to James Monroe on August 8—less than a month after passage of the Ordinance—Virginia Congressman William Grayson stated that the Southern delegates agreed to the anti-slavery clause "for the purpose of preventing Tobacco & Indigo from being made on the N.W. side of the Ohio, as well as for sevl. other political reasons."[14] Unfortunately, Grayson never specified what he meant by the last phrase—but as Lynd argues in his essay, outlawing slavery *north* of the river seems clearly to imply that plantation agriculture would be free to expand without hindrance into the territories *south* of the river.[15] Before the invention of the cotton gin in 1793, two of the major products of slave labor were tobacco and indigo, so Grayson's comment supports this conclusion. In addition, as I will demonstrate, the inclusion of the three-fifths compromise in the Constitution was probably one of the "other political reasons" Grayson refers to.

The swing state in the voting on the three-fifths compromise was Pennsylvania, whose delegation to the Constitutional Convention changed its stance from rejection to approval between July 11 and 12. As I will show, this switch probably occurred after the delegates in Philadelphia learned that Southern Congressmen were willing to accept a slave-free Northwest Territory. In addition, I believe that Pennsylvania's acceptance of the three-fifths ratio was at least partially influenced by the possibility of the enormous profits to be made buying and selling land in the territory north of the Ohio River— among the Pennsylvania delegates at the Convention were some of the greatest "plungers" of the period. One of the more popular activities in the early Republic was speculation in land, which later grew into the first American financial bubble. The collapse of this speculative frenzy in the 1790s would put many people in debtors' prison, including people as rich and influential as Robert Morris of Philadelphia, the so-called Financier of the Revolution—who was, in fact, a member of the Constitutional Convention. Another delegate from Pennsylvania—and a close associate of Robert Morris—was James Wilson, whose life ended in 1796 while he was on the run from his creditors (due to real estate investments gone bad), hiding with a young wife in a sweltering inn in North Carolina, even while he was, at the very same time, an Associate Justice of the United States Supreme Court.[16] Gouverneur Morris (no relation to Robert, though they were business partners) was also a Pennsylvania delegate—and as I will show later, it may well have been his vote which was crucial in changing Pennsylvania's position from No to Aye on July 12.

Specifically, one of the important objects of financial speculation was the bottom third of the current state of Ohio—a prime piece of real estate, with frontage on the Ohio River, and to its west the Wabash, which with the Maumee formed the most direct route from Lake Erie to the Mississippi. (The French had called the portage between these two rivers, site of the Miami Villages—now Fort Wayne—the "glorious gate" to the south.)[17] Speaking generally, this was to be the first portion of the public domain of the United States open for sale, with the full Northwest Territory being the ultimate prize. Stretching from the Ohio River north to Lake Superior, and from the border of Pennsylvania west to the Mississippi, this territory encompassed an area greater than the original thirteen colonies. It was the fruit of conquest, ceded to the United Colonies when the British government signed the Treaty of Peace in 1783. A vast resource, it presented immense possibilities for the fledgling Federal government. Over the course of the next four years—for the first time as a sovereign nation—the United States made the decision to expand into land inhabited by the First Peoples. In truth, there's not much said about the Native population in the Northwest Ordinance, only a few sentences promising "utmost good faith … toward the Indians," and stating that "their lands and property shall never be taken from them without their consent."[18] Despite this fine language, the fact was that the Native Americans had neither the desire nor the intention of selling their land—and this inconvenient truth interfered with national plans.

Under the Articles of Confederation, the Federal government had no real taxing power, yet it owed an enormous debt amassed while fighting the Revolutionary War. The only means Congress had to pay this debt was to sell land, and the only land of which it could claim ownership was precisely this territory northwest of the Ohio River. Since the early days of the war, members of Congress had been eyeing the Northwest not only for personal gain, but also as a resource that would help pay the national debt. Three fraudulent treaties since the Revolution—Fort Stanwix in 1784, Fort McIntosh in 1785, and Fort Finney in 1786—had supposedly cleared the Indian title to this land—though the First Nations themselves didn't see it that way. They referred back to the Proclamation of 1763 and the original Treaty of Fort Stanwix in 1768, in which the Crown of England reserved to the Indians all land northwest of the Ohio River, and they insisted that this territory was still theirs. Though Federal negotiators after the war were fond of claiming that the British Crown had surrendered this land in the Treaty of Paris, with no regard for their erstwhile Indian allies, a look at the treaty reveals a stipulation that "there shall be no future confiscations made, nor any prosecutions commenced against any person or persons for, or by reason of the part which he or they may have taken in the present war."[19] Either no Native American qualified as a "person" under the terms of the treaty, or the land which the Nations occupied hadn't legally been their property in the first place. In fact, Chief Justice John Marshall's 1823 decision in *Johnson v. M'Intosh* would state the case for this latter interpretation.[20]

Underlying the Northwest Ordinance and many subsequent pieces of legislation is the so-called Discovery Doctrine, according to which the European nations owned the continent the minute they found it, despite its already being inhabited by people of another skin color. Elucidated by Marshall, this doctrine in fact dates back to a fifteenth-century Pope whose mission it was to Catholicize the New World.[21] Years later this mission of colonization was taken up by the U.S. government, which had its own idea of empire-building. A system of territorial expansion, inaugurated by the Northwest Ordinance, led the way across the continent of North America. How the United States treated the indigenous inhabitants is, along with slavery, one of the two original sins of this nation. When William Lloyd Garrison stated that the Constitution was "a covenant with death and an agreement with hell," he was referring to the institution of slavery, but he might just as well have been referring to this theft of the First Nations' homeland—or of the collusion that tied the two together.[22]

It was a small world in which these dealings took place. The entire population of the United States at that time numbered approximately three million, and many of the men in Congress, in the Convention, and in the state legislatures all knew each other or were bound by personal or political or business connections. Gouverneur Morris of New York, for example—after many years as a bachelor—married a member of the Randolph family of Virginia, a distant cousin of Thomas Jefferson.[23] Nine of the fifty-five delegates to the Convention had graduated from the College of New Jersey (now Princeton). Though separated by distances that took days to traverse, it was possible for people to maintain a close-knit connection by means of social networking. This sort of communication was embodied in the Committees of Correspondence that helped facilitate the Revolution itself.[24]

By the summer of 1787, a group of investors from Massachusetts had formed a company to buy up land north of the Ohio River, and the purchase money would be a windfall to the impoverished Federal government. But such a venture would be too risky unless a suitable political structure was in place for the territory—so these investors, who had styled themselves the Ohio Company, were eager for the passage of an ordinance laying out the form of such a government. Their spokesman was Manasseh Cutler, from Ipswich, sometime preacher, sometime botanist, sometime chaplain to the Army of the Revolution. One of the many nineteenth-century biographers of this tireless proponent of the Ohio Company gives us this accolade: "For diversity of good gifts, for their efficient use, and for the variety of modes of valuable service to his country and to mankind, I doubt whether Manasseh Cutler has his equal in American history."[25] These days Cutler would be called a lobbyist, and at the beginning of July 1787, he drove his single-seater carriage down from Ipswich to New York City, where he submitted a purchase proposal to the Confederation Congress:

> It may illustrate the difference between that time and this to say that he accomplished his journey with commendable dispatch, being only twelve days on the road, and that he traveled in his own sulky—a vehicle probably unknown by name to some of my younger readers—a two-wheeled one-horse chaise, wide enough only for a single person—in my boyhood much used by physicians and ministers on their professional rounds. Dr. Cutler carried no less than forty-two letters of introduction, from the Governor of Massachusetts, the President of Harvard College and other distinguished men.[26]

Cutler spent the next few days meeting with various members of Congress—including Nathan Dane, from Beverly, Massachusetts (just a few miles from Ipswich), whom Cutler had known for years—and on Tuesday evening, July 10, Cutler proceeded to Philadelphia, where over the course of the next three days he met with various members of the Constitutional Convention—including Ben Franklin, no stranger himself to the fruitful world of land speculation.

By the close of business on Friday, July 13, Congress had voted to exclude slavery from the Northwest Territory, and the Constitutional Convention had determined that Southerners would have representation in Congress—

and in the Electoral College—based upon a population count which included three-fifths of their slaves. What follows in this book is a close examination of these two events of July 1787—and of their historical context—showing beyond a reasonable doubt how an arrangement linking the two could have occurred, and why.

CHAPTER 1

The Year 1787 Had Started

That something is necessary, none will deny; for the situation of the general government, if it can be called a government, is shaken to its foundation, and liable to be overturned by every blast. In a word, it is at an end; and, unless a remedy is soon applied, anarchy and confusion will inevitably ensue.

—George Washington[1]

The year 1787 had started with the long shadow of Shays' Rebellion stretching across the winter landscape. The Springfield Armory was the site of the first shooting incident of the rebellion, when an angry mob, many of them former soldiers, tried to seize the armory to facilitate their revolt against Massachusetts taxes. These men had been given scrip for payment, back in the bad old days following the peace treaty with Great Britain, and due to poverty and hunger—many of them not even having the means to pay their way home—they sold these certificates for pennies on the dollar to well-heeled investors. Now the Massachusetts legislature, heavily weighted toward the eastern districts, had imposed a tax to pay off these certificates at face value. A few rich men in Boston would benefit, and the western dirt farmers, the men who had sold those certificates, would have to pay good money—gold and silver—to support these payments. Farms were foreclosed upon, and the farmers, massing at the courthouse, had stopped the sheriff's sales. Now they were going further along the road of revolution. (The right to bear arms meant that they could have a musket at home, but the real tools of war, the artillery, remained under lock and key in the armory.) To their way of thinking, they had fought the long war against Britain to throw off the shackles of rich men and the debt they brought with them. On this winter afternoon they gathered at the armory.

A few members of the militia were still loyal to the government, and their commander, William Shepard, had lined them up with field artillery against the mob. At first he ordered his men to fire above the heads of the crowd, but a blast failed to scare these seasoned veterans. They couldn't believe that their former comrades would, in fact, turn the artillery against them. One volley into the crowd, which killed and wounded several men, convinced them otherwise. The mob dispersed, to fight—unsuccessfully— another day.[2]

The fear of open revolt caused by Shays' Rebellion was one of the reasons that George Washington, for one, agreed to come out of retirement to attend the Constitutional Convention, as it brought to a fine point the realization that the current Federal government was unable to raise an army sufficient to suppress rebellion, whether it be by disgruntled veterans, or slaves forbidden to walk the roads at night without a pass—or by Native Americans whose land was being stolen by white settlers. (Only a new Constitution, which gave taxing power to Congress, enabled the formation of an army that, in 1794, at the Battle of Fallen Timbers, finally defeated the Western Indian Confederacy and opened Ohio to white settlement.)

To Henry Knox, however—Secretary at War in the Confederation government—local taxes were only the tip of the iceberg for the rebels:

> That taxes may be the ostensible cause is true, but that they are the true cause is as far remote from truth as light from darkness. The people who are the insurgents have never paid any or but very little taxes. But they see the weakness of government: they feel at once their own poverty compared with the opulent, and their own force, and they are determined to make use of the latter in order to remedy the former.[3]

In Knox's opinion, which he shared with George Washington, the insurgents wanted far more than tax relief; in fact, their "leveling spirit" was a threat to all private property.

> Their creed is, that the property of the United States has been protected from the confiscations of Britain by the joint exertions of all, and therefore ought to be the common property of all; and he that attempts opposition to this creed is an enemy to equality and justice, and ought to be swept from the face of the earth. In a word, they are determined to annihilate all debts public and private, and have agrarian laws, which are easily effected by the means of unfunded paper money.[4]

In the face of this threat, the Confederation government was too weak to prevail.

> This dreadful situation, for which our government have made no adequate provision, has alarmed every man of principle and property in New England. They start as from a dream, and ask what can have been the cause of our delusion? What is to give us security against the violence of lawless men? Our government must be braced, changed, or altered to secure our lives and property. We imagined that the mildness of our government and the wishes of the people were so correspondent that we were not as other nations, requiring brutal force to support the laws.
> But we find that we are men—actual men, possessing all the turbulent passions belonging to that animal—and that we must have a government proper and adequate

for him.... Something is wanting, and something must be done, or we shall be involved in all the horror of failure, and civil war without a prospect of its termination.

Colonel Josiah Harmar was the commander in chief of Federal forces after the Revolution, but the entire military establishment at this time consisted of "one regiment of infantry of eight companies" and "one battalion of artillery"—and most of these troops were posted along the western frontier.[5] Since the Federal government's power to levy taxes under the Articles of Confederation was limited to the "requisitions" it could demand of the States (without any power of enforcement), this remained the state of affairs right up until the new government was formed under the Constitution, and yet this meager force was expected not only to guard the armories out east but also to keep peace along the frontier. Though armed troops were needed to put down the insurrection in Massachusetts, the local militia couldn't be trusted—many of them sympathized with Shays, or were themselves "Shaysites"—so bankers and merchants in Boston raised a private army, under the command of General Benjamin Lincoln. The brief rebellion ended with total defeat of the rebels.[6]

That was the good news—but on the other hand the national treasury lacked enough cash even to make interest payments on the foreign debt, which was essential if the young Republic were to continue borrowing money.[7] As James Madison wrote the Governor of Virginia, "Our situation is becoming every day more & more critical ... and people of reflection unanimously agree that the existing Confederacy is tottering to its foundation."[8] There was a pervasive anxiety among men of property that the troubles which took place in Massachusetts could spread to other states. As Congressman William Irvine wrote his fellow Pennsylvanian, Josiah Harmar, "Under the present Government it is much to be feared that insurgency & rebellion may pervade more States than Massachusetts."[9]

In fact, just as the insurgents in Massachusetts were growing increasingly hostile, American settlers in the Kentucky District of Virginia revealed their own independent streak. In 1784, Spain had closed passage of the Mississippi River to American traffic below Natchez.[10] What the Spanish feared was the loss of their silver mines in the Southwest. They wanted a buffer of a thousand miles of wilderness between the settlers and the mines, as they knew how quickly the American pioneers were expanding their holdings in previously unmapped territory—and they felt that by shutting the Mississippi they would deter western settlement.[11] This had been the main topic of negotiations between the Spanish emissary, Don Diego de Gardoqui, and John Jay, Secretary for Foreign Affairs, since Gardoqui first arrived in New York in 1785.[12] But Congress had become deadlocked on the terms of these negotiations. Northern delegates wished to accommodate the wishes of the King of Spain regarding the Mississippi, in return for most-favored-nation status when it came to selling cod to the growing Spanish market. On the other hand, Virginia and North Carolina had settlements that were continually extending westward across the Appalachian Mountains, and Southern delegates feared that these pioneers—whose only means of selling their agricultural goods was through New Orleans—would shift their allegiance to Spain if the Mississippi were to remain closed.

Since August 1786, the voting in Congress on this issue had been frozen in place, seven votes to five (each state having a single vote in the Old Congress, and Rhode Island often not showing up to be counted). Under the Articles of Confederation, however, treaties required the approval of nine states.[13] Nonetheless, there were rumors in Kentucky that a treaty had already been signed:

> The late commercial treaty with Spain, in shutting up, as it is said, the navigation of the Mississippi, for the term of twenty-five years, has given this western country a universal shock, and struck its inhabitants with an amazement…. To sell us, and make us vassals to the merciless Spaniards, is a grievance not to be borne.[14]

As Washington had written, "The Western settlers (I speak now from my own observation) stand as it were upon a pivot; the touch of a feather, would turn them any way."[15]

David Duncan to Josiah Harmar
9 December 1786
I am well informed the Trade of the Mississippi is stopped for the space of twenty five years, which is longer than I shall live according to the course of things: So the pride & life of the Ohio country is buried & gone at present from us, if a Revolution don't take place in the course of a few years on this side of the mountains. Nothing is more talked of here at present.[16]

In December 1786, the governor of Virginia received a letter from "a few concerned individuals" that indicated outright fighting had broken out in Kentucky.[17] A prime actor in all this turned out to be none other than General George Rogers Clark, the hero of the Revolution who had managed, by capturing British outposts in the Illinois country, to "save" the western territory for the young Republic. As another letter stated, "Clarke is playing Hell. He is raising a Regiment of his own, and has 140 men stationed at Opost … [who have] seized on a Spanish boat worth 20,000 Dollars…. Clarke is eternally drunk, and yet full of design."[18] As Madison assessed the situation in mid–April 1787, "The business with Spain is becoming extremely delicate, and the information from the Western settlements truly alarming."[19]

Anarchy out west demanded the attention of Congress as much as the anarchy in Massachusetts. If the growing population of squatters were to take over the western territory, it would render null and void the hope that land sales could fill the national coffers. As Henry Knox explained to Congress, "If such audacious defiance of the power of the United States be suffered with impunity a precedent will be established, to wrest all the immense property of the Western Territory out of the hands of the public."[20]

Meanwhile, in accordance with an act of Congress, surveyors crossed the Ohio River from the Kentucky District of Virginia to begin a survey of land allotted to Virginia veterans.[21] (The future city of Cincinnati—founded in 1788—would sit smack-dab in the middle of this prime riverfront parcel.) Responding to these signs of encroachment, members of the First Nations showered their displeasure upon the existing Kentucky settlements. As Colonel Levi Todd wrote the governor of Virginia, "Not a week passes without depredations being committed in some part of the District."[22] But when the Westerners asked Congress to provide military support, William Grayson—to whom the requests had been directed—responded that since "there are so many States who are protected (by their situation) from the depredations of the Indians," little help could be expected.[23] The hope for additional Western states to help defend against the First Nations' attacks was probably one of the "other political reasons" that Grayson referred to in his letter about the Northwest Ordinance, saying that "in a few years" he expected the Eastern settlers north of the Ohio would "extend themselves by additional purchases quite to the Mississippi, & thereby form a compleat barrier for our State."[24] These settlers would also perhaps join with their brethren south of the Ohio to agitate for free passage of the Mississippi.

Several Midwestern Indian Nations had met at the Huron Town just south of Detroit, at the end of December 1786, and had sent a lengthy message to Congress indicating their unwillingness to vacate their territory north of the Ohio River. Though this message would not arrive until the summer of 1787, General Richard Butler, Superintendent of Indian Affairs for the Northern Department, reported to the Secretary at War that they had "laboured exceedingly to form a general confederacy among themselves," and Colonel Harmar was warned by an informant that if the Americans "do not agree to their terms ... they intend to begin the war with all their force ... eight thousand men ... from different nations."[25] The situation was grim. Financially constrained, however, Congress could afford only a single regiment of troops to deal with the several dangers the country faced: the new threat from an Indian Confederacy, the possibility of a repeat of Shays' Rebellion in the eastern states, and the growing assertiveness of western settlers to force passage of the Mississippi (and to take for their own the land north of the Ohio that Congress hoped to sell). Many people wished for a stronger central government—that is, one with the power to levy taxes and raise an army. On February 21, 1787, Congress approved a resolution

that on the second Monday in May next a Convention of delegates ... be held at
Philadelphia for the sole and express purpose of revising the Articles of Confederation ... [to] render the federal Constitution adequate to the exigencies of Government and the preservation of the Union.[26]

Despite all this uncertainty and fear, when the Ohio Company share-
holders and directors met in the beginning of March, at the Bunch of Grapes
tavern in downtown Boston, it became clear that there were "many inclined
to become adventurers" out west. It was unanimously resolved, therefore,
that the Directors "make application to the Honorable Congress for a private
purchase of Lands ... adequate to the purposes of the Company."[27] The men
chosen for this task were Generals Samuel Parsons and Rufus Putnam, and
the Rev. Manasseh Cutler. As Cutler wrote to Winthrop Sargent, his friend
and co-investor, "the spirit of emigration never ran higher with us, and the
Ohio lands are held in the highest estimation."[28] Cutler began his lobbying
with a letter to Nathan Dane, Congressman from Massachusetts—who would
later serve on the committee investigating the possible sale of land to the
Ohio Company (and who would also draft the Northwest Ordinance). The
Land Ordinance of 1785 had restricted the sale of public land to the first seven
ranges of townships to be surveyed west of the Pennsylvania border—but
Cutler hoped he could convince Dane of the wisdom of forgoing this stipulation in favor of at least one other sale to a group of "adventurers."[29] As Cutler
stated, this particular purchase would not only help alleviate the national
debt, but in addition these settlers were Northerners, "men of more robust
constitutions, inured to labor, and free from the habits of idleness." In other
words, unlike the Southerners moving into Kentucky, they would not be
slaveholders.

Winthrop Sargent's personal copy of the prospectus of the Ohio Company includes a listing of purchasers who bought shares from him. It is a slim
pamphlet, and on sheets appended to the Articles of Association is a list of
names which includes, among others, Governor James Bowdoin of Massachusetts; General Henry Knox; William Duer of New York, Secretary of the
Treasury Board; New York Assemblyman Alexander Hamilton; Congressmen
Arthur Lee and Edward Carrington from Virginia; and Melancton Smith,
Congressman from New York—in addition to General Rufus Putnam, who
would lead the expedition which founded Marietta in April of 1788.[30] The
spot they chose for their first settlement—after Cutler had spoken with the
Surveyor General, Thomas Hutchins—was at the confluence of the Muskingum and Ohio Rivers, the site of Fort Harmar.[31]

At the end of April 1787, Congress was attempting to determine the best
way of raising cash from western land in order to bolster the nation's finances,
the one hope left Congress—short of a new Constitution—to attain solvency.
As James Madison indicated, this project "involves great difficulties," not least

because of the unruliness of the western settlers.[32] On April 26, the committee appointed "to prepare a plan of a temporary government for such districts, or new states, as shall be laid out by the United States" brought back for consideration a report that, the previous September, had been left as unfinished business.[33] On May 9, this "Ordinance for the government of the western territory" had its second Congressional reading (three readings were necessary before a vote could be taken), after which it was further debated and changes made; these were ordered to be transcribed and printed, and the next day, May 10, the new version was scheduled for its third reading.[34] Also on May 9, Congress first received a proposal from Samuel Parsons, agent for the Ohio Company, in which the Company proposed buying "a tract of country" northwest of the Ohio, for "a sum not exceeding one million of dollars."[35]

This petition from the Ohio Company interrupted the flow of legislation. On May 10, when the Ordinance for the Western Territory was to have its final reading, the Massachusetts delegates requested a postponement, and no further debate took place.[36] The nation's attention being drawn then to the Constitutional Convention in Philadelphia, after May 10 there was no quorum in Congress until the first week of July. This severely limited the ability of the government to conduct business, which as Nathan Dane wrote his colleague Rufus King, "seems to me ... to have a pernicious effect on the public mind and feelings."[37] Exacerbating the problems caused by this lack of political will, a human flood continued down the Ohio River, headed toward Kentucky. As Josiah Harmar recorded, "From the 10th of October, 1786, until the 12th of May, 1787, 177 boats, 2,689 souls, 1,333 horses, 766 cattle, and 102 wagons, have passed Muskingum, bound for Limestone and the Rapids."[38] Colonel Harmar was warned by one of his agents about the probable Indian response to what they considered an invasion of their country:

> They have laid down the boundary to Congress, which is the Ohio River, & say they will be at peace with the Thirteen Fires, if they keep on their own side of the River Ohio, & don't settle or survey on their side of it ... [but] if Congress is determined to sell the lands & have them surveyed, war must be the end of it at last.[39]

CHAPTER 2

Meanwhile in Philadelphia

Speculation in western lands was one of the leading activities of capitalists in those days. As is well known, the soldiers were paid in part in land scrip and this scrip was bought up at low prices by dealers, often with political connections. Furthermore, large areas had been bought outright for a few cents an acre and were being held for a rise in value. The chief obstacle in the way of the rapid appreciation of these lands was the weakness of the national government which prevented the complete subjugation of the Indians, the destruction of old Indian claims, and the orderly settlement of the frontier. Every leading capitalist of the time thoroughly understood the relation of a new constitution to the rise in land values beyond the Alleghanies.

—Charles Beard[1]

Once seated, the delegates at the Constitutional Convention set ground rules for themselves. One of the first steps they take is to attempt to ensure total secrecy from public scrutiny: "That nothing spoken in the House be printed, or otherwise published, or communicated without leave."[2] Not only are the windows closed and nailed shut in the hot Philadelphia summer, to forestall eavesdroppers, but no votes are to be recorded by name, so that the delegates will be able to change their minds without there being a record of what might be considered vacillation. Public relations aside, this is probably a good decision in terms of leading to the best possible outcome—that is, people actually listening to each other and, ideally, coming to a rational decision about what might be best in any particular instance. It is also decided that a quorum will consist of seven states. Voting is to be by states, as it is in the Old Congress, and a majority of states present on any particular day will prevail. Just as in Congressional voting, there must be at least two delegates in agreement from any state for its vote to be counted; otherwise, it is listed as "divided" in the record.

There are, in total, fifty-five delegates who will be present during the summer, though not all of them are there at all times. Thirty-one of these men—for there are no women included—are lawyers. They are meeting in a room approximately forty feet square, seated by threes and fours at tables arranged in a semicircle. James Madison sits in front of them, facing them, taking notes, and behind him, most of the time, sits the Chair of the Convention, George Washington. It is these men who invent the document so important to the course of American history.

> Tuesday, May 29, 1787
>
> His excellency Governor Randolph, a member from Virginia, got up, and in a long and elaborate speech, shewed the defects in the system of the present federal government as totally inadequate to the peace, safety and security of the confederation, and the absolute necessity of a more energetic government.
>
> He closed these remarks with a set of resolutions, fifteen in number, which he proposed to the convention for their adoption [23–24].[3]

Of these proposals—the so-called Virginia Plan—the second and third resolutions are most important to our discussion. (The main author of the plan was James Madison, though since he is busy taking notes, Edmund Randolph is the one who presents it to the delegates.)

> 2nd Resolution: That the rights of suffrage in the National Legislature ought to be proportioned to the Quotas of contribution, or to the number of free inhabitants, as the one or the other rule may seem best in different cases.
>
> 3rd Resolution: That the National Legislature ought to consist of two branches [20].

This is a shot across the bow for the small states, which are used to the unicameral, one-state-one-vote system used in Congress under the Articles of Confederation. What the Virginia Plan proposes is a two-chamber legislature, where representation in one chamber will be proportional to the "quotas of contribution" (in other words, proportional to the wealth of each state, as measured by taxes paid) and in the other will be allocated according to population. In neither chamber, therefore, will states have equal representation.

It was a generally accepted notion at the time that to function most successfully, a legislature should be composed of two separate houses, like the British Parliament—one body elected by the people at large (or at least a portion of the male part of the population) and the other representing wealth and property. This concept was based in part upon the fear that a legislature which contained only a single body of representatives would lack restraint. As John Adams had written in 1776, "A single assembly is liable to all the vices, follies, and frailties of an individual; subject to fits of humor, starts of passion, flights of enthusiasm, partialities, or prejudice, and consequently productive of hasty results and absurd judgments."[4] The second legislative body would serve as a counterweight, and it would be composed of a smaller, more deliberative group of individuals, possessing—it was hoped—more experience and wisdom.[5]

The Convention begins its discussions in what is called "the committee of the whole," a legislative peculiarity by which the whole body can meet and discuss and vote on items without those decisions being binding. The committee of the whole, comprising everyone present, will deliberate and come to a conclusion which is then passed along as a proposal to the very same legislators, who at a later date debate the entire matter again before coming to an ultimate decision. This procedure allows ideas to be floated and considered without necessarily affecting the final outcome. In the case of the Constitution, preliminary decisions could be made concerning some very sticky issues—which would then be revisited in greater detail and controversy. As we shall see.

When the Convention reconvenes a day after Randolph's speech, attention immediately turns to the specific wording of the Virginia Plan: representation in one chamber is to be according "to the number of free inhabitants." This will severely curtail the votes of states like South Carolina and Georgia, where in some coastal districts slaves constitute as much as ninety percent of the population.[6] Keenly aware that this issue is so controversial as to detract attention from the primary question of whether the new Congress, unlike the old, will have proportional representation at all, Madison suggests a somewhat different wording: "that the equality of suffrage established by the articles of Confederation ought not to prevail in the national Legislature, and that an equitable ratio of representation ought to be substituted" [36]. For the small states, which disagree with Madison about the meaning of "equitable," even this is going too far. A small-state delegate, George Reed of Delaware, moves that "the whole clause relating to the point of Representation be postponed"—and so it is [37].

The second resolution in the Virginia Plan states that representation in the other house of Congress (which will later be called the Senate) should be proportional to taxes paid, the so-called quotas of contribution. In the Articles of Confederation, these "requisitions" are based upon "the value of all land within each State granted to or surveyed for any person."[7] Because of problems that arose due to the sticky question of how, and by whom, the assessment of land would occur, Congress in April 1783 approved a change in the Articles. Henceforth, taxes were to be levied

> in proportion to the whole number of white and other free citizens and inhabitants, of every age, sex and condition, including those bound to servitude for a term of years, and three-fifths of all other persons not comprehended in the foregoing description, except Indians not paying taxes.[8]

This language—the first instance of the three-fifths ratio in American constitutional law—was never approved by the legislatures of all thirteen states, which was necessary for amendments under the Articles of Confederation. Nonetheless, four years later, in 1787, the language Randolph uses concerning the "quotas of contribution" contains, by implication, an allusion to the ratio that Congress, after lengthy and heated debate, had already settled upon as a relative value of slave and free labor. To be sure, the actual words Randolph employs on May 30 are ambiguous: "quotas of contribution" might refer to the definition contained in the Articles of Confederation (the value of all land), or it could mean the phrase as redefined in the proposal of April 18, 1783 (containing the rubric "three-fifths of all other persons")—or it could imply that the Convention will in the future decide upon some other means of assessment.[9] In any case, Randolph is stating unequivocally that under the new American constitution, according to the Virginia Plan, one house of Congress will have representation proportional to population, however calculated, and the other will represent wealth, though how that will work in practice is as yet undefined. In this regard, the key question in Philadelphia was how to measure both indexes—population and property—and, specifically, whether (or how) to include slaves in the formulation.

Despite the fact that the states south of the Mason-Dixon line shared a common interest in having their "peculiar species of property" included in any formula of apportionment, there was also an important distinction between them which involved the slave trade. Due to the natural growth of the slave population over the past century and a half, Virginians in 1787 owned too many slaves for the needs of their plantations. This surplus labor, when sold to planters from South Carolina and Georgia, competed with slaves imported directly from Africa. It made sense, therefore, for Virginians to wish to curtail the international slave trade, but that wasn't something the delegates from the Deep South would readily accept, as it would cut the supply and hence raise the price of slave labor. Chief among these delegates was John Rutledge, the former dictatorial governor of South Carolina during the Revolution.[10]

Similarly, though Pennsylvania and Virginia were both large states, and desired to have the influence in national councils that their populations would confer, they also had differing interests—some of which did not involve slavery. For many years, the government of Virginia had attempted to limit property transactions between private citizens—particularly those of other colonies—and the Indian Nations. Before ceding to the Federal government its claim to land northwest of the Ohio River (which occurred in 1784), Virginia claimed as its own all the territory north to the Canadian border.[11] During the Revolution, Virginia attempted to assert eminent domain over the valuable lands beyond the Appalachian Mountains by issuing the Proclamation of 1779, which disallowed all private purchases of land from the Indians, even those which were already on the books:

Be it declared by the General Assembly, that this Commonwealth hath the exclusive right of pre-emption from the Indians, of all the lands within the limits of its own chartered territory.... That no person or persons whatsoever, have, or ever had, a right to purchase any lands within the same, from any Indian nation ... and that such exclusive right or pre-emption, will and ought to be maintained by this Commonwealth, to the utmost of its power.

And be it further declared and enacted ... that all sales and deeds which have been, or shall be made ... by any Indian nation or nations, for lands within the said limits, to or for the separate use of any person or persons whatsoever ... are hereby declared utterly void and of no effect.[12]

In 1773 and 1775, two groups of Pennsylvania investors had arranged to purchase land north of the Ohio River from some friendly chiefs of the Illinois and Piankashaw nations, who claimed to speak for their respective tribes. In 1779, these investors merged into the United Illinois and Wabash Land Company, with claims to some sixty million acres of land, and their president was James Wilson—but these claims were denied validity by the government of Virginia. The point here is that John Rutledge, delegate to the Convention from South Carolina, and James Wilson, delegate from Pennsylvania, both had reasons to distrust the Virginians—and, conversely, to work with each other. Like many other members of the Convention, these two men already knew each other. As one of Rutledge's biographers explains,

On May 18, John Rutledge arrived by boat and was met at the wharf by a messenger from James Wilson who bore a letter inviting him "because of the unprecedented tax on the facilities of our excellent taverns" to become his guest. Rutledge accepted and for the first three weeks of the Convention lived at Wilson's house.[13]

Because each state at the Convention had a single vote, and the small states, banding together, wished to retain their power in any new legislative scheme, the three large states—Massachusetts, Pennsylvania, and Virginia—needed allies in their quest for a majority that would support proportional representation, however allocated. Where would the large states find these allies? If Rutledge posed this question to Wilson, it would have been rhetorical—for the answer was clear to him: Georgia and the Carolinas, the three states of the Deep South. And what was it they would want in return? Wilson might or might not have asked this question—for that too would have been pretty obvious: they wanted to have their "peculiar species of property" considered in any scheme of apportionment, whether by population or wealth. (Due to the value of their agricultural exports—tobacco, rice, and indigo—it was generally considered that the Southern states were the wealthiest in the Union, and a large part of this wealth was their human property.)[14]

It has been asserted, most notably by Richard Barry, and also more recently by David O. Stewart, that Wilson and Rutledge worked closely together throughout the Convention—that in return for the Southerner's support regarding proportional representation, Wilson offered to promote a system of apportionment which included the slave population.[15] We will soon see how James Wilson and John Rutledge might have engineered a means to accomplish their goals.

CHAPTER 3

Beginning with the Treaty of Lancaster

Consider, Brethren, that the People of Virginia are like the leaves upon the trees, very numerous, and you are but a few, and although you should kill ten of their people for one that they kill of yours, they will at last wear you out and destroy you.

—John Penn, Lt. Gov. of Pennsylvania[1]

It is the prevailing opinion of the people in general upon the frontiers, that it is no harm to kill an Indian.

—Col. Josiah Harmar[2]

Beginning with the Treaty of Lancaster, the English colonists in Virginia—previously content to settle on land east of the Appalachian Mountains—revealed a desire for the vast transmontane region. At Lancaster in 1744 (about seventy miles west of Philadelphia) and again in 1752 at Logstown (a short way down the Ohio from the current location of Pittsburgh), the Iroquois defended their rights to the land west of the mountains—but Crown and colonists would later claim that the Indians, at Lancaster, had signed away their rights entirely.

The position of the Iroquois, or Six Nations, was clear:

All the world knows we conquered the several Nations living ... on the back of the great mountains of Virginia; [they] feel the effects of our conquests, being now a part of our nations, and their lands at our disposal.

We know very well, it hath often been said by the Virginians, that the Great King of England, and the people of that colony, conquered the Indians who lived there, but it is not true ... [and] if the Virginians ever get a good right to it, it must be by us.[3]

Likewise, the Royal Governor of Virginia asserted the counterclaim:

It is true that the Great King holds Virginia by right of conquest, and the bounds of that conquest to the westward is the Great Sea.

If the Six Nations have made any Conquest over Indians that may at any time have lived on the West-side of the Great Mountains of Virginia, yet they never possessed any Lands there that we have ever heard of. That part was altogether deserted, and free for any people to enter upon, as the people of Virginia have done, by Order of the Great King, very justly.

As it turned out, there was—to put it politely—a crucial misunderstanding about the final terms of the treaty. While it was true that the Six Nations deeded land to the English extending as far as "the setting sun," the elders would insist that by this they meant only as far the Appalachians, since viewed from the east side of the mountains (where Lancaster was situated) the sun would set into the mountains. Virginia, on the other hand, insisted that the wording meant *all the way* westward—that is, as far as their royal charter extended—or at least as far as the Mississippi, since further west, even the Crown admitted, lay Nouvelle France.

In 1748, under the titular leadership of Thomas Lee—the sire of the famous Lee family, father of Arthur and Richard Henry, and grandfather of Robert E.—a group of Virginians formed the Ohio Land Company, whose business it was to scope out and begin to develop the best land in the upper Ohio Valley. For this purpose the royal government granted them five hundred thousand acres, mostly south of the Ohio River and east of the Kanawha, in return for which they promised to erect a fort at the Forks of the Ohio (now Pittsburgh) and settle a certain number of families on the land. As Jared Sparks describes it,

> The object of the Company was to settle the lands, and to carry on the Indian trade upon a large scale. Hitherto the trade with the western Indians had been mostly in the hands of the Pennsylvanians. The Company conceived that they might derive an important advantage over their competitors in this trade, from the water communication of the Potomac and the eastern branches of the Ohio, whose headwaters approximated each other.[4]

Sparks continues with a description of the proceedings at Logstown, a conference undertaken by Virginia at the Company's request, because "no attempt at establishing settlements could safely be made without some previous arrangements with the Indians." On June 13, 1752, "the Indians agreed not to molest any settlements that might be made on the south-east side of the Ohio … [but] took care to disclaim a recognition of the English title to any of these lands." As one of the elders told the Virginians,

> We are well acquainted that our chief council at the treaty of Lancaster, confirmed a deed to you for a quantity of land in Virginia, which you have a right to; but we never understood, before you told us yesterday, that the lands then sold were to extend farther to the sun-setting than … the other side of the Alleghany Hill.[5]

Sparks concludes: "Hence it appears that the Indians west of the Ohio, who inhabited the lands, had never consented to any treaty ceding them to the

English, nor understood that this cession extended beyond the Alleghany Mountains."

This episode of the Ohio Company is only one of a series of acquisitions by pre-Revolutionary land companies formed to take advantage of the Crown's largesse with its American domain. By 1760, the Governor's Council of Virginia had given away more than three million acres of western land both to groups and individuals.[6] And these grants by the Crown were not just limited to Virginia. Along with the Ohio Company were a flock of other names: Loyal, Susquehannah, Transylvania, Indiana, Mississippi—and yet another land company with the name Ohio, the so-called Grand Ohio Company, favorite of London and Philadelphia investors. This last group of men went so far as to propose the formation of a western colony with the name Vandalia, whose cause Ben Franklin espoused before King and Parliament shortly before the onset of the Revolution—with little success because of the worsening political climate that preceded the outbreak of hostilities.[7]

The world of Thomas Lee's Ohio Company revolved in great part around tobacco, whose planters required an ever-increasing supply of land. Until John Rolfe—perhaps with the assistance of his wife Pocahontas—figured out how best to cultivate the seeds which carried the scent of sweet tobacco to the rest of the world, the colony of Virginia was almost given up for dead.[8] Mortality was high, and there was nothing but memories to send back to the mother country. Once tobacco arrived on the scene in a form palatable to European tastes, all was changed; in a couple of years tobacco was being grown most everywhere it could.

But tobacco is hard on the soil, and at the time not much was known about replenishment and soil management—and in any case it was far cheaper and easier just to abandon the old homestead and move slightly west, to new country, where you could start all over with fresh dirt. This land, to be sure, had recently been the home of Native men and women, and the animals they depended on for food and other essentials of life (the shoulder bone of a deer makes a good hoe, if you don't have a piece of metal handy). But the land stretched off westward in waves of low undulating hills until you hit the mountains … and across the mountains lay even more land.

These English-speaking settlers wanted land of their own to live on and to farm. For religious communities fleeing intolerance, or young men whose older brothers inherited the family business, the provinces of America beckoned. While the French had been content to extract the furs from North America and to keep the English colonists hemmed in along the seaboard, the English saw the New World as a place to dump their excess of young men, who were filling up the prisons and overtaxing the gallows, and who might be put to better use sending some useful product, of whatever sort, back to the homeland. Tobacco was only one of these products: fur, fish, timber, and grain were among the others. At their peak, the number of French men and women in North America could be numbered in the thousands, whereas by the time of the Seven Years' War, in the mid-eighteenth century, the population of the mainland English colonies was closer to one million. Furthermore, the English colonists had a very different idea from the French of what constituted the proper use of land in America. Overtly chauvinistic, one nineteenth-century historian of the west makes the following characterization:

> The French settlers indulged no ambitious visions, and laid no plans, either for territorial aggrandizement or political domination. They made no attempt to acquire land from the Indians, to organize a social system, to introduce municipal regulations, or to establish military defences....
>
> Their houses were comfortable, and they reared fruits and flowers; evincing, in this respect, an attention to comfort and luxury, which has not been practised among the English or American first settlers; but in the accumulation of property, and in all the essentials of industry, they were indolent and improvident, rearing only the bare necessaries of life, and living from generation to generation without change or improvement.[9]

Immigration to Nouvelle France had been severely restricted by the French government, who wanted only troops to contain the English, traders to carry on the fur trade necessary to support the troops, and a few farmers to grow food for the soldiers and priests. The English, the Irish, and the Scots, on the other hand, being more or less free to emigrate, wanted to come and build families and fortunes in the colonies. To accomplish this they desired, first of all, to own their own land, to grow their own crops, to owe no rent, and to work for no boss. Their philosophy, such as it was, can be summed up in the words of John Locke: "As much land as a man tills, plants, improves, cultivates, and can use the product of, so much is his property."[10]

These new Americans had little understanding or respect for the Native view of land tenure, the notion that land was owned by the community and could not be subdivided. It could be *shared* with other nations—and that was what treaties were all about—but ownership according to those treaties did not pass to the members of the other nation. This difference of worldview set the stage for conflict. Alice Beck Kehoe, a scholar of Native history in North America going back as far as the Ice Age, has these scathing words to say about Locke:

> By contrasting Europe's civil society with an alleged wild state of nature in America, Locke asserted it is God's command that Europeans take over the wilderness, labor upon it and by this means make it into private property. Deviously, uncandidly, John Locke ignored decades of his involvement in the actual business of Carolina Colony, where his employers claimed vast lands he knew were already tilled, planted, cultivated, and the products used, by Indians.[11]

What the settlers wanted was their own piece of paradise, as they saw it—the chance to own the land individually, which the Natives thought an absurd concept. And come the settlers did, from England, from Scotland and Ireland, from Europe, where land was prohibitively expensive and already engrossed (as they put it) by the rich and powerful. Here in America, they thought, they could themselves be princes of their own domain. To the large landowner, which in the Southern colonies meant a slave owner, it was as though he lived in a world of his own making, with none but God to hold him accountable:

> Besides the advantage of a pure Air, we abound in all kinds of Provisions without expence (I mean we who have Plantations). I have a large Family of my own, and my Doors are open to Every Body, yet I have no Bills to pay, and half-a-Crown will rest undisturbed in my Pocket for many Moons together. Like one of the Patriarchs, I have my Flocks and my Herds, my Bond-men and Bond-women, and every Sort of Trade amongst my own Servants, so that I live in a kind of Independence on every one but Providence. However tho' this Sort of Life is without expence, yet it is attended with a great deal of trouble. I must take care to keep all my People to their Duty, to set all the Springs in motion and to make every one draw his equal Share to carry the Machine forward. But then 'tis an amusement in this silent Country and a continual exercise of our Patience and Economy.[12]

After the Treaty of Aix-la-Chapelle in 1748, there was an uneasy peace between the French and British on both sides of the Atlantic. When Pehr Kalm, the Swedish-Finnish traveler, journeyed from Albany to Montreal, he had to cross the border between New York and New France, at great personal danger, just north of Saratoga.[13] After the Treaty of Logstown in 1752, the Ohio Company of Virginia sent out surveyors, with plans to build a fort and settle land at the Forks of the Ohio—and in due time the French got wind of this from the Indians. In response as well to the growing presence of English traders in the area, the French embarked upon a plan to build a series of forts between Lake Erie and the Mississippi, to solidify their control of the Ohio Valley. It was amid the uncertainty of this situation that George Washington was sent by Robert Dinwiddie, the Royal Governor of Virginia, to deliver a message to the French commanding officer at Fort Le Boeuf in the autumn of 1753 (at the current location of Waterford, Pennsylvania). In short, said Washington, a French presence continuing on what the British Crown considered British soil would be cause for future conflict.

The following spring, a company of Virginia militia were sent to erect a fort at the Forks of the Ohio, but on April 17, 1754, a much larger force of French soldiers arrived there and under the threat of overwhelming numbers, the British-American contingent surrendered. This marked the beginning of hostilities in what became known in the colonies as the French and Indian War. In fact, it became a world war—the Seven Years' War—and the theater of operations stretched from America to India. Washington himself was present (and perhaps gave the order) when the first shots were fired on May 28, less than a hundred miles southeast of the Forks.[14] His later experience in the war, during which he reached the rank of colonel, formed the basis for his command of the American forces during the Revolution.

Despite early French victories in America, their fleet proved inferior to the British navy, which managed to capture the Fortress at Louisbourg, Nova Scotia, and effectively blockade the mouth of the St. Lawrence Seaway. Thus deprived of goods to trade with the Indians, the French lost the support of the Midwestern nations—and without the support of Native warriors, they realized that their position at the Forks of the Ohio was indefensible. In what would become known in future wars as "strategic withdrawal," the French burned Fort Duquesne in December 1758 and retreated from the Ohio River, which they called La Belle Rivière. As the French governor-general reported to Versailles,

> All the garrisons belonging to our posts on the Beautiful river are retiring to Detroit with as much provisions, artillery, ammunition and merchandise as they can stow away in the bateaux; the surplus was given to the Indians.... All the nations of the Beautiful river witnessed with sorrow the departure of the French.[15]

The war ended with the Treaty of Paris in 1763, which transferred "ownership" of the entire half of the North American continent to the King of England. This created a power vacuum along the Ohio River valley into which the British colonists were eager to intrude. The First Nations, who had thrown their lot in with the French—thinking that in this way they could preserve their rights to their land—were tossed to the wolves in the treaty. No mention was made of them (and they would remember this twenty years later, when the same situation occurred in the Peace Treaty of 1783); by European custom, their land was considered to have passed into the hands of the British Crown, just as two decades later it would become subject to the government of the new United States. As the historian Archer Butler Hulbert reminds us, however, "While England now nominally came into possession of all of this portion of New France, the lands on either side of the Ohio River below Pittsburgh were claimed by the Indian Nations inhabiting them."[16]

After peace broke out in 1763, Pittsburgh became a thriving community, the first of the wilderness towns that sprang up to the west of the mountains, beyond the pale of eastern civilization—mostly, at first, male and testosterone-driven, filled with fur traders, Indians, and alcohol—a place where, as it was said, the restraints of civilized society lay lightly on the shoulders of men. The English and their colonies had fallen into the possession of a great span of territory stretching from the Appalachian Mountains to the Mississippi River, and from Florida north to Hudson's Bay. Slightly more than a decade later, as the French foreign minister predicted, war would break out between the mother country and the colonies:

> The consequences of the entire cession of Canada are obvious. I am persuaded England will ere long repent of having removed the only check that could keep her colonies in awe. They stand no longer in need of her protection; she will call on them to contribute toward supporting the burdens they have helped to bring on her; and they will answer by striking off all dependence.[17]

The struggle for control of the Midwest didn't end with the Peace of Paris, and indeed this conflict continued for five more decades, until the death of Tecumseh in 1815 at the Battle of the Thames.[18]

Beginning early in the eighteenth century, the British had figured out how to wage war without levying burdensome taxes, and this went a long way toward making the multiple wars of the eighteenth century more palatable to the taxpaying public. In later years it would become known as deficit financing.[19] With the assistance of the Bank of England, the Crown floated bond issues to maintain and supply a standing army and navy, helping to establish an empire where the sun never set. The downside was that, after the Seven Years' War, the King's government was faced with a debt unheard of in all previous English history, and needed greater sources of revenue to keep control of colonies which extended from Hudson's Bay to southern Georgia, and from New York to Calcutta. To accomplish this, the British devised a twofold strategy in colonial America. First, they would use the colonists to help pay off the wartime debt, changing the tax structure in ways that would prove onerous, and ultimately disastrous—and at the same time they would attempt to keep expenses down by minimizing the conflict between settlers and Native Americans. Toward this end, even before the peace treaty had been signed in Paris in 1763, the British attempted to keep squatters off the land the Crown had inherited from the French:

Proclamation by General Henry Bouquet
30 October 1761

Whereas by a Treaty held at East Town in the year 1758, and since ratified by His Majesty's Ministers, the Country to the West of the Allegany Mountains is allowed to the Indians for their Hunting Ground, and as it is of the Highest Importance to his Majesty's service, the preservation of the peace and a good understanding with the Indians, to avoid giving them any just cause of Complaint, this is therefore to forbid any of His Majesty's subjects to Settle or Hunt to the West of the Allegany Mountains on any Pretence Whatsoever, unless such Persons have obtained leave in Writing from the General or the Governor of the Provinces Respectively and produce the same to the Commanding Officer at Fort Pitt.[20]

Despite the Treaty of Easton, and Bouquet's proclamation which followed it, relations between the Nations and their new self-defined masters quickly deteriorated. Jeffrey Amherst, governor-general of British North

America, was an avowed racist—perhaps best known for giving smallpox-laden blankets to the First Nations—and he carried out restrictive trade policies.[21] In order to impose control, he put an end to the practice of traders going to the Native villages, and instead insisted that the Indians come to the military posts for their needs, which was highly inconvenient when it meant several days or weeks travel through the wilderness. Furthermore, not wanting to arm the Indians for warfare, he cut off the means with which they hunted (having long since adopted firearms in place of bows and arrows), and he considered unnecessary the traditional practice of giving "presents"— trade goods that Crown officials bestowed upon the Indians at treaties and celebrations. The Native Americans, on the other hand, saw these not as outright gifts but rather as what a good ally would provide for the men and women who supplied the furs their European brethren desired, and who looked out for the Englishmen's best interests in the woods. But Amherst was not impressed, and cut off the flow of goods.

At the same time, the First Nations perceived a British threat that had been absent under the French dominion in North America. For years the French had been saying that whereas they, the French, only wanted to do business with the Indians, supplying the good folks of Europe with beaver furs and deerskins in return for trade goods, the English actually wanted to come settle in the New World, and would, little by little, drive the game away and push the Indians off their ancestral lands. The Native Americans, being nobody's fools, saw the truth of this in what had already occurred throughout the seacoast colonies, and—further angered by Lord Amherst's policies— rose up against the British outposts throughout the Midwest in a brief but widespread insurgency known to history as Pontiac's Rebellion, though Pontiac himself was more the instrument than the initiator of the flare-up. Many outposts throughout the region were overcome in bloody attacks—all but Detroit, Niagara, and Pittsburgh, which withstood the onslaught. In a famous incident at Fort Michilimackinac, at the strait between Lakes Michigan and Huron, the Ottawa during a game of lacrosse feigned a search for a ball that had gone over the palisade, and—grabbing tomahawks from their womenfolk who had hidden them beneath their robes—proceeded to pillage the fort, killing all but the French residents they found inside. They left the French unharmed. The Indians wished for the return of Onontio, the governor of New France, whose soldiers had treated them better than the redcoats.[22]

Continuing the policy begun by Bouquet's order separating colonists from Native Americans—made all the more crucial by Pontiac's Rebellion— the King issued the Proclamation of 1763, which defined a line beyond which the colonists must not settle. Essentially, this line snaked down along the Appalachians to the west of towns and settlements already in existence. Beyond the mountains, no man could wield an ax:

Whereas it is just and reasonable, and essential to our Interest, and the Security of our Colonies, that the several Nations or Tribes of Indians with whom We are connected, and who live under our Protection, should not be molested or disturbed in the Possession of such Parts of Our Dominions and Territories as, not having been ceded to or purchased by Us, are reserved to them, or any of them, as their Hunting Grounds.

We do therefore, with the Advice of our Privy Council, declare ... that no Governor or Commander in Chief in any of our other Colonies or Plantations in America ... grant Warrants of Survey, or pass Patents for any Lands beyond the Heads or Sources of any of the Rivers which fall into the Atlantic Ocean from the West and North West.[23]

Furthermore—and this is extremely important in the light of future events—all purchases of Indian land were reserved to the Crown's prerogative, so that "no private Person do presume to make any purchase from the said Indians of any Lands reserved to the said Indians."

The only problem with this edict is that it didn't work. Though it put a temporary stop to the land speculators, as no clear title was possible, there weren't enough English soldiers along the frontier (or in the entire empire, for that matter) to enforce it on the ground. Moreover, the Proclamation created a good deal of ill will among the colonists—since Americans, particularly those who seek out the edges of civilization, don't like being told what they can't do. It would be an overstatement to suggest that the entire run-up to the American Revolution can be explained by this conflict over the western territories, but the desire to throw off the restraint to settlement imposed by the Crown reinforced the animosity already felt by the colonists to every tax measure the British imposed upon them.[24] The soldiers whom the taxes supported were in large measure responsible for keeping the Americans from their western territories—a constant source of insult and irritation.

In the fullness of time, as they say, one thing led to another, a litany that schoolchildren learn in America: the Stamp Act, the Townshend duties, the Tea Party, the Intolerable Acts, the Boston Massacre, the shots at Lexington and Concord—until, on July 3, 1776, the Continental Congress voted to approve the Declaration of Independence, and the United Colonies were reborn as "free and independent states." In the meantime, despite declarations emanating from London, the pressure of settlement continued to force its way beyond the mountains. Men and women who had been captured by the Indians—those who returned to "civilization"—brought with them stories of a paradise to the westward:

Daniel Boone:

We found everywhere abundance of wild beasts of all sorts, through this vast forest. The buffaloes were more frequent than I have seen cattle in the settlements, browsing on the leaves of the cane, or cropping the herbage on those extensive plains, fearless, because ignorant, of the violence of man. Sometimes we saw hundreds in a drove, and the numbers about the salt springs were amazing.

Richard Henderson:

About 50 yards from the river, behind my camp and a fine spring a little to the west, stands one of the finest elms that perhaps nature has ever produced. The tree is produced on a beautiful plain, surrounded by a turf of fine white clover, forming a green to the very stock. The trunk is about 4 feet through to the first branches which are about 9 feet from the ground. From thence it regularly extends its large branches on every side, at such equal distances as to form the most beautiful tree the imagination can suggest. The diameter of the branches from the extreme end is 100 feet, and every fair day it describes a semicircle in the heavenly green around it upwards of 400 feet in circumference.

Felix Walker:

A new sky and strange earth seemed to be presented to our view. So rich a soil we had never seen before; covered with clover. In full bloom, the woods were abounding with wild game—turkeys so numerous that it might be said they appeared but one flock, universally scattered in the woods....

On entering the plain we were permitted to view a very interesting and romantic sight. A number of buffaloes, of all sizes, supposed to be between two and three hundred, made off from the lick in every direction; some running, some walking, others loping slowly and carelessly, with young calves playing, skipping, and bounding through the plain. Such a sight some of us never saw before, nor perhaps never may again.[25]

Heedless of the Proclamation of 1763, the Americans poured forth. And at the same time not a few rich folks "back east" saw their own opportunity: a chance to grow fabulously wealthy by buying enormous tracts of land in advance of the rush of settlement, and being in a cozy position to sell when the settlers arrived:

George Washington to William Crawford
21 September 1767

I offered in my last to join you in attempting to secure some of the most valuable Lands in the King's part which I think may be accomplished after awhile, notwithstanding the proclamation that restrains it at present, and prohibits the settling of them at all, for I can never look upon that proclamation in any other light (but this I say between ourselves) than as a temporary expedient to quiet the minds of the Indians. It must fall, of course, in a few years, especially when those Indians are consenting to our occupying the lands. Any person, therefore, who neglects the present opportunity of hunting out good lands, and in some measure marking and distinguishing them for their own, in order to keep others from settling them, will never regain it.[26]

There began to be so much pressure from the colonists spreading westward that it was decided by the Iroquois Confederacy, otherwise known as the Haudenosaunee or Six Nations, to try to blunt the force on their homeland by deflecting settlement to the south—that is, to the south of the Ohio River. As Chief Abraham of the Mohawks said to Sir William Johnson, British Superintendent of Indian Affairs,

> We have been for some time deliberating on what you said concerning a Line between the English and us, & we are sensible it would be for our mutual advantage if it were not transgressed, but daily experience teaches us that we cannot have any great dependence on the white People, and that they will forget their agreements for the sake of our Lands.[27]

The Six Nations, it will be remembered, claimed ownership of all the lands beyond the mountains by virtue of their victories in a devastating series of Indian wars in the seventeenth century. As William Johnson explained this to the Lords of Trade,

> [The Iroquois] claim by right of conquest all the country, including the Ohio, along the great ridge of Blue mountains at the back of Virginia; thence to the head of Kentucky river and down the same to the Ohio above the rifts; thence northerly to the south end of Lake Michigan; then along the east shore to Missillimackinack; thence easterly across the north end of Lake Huron to Ottawa river and Island of Montreal.[28]

Consequently, as Archer Hulbert tells us, the British conducted the Treaty of Fort Stanwix, in 1768, with the Iroquois, "not with the Delawares and Shawanese and Southern Nations" who actually lived "and hunted there."[29]

Though Johnson was only authorized by the British government to buy the rights to land south of the Ohio as far west as the Kanawha River, the final line he and the Six Nations settled on—the deed was dated November 5, 1768—extended much further west, to the mouth of the Tennessee. This included the Kentucky River as well as the Falls of the Ohio, where Louisville now stands—that is, much of present-day Kentucky and part of Tennessee and West Virginia.[30] Most of this territory was already claimed by both the Shawnees, to the north, and the Cherokees, to the south—both of whom used Kentucky as their hunting grounds and who had in fact fought sporadically against each other for years, thus bequeathing to the future commonwealth the designation of *the dark and bloody ground*.[31] In fact, this same land had been promised to the Cherokee Nation by the Treaty of Hard Labor (signed just three weeks earlier, on October 14).[32] In exchange for all this territory, the Crown gave the Six Nations £10,000 and assorted other gifts. The Shawnees, for whom the Iroquois claimed to be bargaining, got nothing. This tended to increase the animosity which already existed between the Shawnees—and their allies the Delawares and Wyandots—and the Iroquois Confederacy. Memories are long, and this betrayal at Fort Stanwix, for that's how it seemed to the Shawnees, would prove a problem for the First Nations in the future in their attempts to unite against the settlers' encroachment.[33]

Though the land north of the Ohio continued to be Indian Country, it

The Treaty Line established at Fort Stanwix in 1768: all territory north of this line was reserved to the First Nations.

wasn't long before settlers like Daniel Boone took advantage of the new map, "to wander through the wilderness of America, in quest of the country of Kentucky."[34] By the outbreak of the Revolutionary War, according to Archer Hulbert, "the entire southern shore of the Ohio had been abandoned by Indians."[35] By contrast, the area north of the Ohio remained for the most part free of white settlement. In fact, it had been pretty much entirely depopulated during the devastation which accompanied the so-called Beaver Wars of the seventeenth century, during which the Iroquois pushed the other nations westward. These conflicts were occasioned by the overtrapping and consequent depletion of the furbearing creatures in the territory east of the

Appalachian Mountains—all to satisfy the insatiable demands of Europeans for waterproof felt hats.[36] Following the Great Peace of Montreal in 1701, however, the country beyond the Forks of the Ohio filled once again with Native peoples: Wyandots in the north, Delawares, Shawnees, and Mingos in the south, and the Miami and Piankashaw and Illinois Nations to the west.

The Shawnees were the wanderers of America—the only Indian nation whose oral history includes the story of having come across the water (perhaps from Cuba). They had, according to tradition, once occupied the Midwest but had dispersed south and east in response to the Iroquois invasion, wandering for decades until the Miamis invited them to settle on territory just east of the Wabash River.[37] Lower Shawnee Town was then established on the Ohio River at the mouth of the Scioto, but was later moved upstream for security from the groups of warriors, both Native and European, who traveled up and down the Ohio. For years the Shawnees would be at the center of the anvil where the hammer of encroaching Kentucky settlers came crashing northward, and it was they who would give birth to Tecumseh, the last great leader opposing white settlement in the Northwest Territory.

By the middle of the eighteenth century there were villages of different nations close by each other in the Ohio Country—and intermarriages. A pattern of intertribal settlement spread into the territory between the Ohio River and Lake Erie. This was not so much at the level of the towns—"Nonehelema's Town" or "Newcomer's Town"—that were composed of one extended family or clan, but rather the villages of different nations lay scattered about the landscape at particularly beautiful or convenient places, such as the portages between the Ohio and Great Lakes watersheds. At least in the time of which we're speaking, there was no exclusive "Shawnee Territory" or "Delaware Territory" or "Mingo Territory," though different nationalities were more concentrated along certain river valleys. The valley of the Muskingum and its tributaries, for example, was the home of the Delaware Nation (more properly known as the Lenape), the valley of the Scioto that of the Shawnee, and the Miami lay along the Wabash and Miami Rivers. But there were also groupings of these tribes interspersed throughout the region.[38]

Now that villages dotted the landscape, the traders came, white men and women and those of mixed race. Though we know the names of some of these individuals—Richard Butler, Alexander McKee, Matthew Elliott— most of them remain anonymous, a class of men and women who have long since vanished from the woods. We see them in our mind's eye, moccasins on their feet (more comfortable by far on forest paths than western shoes), then deerskin leggings to the thighs to protect their flesh from branches and thorns, and often a broadcloth shirt or the waistcoat of a gentleman, with a blanket worn as overcape, depending on the weather. There were also scattered among the villages tradesmen such as blacksmiths and gunsmiths, who were needed to repair the long rifles so useful for hunting, as well as white men and women who had been captured as children and raised as members of the various nations—and various other individuals who were simply tired of living in the eastern cities. One nineteenth-century historian gives this description of the scene:

> Numbers of white people, it must be noted, had early in the century ... become dispersed among the Ohio tribes in various ways and with diverse fortunes. First of all were the French traders, the *coureurs de bois*, the stragglers and deserters who drifted on the Maumee, the Sandusky, and perhaps the Cuyahoga. They left no annals nor trace, unless it be the axe-marks upon trees, or the rusty relics of guns and skillets, which occasionally puzzle the antiquarians on the lakeshore. There were many refugees also who had left the settlements under a cloud, and some of these renegades became the most ferocious enemies of the early settlers. More than all were the captives, white and black, who had been spared from the stake and adopted as members of the tribes.[39]

With this mixture of whites and Indians, it can well be said that an intercultural society was forming in "the country between," which we have come to call the Midwest. But pressure upon this society was growing in the form of settlers moving across the Appalachians or looking north across the Ohio from Kentucky. Meanwhile, conflict between the British government and the rebellious colonists along the Atlantic Seaboard necessitated a pullback of British troops from the frontier—Fort Pitt, for example, was abandoned in 1772. Just as the retreat of the French had left a power vacuum a decade earlier, so the redeployment of the redcoats left a cauldron out west that was beginning to steam.

CHAPTER 4

Now Back to the Constitutional Convention

Mr. Madison is a character who has long been in public life; and what is very remarkable every Person seems to acknowledge his greatness. He blends together the profound politician, with the Scholar. In the management of every great question he evidently took the lead in the Convention, and tho' he cannot be called an Orator, he is a most agreeable, eloquent, and convincing Speaker. From a spirit of industry and application which he possesses in a most eminent degree, he always comes forward the best informed Man of any point in debate. The affairs of the United States, he perhaps, has the most correct knowledge of, of any Man in the Union. He has been twice a Member of Congress, and was always thought one of the ablest Members that ever sat in that Council. Mr. Madison is about 37 years of age, a Gentleman of great modesty,—with a remarkable sweet temper. He is easy and unreserved among his acquaintance, and has a most agreeable style of conversation.

—William Pierce[1]

In its first, preliminary state, the Convention is meeting as a "committee of the whole"—and therefore nothing the delegates decide at this point is binding, but will instead be referred back to the whole body for further debate. Having been postponed at the end of May, on June 9 the key question of proportional representation again comes up for discussion. The debate is begun by William Paterson of New Jersey, who moves "that the Committee resume the clause relating to the rule of suffrage in the National Legislature" [Farrand, 1:176]. Paterson, a small-state delegate,

considered the proposition for a proportional representation as striking at the existence of the lesser States.... He said there was no more reason that a great individual State contributing much, should have more votes than a small one contributing little, than that a rich individual citizen should have more votes than an indigent one [178–179].

In response to Paterson, James Wilson "entered elaborately into the defence of a proportional representation, stating for his first position that as all authority was derived from the people, equal numbers of people ought to have an equal number of representatives" [179]. Wilson asserts that "this principle had been improperly violated in the Confederation, owing to the urgent circumstances of the time." He goes on to ask, "Are not the citizens of Pennsylvania equal to those of New Jersey? does it require 150 of the former to balance 50 of the latter?" [180]—and he concludes with a challenge: "If the small States will not confederate on this plan, Pennsylvania & he presumed some other States, would not confederate on any other." To give the delegates more time to consider this crucial decision, once again debate is postponed.

This is the heart of the matter. Will the new legislature look like the Confederation Congress, which has been likened to a conclave of foreign ministers of sovereign republics[2]—or will it resemble, for example, the bicameral legislature of Massachusetts, with proportional representation in one house, and the other house reflecting the interests of monied individuals? On Monday, June 11, Abraham Baldwin from Georgia takes his seat at the Convention. Baldwin is originally from Connecticut, went to college at Yale with other so-called Connecticut Wits—one of whom was the poet Joel Barlow, who in fact had married Baldwin's sister—and Baldwin remains close friends with a number of men from Connecticut.[3]

At this point in the debate, Roger Sherman of Connecticut proposes

that the proportion of suffrage in the first branch should be according to the respective numbers of free inhabitants; and that in the second branch or Senate, each State should have one vote and no more. He said as the States would remain possessed of certain individual rights, each State ought to be able to protect itself: otherwise a few large States will rule the rest [196].

The compromise that Sherman suggests will in essence constitute the ultimate solution to the dilemma (though slaves as well as free inhabitants will be counted for representation in the House, and each state will have two votes in the Senate)—but at this point that final decision is more than a month off, and no one in the room knows how the story will end. Immediately, John Rutledge responds to the suggestion that only free men be counted. Rather, he says, "the proportion of suffrage in the first branch should be according to the quotas of contribution. The justice of this rule could not be contested." Pierce Butler, also from South Carolina, "urged the same idea: adding that money was power, and that the States ought to have weight in the Govt. in proportion to their wealth." Butler is an Irish immigrant, a former major in the British army who before the Revolutionary War married a Southern heiress and became, over time, one of the largest slaveholders in the United States. Though he's a delegate from South Carolina, he also has extensive landholdings in Georgia, including two plantations on St. Simons Island.

Two of the large-state men, Wilson of Pennsylvania and Rufus King from Massachusetts, "in order to bring the question to a point, move 'that the right of suffrage in the first branch of the national Legislature ought not to be according the rule established in the articles of Confederation [that is, one vote per state], but according to some equitable ratio of representation.'" John Dickinson—a Philadelphia lawyer who is representing the three "lower counties" of Pennsylvania (which have recently split off to form the state of Delaware)—agrees with Rutledge and Butler that "the actual contributions of the States [should be] the rule of their representation & suffrage in the first branch. By thus connecting the interest of the States with their duty, the latter would be sure to be performed." That is, if the states' representation in Congress was based upon the taxes they paid, they would be sure to pay these taxes—which had been an ongoing problem in the preceding years.

The conversation is becoming more heated—which we know because just as the question is about to be put to a vote, Wilson stands up to read a lengthy comment by Benjamin Franklin—another Pennsylvania delegate—who is too infirm with gout to address the members, but who wishes to add a conciliatory note to the proceedings. He reminds his audience that

> the present method of voting by States, was submitted to originally by Congress, under a conviction of its impropriety, inequality, and injustice. This appears in the words of their Resolution. It is of Sept. 6. 1774. The words are: "Resolved that in determining questions in this Congress each colony or province shall have one vote: the Congress not being possessed of or at present able to procure materials for ascertaining the importance of each Colony" [200].

Franklin also asks that the delegates maintain their sense of courtesy and decorum:

> It has given me a great pleasure to observe that till this point, the proportion of representation, came before us, our debates were carried on with great coolness & temper. If any thing of a contrary kind has on this occasion appeared, I hope it will not be repeated; for we are sent here to *consult* not to *contend*, with each other [197].

Finally, the motion passes that the right of suffrage in the first branch of the national legislature ought to be "according to some equitable ratio of representation" [200]. Then John Rutledge, seconded by Pierce Butler, moves to add the words "according to the quotas of Contribution" [201]. James Wilson, seconded by Charles Pinckney of South Carolina, immediately proposes to substitute the actual language of the 1783 resolution, which includes the three-fifths ratio. This is the first overt mention of the three-fifths ratio at the Constitutional Convention—and is also, in my opinion, the first overt instance of Wilson and Rutledge working together to facilitate their common goals (the fact that both these motions, by Rutledge and Wilson, are seconded by South Carolina delegates serves to support this thesis). Wilson's motion, to be precise, states that

> after the words "equitable ratio of representation" the words following [should be added]: "in proportion to the whole number of white & other free Citizens & inhabitants of every age sex & condition including those bound to servitude for a term of years and three fifths of all other persons not comprehended in the foregoing description, except Indians not paying taxes, in each State," this being the rule in the Act of Congress agreed to by eleven States, for apportioning quotas of revenue on the States [201].

Elbridge Gerry of Massachusetts immediately raises an objection: that slaves, which are property in the South, are included in this formulation, but not "the cattle and horses of the North." Despite this objection, Wilson's resolution passes 9–2, with Massachusetts, Connecticut, New York, Pennsylvania, Maryland, Virginia, the Carolinas, and Georgia in the affirmative, but New Jersey and Delaware voting no.

Then debate moves to a consideration of the second branch, the Senate, and how it would be constituted. When Roger Sherman, seconded by another Connecticut delegate, Oliver Ellsworth, moves that each state have an equal, single vote, as in the Old Congress, that suggestion fails, 5–6:

> Mass. no. Conn. ay. N.Y. ay. N. J. ay. Pa. no. Del. ay. Md. ay. Va. no. N.C. no. S.C. no. Geo. no [201–202].

By themselves, the large states—Massachusetts, Pennsylvania, Virginia—can't prevail against the small states, who would like equal representation in both houses of Congress, so they need the support of at least three of the other states. Wilson's motion for proportional representation in the first chamber based on population, including three-fifths of the slaves, is supported by the southern small states, Georgia and the Carolinas, though two other small states, New Jersey and Delaware, oppose it. Even more significantly, Sherman's motion for equal representation in the Senate is supported by all the small states *except those three from the Deep South*. Consequently, when the Committee of the Whole reports on June 13 a list of items to be debated in the full Convention, and there decided upon in a binding fashion, proportional representation is the tentative rule for both houses of Congress:

> [Resolution 7.] That the rights of suffrage in the 1st. branch of the National Legislature, ought not to be according to the rule established in the articles of confederation but according to some equitable ratio of representation, namely, in proportion to the whole number of white & other free citizens & inhabitants, of every age sex and condition, including those bound to servitude for a term of years, & three fifths of all other persons, not comprehended in the foregoing description, except Indians not paying taxes in each State.

And:

[Resolution 8.] That the right of suffrage in the 2d. branch of the National Legislature ought to be according to the rule established for the first [236].

At the end of June, the delegates begin to meet "in Convention," rather than as the Committee of the Whole. In the ensuing weeks, when decisions are made as to what will go into the final document, much of the debate focuses on the dispute involving proportional and equal representation—all the earlier polite discussions being mere preamble for the rough and tumble of these sessions. These votes are for real, and perhaps forever—or at least until an amendment is approved by two-thirds of both Houses of Congress and three-fourths of the state legislatures. The conflict between the large and small states takes center stage, and only slowly does the compromise emerge— nowadays it's hard to imagine the country without it—whereby the two houses of Congress have different schemes of representation.

On June 27, John Rutledge, taking the bull by the horns, proposes postponing debate over the sixth resolution, which concerns the powers of Congress, to take up the seventh and eighth, which deal with what he calls the "most fundamental points"—that is, "the rules of suffrage in the two branches" [436]. This motion is approved without debate. Then, according to James Madison (who uses the passive voice), it was proposed that "suffrage in the first branch should be according to an equitable ratio." Here ensues a massive debate, which continues for several days, involving the benefits of proportional representation as opposed to voting by state. One of the speakers is Luther Martin, from Maryland, a man taken to heavy drinking and long-winded diatribes—and a firm believer in states' rights:

> Mr. Luther Martin contended at great length and with great eagerness that the General Government was meant merely to preserve the State Governments ... that its powers ought to be kept within narrow limits; that if too little power was given to it, more might be added; but that if too much, it could never be resumed ... that an equal vote in each State was essential to the federal idea, and was founded in justice & freedom, not merely in policy ... that the States like individuals were in a State of nature equally sovereign & free ... that the States being equal cannot treat or confederate so as to give up an equality of votes without giving up their liberty: that the propositions on the table were a system of slavery for 10 States ... [437–438].

This speech lasts for more than three hours, and at the end of that time Martin is too exhausted to finish. The next day, as James Madison reports, "Mr. L. Martin resumed his discourse, contending that the Genl. Govt. ought to be formed for the States, not for individuals" [444]. Finally, Jonathan Dayton of New Jersey and John Lansing of New York (whose population still puts it among the small states) move "to strike out 'not' so that the seventh article might read that the rights of suffrage in the 1st branch ought to be according to the rule established by the Confederation" [445]—that is, an equal vote for each state. Back to square one.

On June 29, after more fruitless discussion, Dr. William Johnson, the president of Columbia College and a delegate from Connecticut, states that "the controversy must be endless whilst gentlemen differ in the grounds of their arguments" [461]. Despite occasional prescient comments that the real conflict lies not between the large and small states but rather between North and South, the main thrust of controversy still involves proportional rather than equal representation. In the face of increasing acrimony, men worry that the Convention will fail in its task and the United States quite literally come apart at the seams. James Madison "entreated the gentlemen representing the small States to renounce a principle which was confessedly unjust … [and] to ponder well the consequences of suffering the Confederacy to go to pieces" [464].

Alexander Hamilton, a believer in the strongest possible Federal government, then observes that the small states are interested in "power" rather than "liberty"—because "there could not be any ground for combination among the States whose influence was most dreaded" [466]. Which is to say: the interests of Massachusetts, Pennsylvania, and Virginia are so diverse that they couldn't possibly agree about anything they'd want to force upon the rest of the states (other than proportional representation itself), and the small states are only interested in maintaining the unjust influence they have in a system whereby Delaware, for example, with forty thousand inhabitants, has the same weight as Pennsylvania with ten times that number.[4] Hamilton suggests that "the only considerable distinction of interests lay between the carrying & non-carrying States, which divide instead of uniting the largest States"—or in other words, between the Northern states, whose economy is based upon trade, and the Southern states, whose economy depends on the agricultural products produced by slaves. Gerry of Massachusetts agrees with him, stating that he "was a member of Congress at the time the Federal articles were formed," and only voted for equal representation "against his judgment, and under the pressure of public danger, and the obstinacy of the lesser States." He fears that the Confederation is dissolving, and "lamented that instead of coming here like a band of brothers, belonging to the same family, we seem to have brought with us the spirit of political negotiators" [467].

Finally, the delegates approve a resolution "that the rule of suffrage in the first branch ought not to be according to that established by the Articles of Confederation" [468]. The states voting aye are Massachusetts, Pennsylvania, Virginia, North Carolina, South Carolina, and Georgia—once again, the three large states and their Southern allies. Ellsworth, from Connecticut, then moves that "the rule of suffrage in the second branch be the same with that established by the Articles of Confederation" [468]. He hopes a compromise can take place, stating that the nation is in fact a twofold entity, partly "national" and partly "federal":

The proportional representation in the first branch was conformable to the national principle & would secure the large States against the small. An equality of voices was conformable to the federal principle and was necessary to secure the Small States against the large. He trusted that on this middle ground a compromise would take place. He did not see that it could on any other [468–469].

Baldwin of Georgia now speaks up. He plans to vote against Ellsworth's motion for equal representation in the second branch, he says—and the reason for this is simple: "He thought the second branch ought to be the representation of property, and that in forming it therefore some reference ought to be had to the relative wealth of their Constituents" [469–470]. This speech is consistent with the Southerners' desire for a scheme of apportionment that will take into account their human property.

Debate continues on Ellsworth's proposal. Madison asserts on June 30 that the real distinction between the states is not that they "were divided into different interests ... by their difference of size," but rather

by other circumstances, the most material of which resulted partly from climate, but principally from the effects of their having or not having slaves. These two causes concurred in forming the great division of interests in the United States. It did not lie between the large & small States: it lay between the Northern & Southern, and if any defensive power were necessary, it ought to be mutually given to these two interests [485–486].

Seeing the direction the debate is taking, Franklin once again introduces the spirit of conciliation: "When a broad table is to be made, and the edges of planks do not fit, the artist takes a little from both, and makes a good joint. In like manner here both sides must part with some of their demands, in order that they may join in some accommodating proposition" [488].

Rufus King then observes that "the simple question" is "whether each State should have an equal vote in the 2d. branch." He is, moreover, "filled with astonishment" that the delegates are ready to sacrifice national existence "to the phantom of *State* sovereignty" [489]—Luther Martin, for example, stating that he "would never confederate if it could not be done on just principles" [490]. Gunning Bedford of Delaware argues that there is "no middle way between a perfect consolidation and a mere confederacy of the States" [490]. (The word *consolidation* at the time was used as a pejorative term that, to many people, had the same sense as *totalitarian* does these days.) Bedford continues:

The little States are willing to observe their engagements, but will meet the large ones on no ground but that of the Confederation. We have been told with a dictatorial air that this is the last moment for a fair trial in favor of a good Government. It will be the last indeed if the propositions reported from the Committee go forth to the people [492].

Bedford may in fact be aware of the coalition that had been put together between the three large states and the three states of the Deep South—and his use of *dictatorial* may be an allusion to John Rutledge's alleged wartime role as the "Dictator of South Carolina."[5] There are probably others at the Convention who share this knowledge, but Bedford is the one who puts it into words. Interestingly, this speech isn't recorded by Madison, but rather by Robert Yates of New York (Abraham Yates's brother), according to whose notes Bedford asserts that the states of the Deep South have aligned themselves with the large states:

> Even the diminutive state of Georgia has an eye to her future wealth and greatness—South Carolina, puffed up with the possession of her wealth and negroes, and North Carolina, are all, from different views, united with the great states [500].

The Convention adjourns that Saturday, June 30, on a note of dissension, with no vote having taken place. The delegates have until Monday to think things over. George Mason writes Beverly Randolph, the acting governor of Virginia, that the situation is "now drawing to that point on which some of the fundamental principles must be decided, and two or three days will probably enable us to judge ... whether any sound and effectual system can be established or not."[6]

On Monday, July 2, a crucial vote takes place, and Ellsworth's motion to allow each state equal representation in the second branch fails in a tie vote. It is opposed by the usual coalition of Massachusetts, Pennsylvania, Virginia, North Carolina, and South Carolina—but surprisingly, Georgia's ballot is divided [510]. The alliance that has, so far, opposed equal state representation even in one chamber of Congress, even as part of a compromise, is showing some decay. Despite what Baldwin said three days previously, he doesn't in fact vote against the proposal for equal representation. (Notably, on this important occasion Madison actually recorded individual votes.) The math is simple: two Georgia delegates who are also members of Congress, William Few and William Pierce, have left Philadelphia for New York, so there will be a quorum in Congress to vote on important business. This leaves only two Georgia delegates in Philadelphia, William Houston and Abraham Baldwin— and since Baldwin votes *for* Ellsworth's proposal, the Georgia vote is split. Though a tie vote in this case has the same result as a negative vote—that is, the compromise fails to pass—the voting indicates cracks in a previously intact voting block. It is probable that Baldwin's Connecticut roots and close connection to William Johnson influenced his vote, and that perhaps he has taken Gunning Bedford's warnings seriously—perhaps he has realized, after talking with the Connecticut delegates, that, as Luther Martin said later, "we [of the small states] would go home, and thereby dissolve the convention, before we would give up the question."[7] In any case, according to Baldwin's biographer, "no record indicates that Baldwin ever referred to this maneuver publicly."[8]

At this juncture, Charles Pinckney, from South Carolina, expresses his anxiety: "Congress have failed in almost every effort for an amendment of the Federal system. Nothing has prevented a dissolution of it, but the appointment of this Convention; & he could not express his alarms for the consequences of such an event" [511]. Another Carolina delegate, General Charles Cotesworth Pinckney (cousin to the younger man), proposes that, in order to arrive at a solution—"the States being exactly divided on the question for an equality of votes in the 2d. branch"—a Grand Committee be appointed consisting of a member from each State, "to devise & report some compromise" [511].

This motion passes with little opposition, Sherman agreeing that the Convention is "now at a full stop" [511], and Hugh Williamson of North Carolina saying that "if we do not concede on both sides, our business must soon be at an end" [515]. To give the committee sufficient time to deliberate, the Convention adjourns until Thursday, July 5. The committee elected by the delegates consists of Elbridge Gerry of Massachusetts, Oliver Ellsworth of Connecticut, Robert Yates of New York, William Paterson of New Jersey, Benjamin Franklin of Pennsylvania, Luther Martin of Maryland, George Mason of Virginia, William Davie of North Carolina, John Rutledge of South Carolina, and Abraham Baldwin of Georgia [516]. (New Hampshire and Rhode Island are absent from the Convention.) While the committee meets, the other delegates take a day off for the Fourth of July. However uncertain the future looks, the new nation celebrates the fact that it has survived until its twelfth year.

Frustrated and "deeply distressed" by the lack of progress at the Convention, Alexander Hamilton has departed Philadelphia to pursue private business in New York—but on July 3 he writes his friend and mentor George Washington that he will return if he has "reason to believe that my attendance at Philadelphia" would aid in "rescuing the American empire from disunion, anarchy, and misery."[9]

CHAPTER 5

A Brief History
of the United Illinois
and Wabash Land Company

In the United States there is an immense quantity of land, rich, well-situated and in a salubrious climate. This land lies useless and unimproved from the want of labour and capital and stock.

In Europe there is an abundance of labour and capital and stock; but rich and well-situated land cannot be obtained, unless at a very high price.

A plan, by which the surplus labour and stock and capital of Europe would be employed on the unimproved lands of the United States, must be eminently advantageous to both.

It might be carried on to an extent, and with a degree of certainty and system unknown to transactions of any other kind: and the profits of it would be greater than those, which could be expected from any continued series of mercantile speculations....

The extent of the plan may be measured by the millions of acres, which could be furnished by the United States; and by the millions of men and of money which could be furnished by Europe.

—James Wilson[1]

In 1773—despite the Proclamation of 1763, which prohibited settlement in or ownership of land to the west of the Appalachian Divide—a group of investors, dealing through an individual named John Murray, transacted a purchase of land just east of the Mississippi River from some friendly chiefs of the Illinois Nation who claimed to speak for the tribe. Two separate parcels were involved: one along the Illinois River upstream from its mouth, and one at the confluence of the Ohio and Mississippi. These investors included the Gratz and Franks brothers of Philadelphia, and across the Atlantic, their cousins the Franks brothers in London, all well-established merchants. They called themselves the Illinois Company, and included as well Robert Morris, who would later become known as the Financier of the Revolution (and later still was a delegate to the Constitutional Convention), and Silas Deane, an American purchasing agent who accompanied Ben Franklin to Paris on his wartime diplomatic mission. Two years later, in 1775, another group of investors—including many of the same men—purchased two more parcels of land from some Piankashaw chiefs, and this group styled itself the Wabash Company. These two parcels, a good deal further east than the Illinois Company's land, lay adjacent to the settlement at Vincennes (one north and one south of it), along both banks of the Wabash River.[2]

These two companies, as we've seen previously, joined forces in 1779 and became the United Illinois and Wabash Land Company. Their president, James Wilson, was also their largest shareholder, and his one-and-a-half shares would entitle him to at least a million of the acres the company claimed, if their title to the land were approved.[3] That same year, however—as we've also seen—the recently independent Commonwealth of Virginia, which had not yet ceded its claim to the territory north of the Ohio River, issued a proclamation outlawing individual land purchases from the Indian Nations, and subsequently denied the claims of the Illinois and Wabash Company. After this, the company took its fight to Congress, but until the end of the war Congress had other matters to deal with.

From the very start of the Revolution, the "empty" land of the west had figured greatly in the Patriots' vision. In *Common Sense*, Tom Paine explained why the time was ripe for independence:

> Another reason why the present time is preferable to all others, is, that the fewer our numbers are, the more land there is yet unoccupied, which, instead of being lavished by the King on his worthless dependents, may be hereafter applied, not only to the discharge of the present debt, but to the constant support of government. No nation under heaven hath such an advantage as this.[4]

The new Federal government, as Paine suggested, viewed in land a valuable and unique resource with which to pay off war debts—but before the fledgling Republic could take advantage of this enormous territory, the individual states first had to yield their claims. Some states, such as Virginia, had claims to this land based upon their colonial charters, but others, such as Maryland and Pennsylvania, were lacking in this regard—the so-called landless states. It's important to note here that even early in the war, Congress intended that this territory—despite its status as "Indian Country" following the Treaty of Fort Stanwix—would ultimately be divided into states equivalent in nature to the original thirteen:

Tuesday, October 10, 1780

Resolved, That the unappropriated lands that may be ceded or relinquished to the United States, by any particular states ... shall be granted and disposed of for the common benefit of the United States and be settled and formed into distinct republican states, which shall become members of the federal union, and have the same rights of sovereignty, freedom and independence, as the other states.[5]

Furthermore, according to Congress, "no purchases and deeds from any Indians or Indian Nations, for lands within the Territory to be ceded or relinquished ... shall be deemed valid or ratified by Congress"—which boded ill for the Illinois and Wabash claims. This resolution was supported vociferously by Maryland, whose delegates made the "landed" states' promise to relinquish their claims a sine qua non for Maryland's approval of the Articles of Confederation. In fact, the main impediment to the final passage of the Articles in 1781 consisted of this disagreement about the western lands; the Articles only took effect once they were ratified by *all* the states, and the last state to do so was Maryland.[6]

Though the war in the east for the most part ended in the fall of 1781 with Cornwallis's surrender at Yorktown, it continued throughout 1782 in the area west of the Appalachians. There was a particularly brutal massacre by American militia of ninety-two unarmed Christian Indians—entire families cudgeled to death, one by one, in the church of the small community of Gnadenhutten (in present-day Ohio), to which they'd returned to harvest their corn in the midst of a brutal winter.[7] And the following summer, Indian warriors—on an expedition of revenge against the Kentucky settlements—ambushed and killed more than seventy Kentucky militiamen, among them one of Daniel Boone's sons, at a river crossing known as Blue Licks. Animosities out west were still running high when the peace treaty was ratified in 1783.

Simon Girty had been a trader and translator before the war, working out of Pittsburgh. Along with two other traders, Alexander McKee and Matthew Elliott, he went over to the British side, believing that the Indians, among whom he had been raised, would probably get better treatment under a British government than they would if the Americans prevailed in the struggle. He and several other British soldiers accompanied the Native warriors on their expedition to Kentucky, and before the Battle of Blue Licks, Girty exhorted the warriors:

> Brothers, the intruders ... are planting fruit trees and ploughing the lands where not long since were the cane break and the clover field. Were there a voice in the trees of the forest, or articulate sounds in the gurgling waters, every part of this country would call on you to chase away these ruthless invaders, who are laying it waste. Unless you rise in the majesty of your might, and exterminate their whole race, you may bid adieu to the hunting ground of your fathers, to the delicious flesh of the animals with which they once abounded, and to the skins with which you were once enabled to purchase your clothing and your rum.[8]

One of the final accomplishments of the Revolutionary War years, if one can call it that, was an item that would only add to the Native Americans' displeasure—the completion of Mason and Dixon's line separating Pennsylvania from Virginia. In October 1767, those two English surveyors had been told by a representative of the Six Nations not to proceed "one step further" when they got as far as the Great Warrior's Path along the west side of the Allegheny Mountains, and it still wasn't clear where Pennsylvania ended and Virginia began.[9] Fifteen years later, in November 1782, surveyors from Virginia and Pennsylvania finally extended the line to its terminus at the southwest corner of Pennsylvania, and from there ran the Pennsylvania boundary north to the Ohio River.[10] This so-called Geographer's Line now like a stiletto pierced to the heart of Indian Country, and—having established what surveyors call a Point of Beginning—it would allow Americans to begin the task of parceling out the entire Northwest Territory. From that moment, the First Nations in the Midwest can date their dispossession.

Also in 1782, with the war winding down, Congress could turn its attention to the claim of the United Illinois and Wabash Land Company to their purchases in the Ohio Country. This claim was summarily dismissed by a committee, because "the said purchases were made of certain Indians without any public treaty or other proper act of notoriety."[11] When the war ended, as when it began, Congress was still looking at the western territory as a common resource which "if properly managed ... will be a means of restoring national credit."[12] In 1784, when Virginia followed the recommendation of Congress and ceded its territory north of the Ohio to the Federal government, its delegates wanted Congress to affirm Virginia's previous ownership of the territory, which was the state's legal basis for voiding the claim of the Illinois and Wabash Company. Congress, however—divided into factions by delegates having interests in several different land companies—chose not to do so.[13] This left the door open for James Wilson to keep pressing for validation of the Company's legal ownership, and even after Wilson's death in 1796 the Company continued to press its claim, though it was consistently denied by Congress.[14] Finally, the matter ended up in the Supreme Court of the United States, in the famous case of *Johnson v. M'Intosh,* where in 1823 the issue would be settled and the claim finally disallowed.[15]

The United Illinois and Wabash Company wasn't alone in its desire for Ohio Country land. The Treaty of Paris left the new nation with an enormous domain, extending westward to the Mississippi and north as far the Great Lakes, which formed a watery roof over the Midwest—but there was no mention in the Treaty of the Indians' right to any of that territory. Now that the bullets had stopped, Americans began looking at the western country with hopes and expectations. As George Washington wrote Rufus Putnam in the beginning of June 1783, "I am endeavoring to do something with the lands I now hold and have held in that country these twelve or fourteen years."[16]

When news of the peace first arrived in Indian Country, it didn't take the Nations long to realize that they'd drawn the short straw, despite the terms of the Treaty of Fort Stanwix which the Haudenosaunee had made with the Crown in 1768, and despite the fact that many nations had remained loyal and fought long and hard on the side of the British. As one general wrote to Frederick Haldimand, governor of Quebec,

> The Indians from the surmises they have heard of the boundaries, look upon our conduct to them as treacherous and cruel; they told me they never could believe that our King could pretend to cede to America what was not his own to give, or that the Americans would accept from him what he had no right to grant.[17]

In June 1783, at an Indian Council at Detroit—which still remained in British hands—a member of the Ouiatenon Nation summed it up this way to the commanding officer: "Father! ... in endeavoring to assist you it seems we have wrought our own ruin."[18] Nonetheless, Sir John Johnson of the British Indian Agency—son of William Johnson—tried to reassure the Crown's sometime allies:

> You are not to believe or even think that by the line which has been described, it was meant to deprive you of an extent of country of which the right of soil belongs to you and is in yourselves as sole proprietors ... neither can I harbor an idea that the United States will act so unjustly or unpolitically as to endeavor to deprive you of any part of your country under the pretense of having conquered it.[19]

Despite what the English wanted the Indians to believe, the Americans had other ideas. After the war, an economic depression along the eastern seaboard had the effect of pushing even more people to seek a new home across the mountains. Joseph Hadfield, an English merchant visiting the United States to try to collect on his father's accounts, described in his journal "the distraction and low state of public and private credit, owing to the number of failures which daily take place."[20] As the country was in no financial condition to wage further war, Congress needed to ensure that peace prevailed with the Midwestern nations. Even so, the Americans from the start took a belligerent tone with their neighbors:

> *Resolved*, That the Secretary at War take the most effectual measures to inform the several Indian Nations, on the frontiers of the United States ... that unless they immediately cease all hostilities against the citizens of these states, and accept of these friendly proffers of peace, Congress will take the most decided measures to compel them thereto.[21]

It was clear to some foresighted people what the future held, one American general reporting to another that, in July and August alone, "great numbers of men have crossed the Ohio, and have made actual settlements in different places from the Muskingum to the Wabash. This will, in all probability, renew the Indian war."[22] Similarly, George Washington had concerns about allowing a wide extended country to be over run with land jobbers, speculators, and monopo-lisers or even with scatter'd settlers.... For the people engaged in these pursuits with-out contributing in the smallest degree to the support of government, or considering themselves as amenable to its laws, will involve it by their unrestrained conduct, in inextricable perplexities, and more than probable in a great deal of bloodshed.[23]

In short, it was essential that squatters remain on the south side of the Ohio. Following this line of reasoning, on September 22, 1783, Congress issued a proclamation to "prohibit and forbid all persons from making set-tlements on lands inhabited or claimed by Indians."[24] A proclamation, how-ever, was all Congress could muster. In reality, there was barely enough money in the coffers to pay for a scattering of troops to keep the peace between the Indians and the encroaching settlers—despite the hope that Federal land sales would lift the country out of debt and allow the new Republic to take its place among the great nations of the world. According to one congressman, "if we consider the value of our western territory which contains an extent of nearly five hundred thousand square miles ... our present debt ... [is] but a mere baggatelle to the wealth of this Country."[25] For the time being, however, faced with a chronic shortage of cash, Congress—with a single regiment of sol-diers—needed somehow to keep settlers and Indians from killing each other all along the frontier:

We had before us authentic information of continual & extensive emigrations made into a Country which unless otherwise dispos'd of, would not only remain profitless to the United States, but would become a prey to lawless banditti & adventurers, who must necessarily have involv'd us in continued Indian wars.[26]

Unfortunately, no law-abiding buyer would purchase western land while a state of war existed—but to raise money for more troops to keep the peace, the states had to grant to the Federal government the all-important right to levy taxes. If that occurred, sales of western land would yield a windfall.

CHAPTER 6

Under the Articles of Confederation

Our situation is truly delicate and critical. On the one hand, we stand in need of a strong federal government, founded on principles that will support the prosperity and union of the Colonies. On the other, we have struggled for liberty and made costly sacrifices at her shrine and there are still many among us who revere her name too much to relinquish, beyond a certain medium, the rights of man for the dignity of government.

—Mercy Warren[1]

Under the Articles of Confederation, the United States had no power to levy taxes. Its only source of revenue was to "requisition" the thirteen states. In its yearly budgets, Congress stated the amounts that each state was to provide for the common treasury—but there was no enforcement procedure. Funds were slow in coming; more often than not, the money never came at all.

From the very beginning of the Republic, the questions of taxation and representation proved vexing to the members of Congress, in large part due to the issues raised by chattel ownership of human beings. To begin at the beginning: after hostilities broke out between Crown and colonies, it quickly became apparent that this was a desperate situation. Colonial militias alone could not defeat the British war machine—but how would the new nation raise an army, how would it pay its bills? There was a need for some sort of central government to run the show. Even the Continental Army, at best, could only stave off defeat long enough for the English people to grow weary of war. Only by *not losing* the war could George Washington and his troops succeed in winning it—but for this they would need financial and military assistance from the French government, and loans from Dutch bankers. Long before Cornwallis's surrender at Yorktown, it was necessary that there be a system of government in place for the thirteen disparate colonies.

Due to what they saw as a long history of oppression by the Crown, the Revolutionaries were opposed to a strong governing power, and hesitant to give the new national government the power to levy taxes. A system was needed that would somehow induce individual states to willingly part with their cash. Equally urgent was the question of how to apportion representation in the new national legislature. As John Adams commented in September 1774, "If we vote by Colonies, this method will be liable to great inequality and injustice; for five small Colonies, with one hundred thousand people in each, may outvote four large ones, each of which has five hundred thousand inhabitants."[2] That same month, the Continental Congress arrived at the initial compromise that did indeed give each colony one vote, though there had to be at least two delegates in agreement for this vote to be counted:

> Resolved, That in determining questions in this Congress, each Colony or Province shall have one Vote.—The Congress not being possess'd of, or at present able to procure proper materials for ascertaining the importance of each Colony.[3]

This was a stopgap measure that pleased few people, least of all the delegates from the largest states of Massachusetts, Pennsylvania, and Virginia. But it was the best they could do at the time, for the very reasons that later beset the men at the Constitutional Convention: whether to count slaves, and whether (or how) to include wealth in the formula for apportionment—including, of course, the wealth represented by human property. As Patrick Henry said in the debates on September 5, "Slaves are to be thrown out of the question, and if the freemen can be represented according to their numbers, I am satisfied." Thomas Lynch of South Carolina responded that he differed "in one point from the gentleman from Virginia, that is, in thinking that numbers only ought to determine the weight of Colonies." In Lynch's opinion, "it ought to be a compound of numbers and property that should determine the weight of the Colonies."[4] The method that Congress settled upon, one vote per state, was considered a temporary solution, and "an entry was made on the Journals to prevent its being drawn into precedent in future."[5]

After the shooting war broke out at Lexington and Concord the following April, Congress had to decide how to apportion the expenses of a military struggle. Quite literally under the gun, Congress resolved on July 29, 1775, "That the proportion or quota of each colony be determined according to the number of Inhabitants, of all ages, including negroes and mulattoes in each colony."[6] When the time came to make this a more formal agreement in the Articles of Confederation, questions arose. There were disagreements about the best way to assess the population—specifically, whether a slave should be counted the same as a free person. Though every state contained slaves and slaveholders, attitudes differed based upon the size of a given state's slave population, which ranged from small in New England to considerable in the South (nearly fifty percent in Virginia and well over that in South Carolina: eighty to ninety percent in some coastal districts). Those from the South believed that a slave's labor was less valuable than that of a free man or woman, as he or she had no incentive to work, other than the lash, while those in the North generally felt that population was to be considered a placeholder, so to speak, for the financial clout of the province—and therefore slaves should be counted the same as free whites in the equation.[7]

Reading the accounts of these early debates we see foreshadowings of the arguments from Philadelphia in 1787, sometimes from the very same people: Roger Sherman from Connecticut, James Wilson from Pennsylvania. From the start, we see disagreements that will arise again in the course of the next decade—how to count population, how to measure the relative worth of free and slave labor. We should note that here in the discussions over taxation, the Northerners wanted slaves counted fully with white men, and the Southerners wanted to reduce their relative value. This sentiment would be reversed when it came to apportionment for voting purposes: in the Constitutional Convention, the Southerners wanted slaves counted fully, and the Northerners would have preferred that they not be counted at all.

Furthermore, in these debates of 1776, we see the Southern delegates threatening secession, *even before there is any formal nation to secede from.* As Thomas Lynch said, "If it is debated whether [our] slaves are [our] property, there is an end of the confederation."[8] Franklin's reply to this is trenchant: "Slaves rather weaken than strengthen the State, and there is therefore some difference between them and sheep; sheep will never make any insurrections." In fact, the fear of slave insurrections was common currency below the Mason-Dixon line. There were slave patrols out at night to make sure that black folks didn't meet in the woods to plan revolt, as had already occurred in the Stono Rebellion in Georgia, in 1739. These patrols were drawn from the able-bodied men in the state militias, and the fear was so prevalent that slaves would take control of the armories before the alarm could be sounded that each patrol member was obligated to keep his firearm at home.[9] From this point of view the right to keep deadly weapons in one's house was not so much to fight off foreign invaders or a Federal army moving in from out of state—since for that purpose arms could be kept under lock and key in the local armories, to be distributed when enemy ships were spied on the horizon—but rather to guard against an "enemy" much closer to home.

So rancorous did the debate get in 1776 over the relative value of slave and free labor that Congress decided finally to scrap the whole notion of basing taxes upon population and instead assess each state according to the value of all surveyed real estate. This method also presented a problem, however: who would assess it and by what standard? Though this issue was clear from the start to the members of Congress (and ultimately proved to be intractable), the racial problem in counting population was so difficult that even a potentially corrupt system seemed preferable, or at least it was one that the delegates could agree upon. Not until October 1777 did Congress finalize the means by which to apportion expenses. The costs of government were to be shared as defined in Article 8 of the Articles of Confederation:

> All charges of war, and all other expenses that shall be incurred for the common defense or general welfare, and allowed by the United States in Congress assembled, shall be defrayed out of a common treasury, which shall be supplied by the several States in proportion to the value of all land within each State, granted or surveyed for any person, as such land and the buildings and improvements thereon shall be estimated according to such mode as the United States in Congress assembled, shall from time to time direct and appoint.[10]

It should be noted here that the taxes were to be assessed and collected by state, not Federal authorities. Nor were there any enforcement procedures: the Federal government could requisition, but lacked the means to force collection of those monies should any or all of the state governments prove to be deadbeats. In fact, this property-based method of tax assessment was unworkable from the start; not only did the value of land vary considerably from North to South, but there was also a natural tendency to downgrade one's own tax assessment at the expense of one's neighbors. *Quis custodiet ipsos custodes?* Who would supervise the assessors?—or rather, if the states themselves supervised them, who was to keep the states from soft-pedaling the amounts they owed? These questions were never answered and the assessments, let alone the money, never materialized.

The flip side of the question of valuation for tax assessment was that of how to assess the importance of each state for voting purposes. As John Adams wrote his wife, Abigail, "One great question is, how we shall vote—whether each Colony shall count [as] one; or whether each shall have a weight in proportion to its number, or wealth, or exports and imports, or a compound ratio of all?"[11] The initial decision to give each colony one vote—made in 1774 under the pressure of circumstance—was restated in 1776 in the draft Articles of Confederation. In the debates over this item, we see the same arguments that would appear eleven years later in the Constitutional Convention. As Samuel Chase of Maryland summarized the situation, "the larger colonies had threatened they would not confederate at all if their weight in Congress should not be equal to the numbers of people they added to the confederacy; while the smaller ones declared against a union if they did not retain an equal vote for the protection of their rights."[12] And Roger Sherman proposed the solution that he would again propose in 1787: "The vote should be taken two ways; call the Colonies, and call the individuals, and have a majority of both."[13]

In the end, not being able to agree upon a means to allocate power proportionately to either wealth or population, Congress in Article 5 retained the formulation first settled upon in 1774, with the word *colony* changed to *state*: "In determining questions in the United States in Congress assembled, each State shall have one vote."[14] Furthermore, as finally determined in Article 9, Congress could make no important decisions, such as borrowing money or going to war, or entering into treaties and alliances, "unless nine States assent to the same." As for amending the document, Article 13 stated that no alteration was possible "unless such alteration be agreed to in a Congress of the United States, and be afterwards confirmed by the legislatures of every State." Since any change would require a unanimous decision, such amendments were a virtual impossibility. Even the consent of nine states, necessary for important fiscal and diplomatic decisions, would turn out to be pretty much beyond the reach of this legislative body.

There was another pressing issue in August 1776, and that was the problem of attracting troops to the army, which at that moment was having a devil of a time contending with British forces in the Battle of Long Island. Washington was forced to give way, and only by the slimmest of chances did he manage to withdraw his troops across the Hudson River to the relative safety of New Jersey. From this juncture, therefore, date the land bounties given for military service. On September 16, 1776, it was resolved "that Congress make provision for granting lands ... to the officers and soldiers who shall so engage in the service, and continue therein to the close of the war."[15] The amounts of land ranged from five hundred acres for a colonel down to one hundred for each noncommissioned officer and soldier. These land bounties would prove to be of immense importance in the postwar settlement of the western territories.

By 1783 the war was finished and it had become clear that the system designed to raise money for the Federal government was unworkable. Quite simply, the states had not responded adequately to the requisitions that Congress had imposed under the Articles of Confederation, and during the winter and spring of that year Congress focused on a better way of raising money. The new nation was faced with war debts in the neighborhood of forty million dollars—not including the debts of the various states, which constituted several more tens of millions—as well as the ongoing expenses, civil and military, of the Federal government. (These were enormous sums in the eighteenth century for a government unable to levy taxes, two orders of magnitude greater than the figures themselves would suggest: that is, *billions* in twenty-first-century dollars.) The country's credit was exhausted, and creditors, both domestic and foreign, were demanding a repayment scheme before they would commit to more loans.[16]

From the states' point of view, however, they had no "extra" money to forward to Congress, for they themselves were facing huge debts, having borne the expense of raising and supplying militia—and the taxpayers, as in western Massachusetts, were on the verge of revolt.[17] By this time the so-called Impost, a five percent duty on imports—the approval of which required a unanimous vote of the states—had already gone down to defeat once, in 1781.[18] This would have enabled the Federal government to levy taxes directly, rather than merely continue to request money from the states. But fear abounded that if the Federal government were to get that power, and with it the ability to support an army independent of state support—who knew what the end result would be? As Arthur Lee of Virginia expressed his opposition, "No one who had ever opened a page or read a line on the subject of liberty, could be insensible to the danger of surrendering the purse into the same hands which held the sword."[19] And his colleague George Mason, close friend of George Washington and future delegate to the Constitutional Convention, shared this sentiment: "When the same man or set of men holds both the sword and the purse, there is an end of liberty."[20]

In 1783, the effort in Congress to raise money was twofold: first, to amend the proposal to tax imports so that all the states might accept it this time around, and also to find a way of assessing yearly requisitions that might prove more workable than a tax on real estate. Congress returned to the old debate about assessing taxes on the relative size of the states' population, which would be an easier index to measure if they could figure out whom to count. Since requisitions, under the existing rubric, were applied to each state in proportion to the monetary value of its real estate, it seemed only fair to assess a population with the same thing in mind—that is, the value of a person's labor. And here the debate, once again, centered around the "peculiar species of property"—which is to say, the relative worth of slave and free labor. Northerners, as previously, would have liked to count slaves equally with other inhabitants for tax purposes, but Southerners, once again, demurred. After lengthy and acrimonious debate, Congress settled upon the compromise ratio of three freemen to every five slaves. In this way, the three-fifths compromise became enshrined in American legislation four years before the Constitutional Convention. At this time, it pertained only to taxation, and the arguments ended up being turned on their head in 1787 when the debate involved apportionment for voting purposes.

In 1783, Congress was meeting in the State House in Philadelphia, and the speakers, many of them, were the same individuals who would four years later be heard in the very same building—John Rutledge and James Wilson and James Madison, to name three. The questions raised here—involving money and power, and how to reconcile the two—would reverberate throughout the next four years until, in 1787, they could no longer be denied, and the solutions, such as they were, would pass into the legal structure of the

Federal government. Just as four years hence, James Madison in 1783 took copious notes for posterity's sake, and he is for this reason instrumental in what we now know about the political evolution of this country. Because of his scribbling efforts, we can listen in on the first discussion of what would later become the three-fifths compromise in the Constitution.

On March 27, Madison assessed the difficulty, saying that he "thought the value of land, could never be justly or satisfactorily obtained; that it would ever be a source of contentions among the States ... unless exchanged for a more simple rule."[21] In response, James Wilson reminded the members that "he was in Congress when the Article of Confederation directing a value of land was agreed to," and that the problem in choosing population as a means of assessment then lay in "the impossibility of compromising the different ideas of the Eastern and Southern States as to the value of Slaves compared with the Whites." And so the matter was sent to committee, where the discussion, once again, returned to the relative value of free and slave labor. On March 28, the committee reported back.

Here is the account as taken directly from Madison's notes:

The Committee last mentioned reported that two blacks be rated as equal to one freeman.

Mr. Wolcott [Connecticut] was for rating them as 4 to 3.

Mr. Carroll [Maryland] as 4 to 1.

Mr. Williamson [North Carolina] said he was principled against slavery; and that he thought slaves an incumbrance to Society instead of increasing its ability to pay taxes.

Mr. Higginson [Massachusetts] as 4 to 3.

Mr. Rutledge [South Carolina] said, for the sake of the object he would agree to rate slaves as 2 to 1, but he sincerely thought 3 to 1 would be a juster proportion.

Mr. Holten [Massachusetts] as 4 to 3.

Mr. Osgood [Massachusetts] said he could not go beyond 4 to 3.

On a question for rating them as 3 to 2 the votes were:

N.H., ay. Mas., no. R.I., divided. Cont., ay. N.J., ay. Pa., ay. Delr., ay. Maryd, no. Virga., no. N.C., no. S.C., no. [5 aye, 5 no, 1 divided.]

After some further discussions on the report in which the necessity of some simple and practicable rule of apportionment came fully into view, Mr. Madison said that in order to give a proof of the sincerity of his professions of liberality, he would propose that Slaves should be rated as 5 to 3.

Mr. Rutledge [South Carolina] seconded the motion.

Mr. Wilson [Pennsylvania] said he would sacrifice his opinion to this compromise.

Mr. Lee [Virginia] was against changing the rule, but gave it as his opinion that 2 slaves were not equal to 1 freeman.

On the question for 5 to 3 it passed in the affirmative:

N.H. ay. Mass. divided. R.I., no. Cont. no. N.J. ay. Pa., ay. Maryd, ay. Va. ay. N.C. ay. S.C. ay. [7 aye, 2 no, 1 divided.][22]

Finally, on April 18, 1783, Congress passed the proposal to alter Article

8 of the Articles of Confederation, and it was sent out to the states for approval. Though it was never ratified by all thirteen, and hence did not become the law of the land, it introduced the three-fifths ratio to the country at large:

> All charges of war, and all other expenses, that have been, or shall be, incurred for the common defence or general welfare, and allowed by the United States in Congress assembled ... shall be defrayed out of a common treasury, which shall be supplied by the several states in proportion to the whole number of white and other free citizens and inhabitants, of every age, sex, and condition, including those bound to servitude for a term of years, and three-fifths of all other persons not comprehended in the foregoing description, except Indians not paying taxes.[23]

CHAPTER 7

Philadelphia in July

Mr. Wilson ranks among the foremost in legal and political knowledge. He has joined to a fine *genius* all that can set him off and show him to advantage. He is well acquainted with Man, and understands all the passions that influence him. Government seems to have been his peculiar Study, all the political institutions of the World he knows in detail, and can trace the causes and effects of every revolution from the earliest stages of the Grecian commonwealth down to the present time. No man is more clear, copious, and comprehensive than Mr. Wilson, yet he is no great Orator. He draws the attention not by the charm of his eloquence, but by the force of his reasoning. He is about 45 years old.

—William Pierce[1]

In Philadelphia, the Convention reconvenes a day after the July 4 recess. The Grand Committee has considered the clause about apportionment, and Elbridge Gerry reports a proposal which has come to be known as the Great Compromise: "That in the first branch of the Legislature each of the States now in the Union shall be allowed one member for every 40,000 inhabitants of the description reported in the seventh resolution of the Committee of the whole House"—which is to say, including the three-fifths ratio—and "in the second Branch of the Legislature each State shall have an equal Vote" [Farrand, 1:524].[2] Significantly, this proposal does not apply to future states to be formed out of the western territory.

This is an all-or-nothing deal: part of the report states that the "propositions be recommended to the Convention, on condition that both shall be generally adopted" [524]—and it also includes protection for the wallets of the large states in the proscription that "all bills for raising or appropriating money ... shall originate in the first branch of the Legislature" [524]. James Madison indicates in his notes that the whole compromise had been suggested to the Committee by Ben Franklin [526].

However, Madison doesn't like the compromise: "He conceived that the

Convention was reduced to the alternative of either departing from justice in order to conciliate the smaller States ... or of displeasing these by justly gratifying the larger States" [527–528]. He also warns the Convention that they will need to produce a document that a majority of people in the states will approve, and that it would be "in vain to purchase concord in the Convention on terms which would perpetuate discord among their Constituents" [528]. Gouverneur Morris, another large-state delegate, also disapproves of the proposal. As Madison reports, he "thought the form as well as the matter of the Report objectionable.... He conceived the whole aspect of it to be wrong."

> He came here as a Representative of America; he flattered himself he came here in some degree as a Representative of the whole human race; for the whole human race will be affected by the proceedings of this Convention. He wished gentlemen to extend their views beyond the present moment of time; beyond the narrow limits of place from which they derive their political origin [529].

And like Madison, Morris issues a warning, though this goes beyond the fear that the country will reject the Constitution:

> This Country must be united. If persuasion does not unite it, the sword will. He begged that this consideration might have its due weight. The scenes of horror attending civil commotion can not be described, and the conclusion of them will be worse than the term of their continuance. The stronger party will then make traitors of the weaker; and the Gallows & Halter will finish the work of the sword [530].

This is the first time at the Convention that the abyss opens before the men, that they are confronted openly with the possibility of what might arise if they fail in their task. Elbridge Gerry, from Massachusetts, agrees that the situation is indeed dire: "If we do not come to some agreement among ourselves some foreign sword will probably do the work for us" [532].

Sharing this concern, Gunning Bedford of Delaware favors the proposal: "The condition of the U. States requires that something should be immediately done. It will be better that a defective plan should be adopted, than that none should be recommended" [532]. Another small-state man, Oliver Ellsworth of Connecticut, also lauds the report of the Grand Committee, saying that "he had not attended the proceedings of the Committee, but was ready to accede to the compromise they had reported. Some compromise was necessary; and he saw none more convenient or reasonable" [532]. Finally, George Mason, a delegate from Virginia who was also a member of the Grand Committee, states that the report "was meant not as specific propositions to be adopted, but merely as a general ground of accommodation." He too insists on the necessity of compromise:

> There must be some accommodation on this point, or we shall make little further progress.... It could not be more inconvenient to any gentleman to remain absent

from his private affairs, than it was for him: but he would bury his bones in this city rather than expose his Country to the Consequences of a dissolution of the Convention without anything being done [533–534].

Given what Mason says here, it is ironic that he was one of the men who did not sign the final document.

The delegates now turn specifically to the clause having to do with the first branch—that is, the ratio of one member for every forty thousand inhabitants. And it is here that Gouverneur Morris, delegate from Pennsylvania and one of the wealthiest men in the nation, speaks up in defense of the rights of property. He objects to using population as the "scale of apportionment," and thinks property ought also to be taken into account:

Life and liberty were generally said to be of more value, than property. An accurate view of the matter would nevertheless prove that property was the main object of Society ... which could only be secured by the restraints of regular Government. These ideas might appear to some new, but they were nevertheless just. If property then was the main object of Govt. certainly it ought to be one measure of the influence due to those who were to be affected by the Government [533].

As I've suggested, this is a topic also close to the heart of the delegates from Georgia and the Carolinas—and by extension to James Wilson, who is attempting to forge an alliance with the Southern delegates. Though Wilson will argue against taking property into account in any way but by the counting of population, he is well aware that it is a key element in the Southerners' thinking.

Gouverneur Morris then raises the issue of western territory, and the "range of New States which would soon be formed in the west," which have been left out of the proposal concerning apportionment. Specifically, he says that they "will have an interest in many respects different.... Provision ought therefore to be made to prevent the maritime States from being hereafter outvoted by them" [533–534].

John Rutledge agrees: "The gentleman last up had spoken some of his sentiments precisely. Property was certainly the principal object of Society. If numbers should be made the rule of representation, the Atlantic States will be subjected to the Western" [534]. Rutledge then moves to postpone the first clause of the report "in order to take up the following, *viz.*, 'That the suffrages of the several States be regulated and proportioned according to the sums to be paid towards the general revenue by the inhabitants of each State respectively.'" In making this proposal, Rutledge has attempted to bring the debate back to the important notion—crucial to him and his colleagues from the South—that wealth (including slave property) be included in any scheme of apportionment.

At this point, John Lansing's notes of the Convention—which are not included in Farrand's *Records*—quote a statement that Pierce Butler makes while seconding Rutledge's motion, a speech that Madison, in fact, omits in his notes. According to Lansing, Butler tells the assembly, "You may either take this Rule or [the] whole Number of Whites and Slaves."[3] As I read this, it seems a belligerent, in-your-face sort of comment, rejecting any notion of compromise. Butler was probably speaking loudly when he said it, and one imagines that it would have been a hard comment for Madison to miss. Perhaps he felt that his account would be inflammatory enough without it. (In fact, James Madison didn't allow his notes to become public until after his death in 1837.)

Responding to Gouverneur Morris and John Rutledge's desire to limit the influence of future western states, George Mason now states that "he was himself decidedly of opinion that if they made a part of the Union, they ought to be subject to no unfavorable discriminations. Obvious considerations required it" [534]. Mason's words can be interpreted in the light of his being a very rich, slave- and land-holding Virginian, owning tens of thousands of acres of Kentucky land.[4] His "obvious considerations" no doubt refer to the threat of secession expressed by many westerners concerned about free navigation of the Mississippi. Edmund Randolph, another Virginian, concurs with Mason [534]. In part because the area north of the Ohio River is still Indian Country, it's generally expected at the time that the bulk of internal "migration" will occur south of the Ohio River—as is already happening in Kentucky—and that new states will fall into the southern orbit. As Hugh Williamson of North Carolina has written, "The advantages of a temperate climate over a cold one are so obvious that the whole bent of population is to the Southward."[5] But few delegates approve of Rutledge's proposal, which ties voting so rigidly to wealth. His motion fails miserably, 9–1, only South Carolina voting in its favor [534].

Given that well over two centuries have passed since the Convention, it's easy to see the Great Compromise as an inevitability: the Senate with equal voting by state, and the House with proportional representation. But in fact the process unfolded through many days of debate, and anyone who has been in Philadelphia in the summer can attest to the discomfort the delegates must have felt, enclosed in a hot room and burdened as they were by layers of heavy eighteenth-century clothing. They spent a lot of time focused on the issue of representation, and it's no wonder that—exhausted finally by circular arguments—they took the three-fifths ratio, which had been decided upon previously, and applied it to the current circumstance.

On July 6, Gouverneur Morris moves (seconded by James Wilson) to refer to yet another committee that part of the report having to do with "one member for every 40,000 inhabitants," so that they "might absolutely fix the number for each state in the first instance; leaving the Legislature at liberty to provide [in the future] for changes in the relative importance of the States, and for the case of new States" [540]. Elbridge Gerry supports the recommitment, stating that "Representation ought to be in the Combined ratio of numbers of Inhabitants and of wealth, and not of either singly" [541]. Rufus King, Gerry's colleague from Massachusetts, agrees "that the number of inhabitants was not the proper index of ability & wealth; that property was the primary object of Society; and that in fixing a ratio this ought not to be excluded from the estimate."

King goes on to raise the issue of future western states that Gouverneur Morris has already referred to:

> With regard to New States, he observed that there was something peculiar in the business which had not been noticed. The U.S. were now admitted to be proprietors of the Country northwest of the Ohio. Congress by one of their ordinances have impoliticly laid it out into ten States, and have made it a fundamental article of compact with those who may become settlers, that as soon as the number in any one State shall equal that of the smallest of the thirteen original States, it may claim admission into the Union [541].

Because, as King states, the smallest state—Delaware—contains fewer than thirty-five thousand inhabitants, it's possible that "if this plan be persisted in by Congress, ten new votes may be added, without a greater addition of inhabitants than are represented by the single vote of Pennsylvania." Furthermore, he says, "the plan as it respects one of the new States is already irrevocable, the sale of the lands having commenced, and the purchasers and settlers will immediately become entitled to all the privileges of the compact."

There are many items of interest in this speech. First, we should note that King agrees with Morris that property must be represented in at least the first apportionment of seats in Congress; then he talks about future states to be formed in the western territory—and he is speaking of their influence in the current Congress or in the proposed Senate, where according to the latest proposal each state will have a single vote. The ordinance he speaks of is that of 1784, which allows for ten potential states north of the Ohio River. This is one reason that ninety miles away in New York City, Congress would the following week finalize a new ordinance for the western territory, and this time around western states north of the Ohio would be limited to five in number (and Congress would have a good deal more control over the interregnum period between the establishment of a territory and its admission as a state). In later years, the question of the authority of Congress over the territories—particularly as it regarded slavery—would become a hotly disputed item. In 1787, however, it's quite clear that a majority of delegates, both in New York and Philadelphia, felt Congress had the power to establish any sort of condition it wanted in territory still to be admitted to the Union.

In the last point King makes, he refers to land sales that have already "commenced." It's not clear what he's referring to, as the contract between the Ohio Company and the United States won't be finalized until July 27, and the first public sales under the Land Ordinance of 1785 won't take place until later that fall.[6] Manasseh Cutler at this time was just arriving in New York City to carry on his lobbying activities. Perhaps King is referring to the fact that negotiations between the Ohio Company and Congress are already underway.

After King, Pierce Butler from South Carolina speaks up. Once again, he wants to be sure that Southerners' property is included in the measure of apportionment:

> He was persuaded that the more the subject was examined, the less it would appear that the number of inhabitants would be a proper rule of proportion.... He contended strenuously that property was the only just measure of representation. This was the great object of Government: the great cause of war, the great means of carrying it on [542].

Charles Pinckney then disagrees with his fellow South Carolinian, saying that "the value of land had been found on full investigation to be an impracticable rule" and he concludes that "the number of inhabitants appeared to him to be the only just and practicable rule." But then he asserts, in accord with Butler's comment a day earlier, that in the counting of population, "blacks ought to stand on an equality with whites" [542].

Gouverneur Morris's motion to send this most important of clauses to a committee passes the house, and the "Committee of Five" is selected by ballot: Gouverneur Morris, Nathaniel Gorham of Massachusetts, Edmund Randolph, John Rutledge, and Rufus King—two men from Massachusetts, one Virginian, one New Yorker who is serving as a delegate from Pennsylvania, and one delegate from South Carolina. We should take a moment here to remember that all these comments are coming to us from the pen of James Madison, who sat at the front of the Convention, facing the members (just slightly beneath the dais on which Washington sat as chairman), feverishly taking notes. Since he was unable to indicate the various intonations that carry meaning along with the words themselves, we can only imagine the heated voices in a hot room, each one perhaps louder than the last, accompanied by sharp glances and an occasional grin or grimace. We can only imagine the depth of emotion that the delegates bring to these issues, each man representing part of a polity that has only in recent years begun to think of itself as a single nation.

The Convention then turns to the clause "relating to an equality of votes in the second branch" [543]. Quite reasonably, Franklin suggests that this question can't be considered by itself, but rather needs to be discussed in relation to the clause just committed, and it's decided finally, after considerable debate, to postpone consideration of this second topic as well [553]. Over the first weekend in July, the Convention awaits the report of the Committee of Five.

CHAPTER 8

History of the Anti-Slavery Clause

We have seen the mere distinction of colour made in the most enlightened period of time, a ground of the most oppressive dominion ever exercised by man over man.

—James Madison[1]

Mr. Madison told me, that if he could work a miracle, he knew what it should be. He would make all the blacks white; and then he could do away with slavery in twenty-four hours.

—Harriet Martineau[2]

No sooner was the ink dry on the provisional treaty with Great Britain—word of which arrived in Philadelphia on March 12, 1783—than some officers and soldiers attempted to take advantage of the promises of land made to them at the start of the war.[3] That spring, the first active movement to settle the area north of the Ohio River began to form. From the very beginning, some of these ideas involved the future prohibition of slavery. On April 7, Timothy Pickering of Massachusetts, former quartermaster general of the Continental Army, enclosed in a letter to Samuel Hodgdon certain "propositions for settling a new state by such officers and soldiers of the Federal Army as shall associate for that purpose ... [t]he total exclusion of slavery from the State to form an essential and irrevocable part of the Constitution."[4] This movement proceeded on June 16 with a petition to Congress—signed by 288 former officers of the Continental Army—which began by reminding Congress of its prewar pledge of land to soldiers or their heirs, and stating that "your petitioners are informed" that a certain parcel of land north of the Ohio River—and encompassing most of the current state of Ohio—"is a tract of country not claimed as the property of; or within the jurisdiction of any particular state in the Union." The petition concluded by requesting that Congress "procure the aforesaid lands of the Natives" for the benefit of "all officers & soldiers who wish to take up their lands in that quarter"—and suggested that this settlement would be "of lasting consequence to the American Empire."[5]

George Washington lent his support to this endeavor, writing the President of Congress that this particular piece of land "ought to be the first settled in preference to any other," and that "it cannot be so advantageously settled … as by the disbanded officers and soldiers of the Army." His thinking was that "a settlement formed by such men would give security to our frontiers" and would be the most likely means to "induce" the Indians "to remove into the illimitable regions of the West," enabling the Americans "to purchase upon equitable terms … their right of preoccupancy."[6] It should be noted here that Washington's letter referred to the *purchase* of lands from the First Nations, and the petition used the somewhat more ambiguous term *procure*—since nothing at all could be accomplished before Congress had acquired the land from its current inhabitants. Of course, this presumed that the Indians would be willing to sell, and that the states such as Virginia would cede their claims to western lands. Furthermore, for the land to have value for settlers and investors, there had to be at least a modicum of security, which meant not only that the current inhabitants had to be dispossessed but also that a plan of government had to be established for the new territory—providing protection from Indians and squatters alike.

On December 20, 1783, the Virginia House of Burgesses acted to "convey, transfer, assign and make over unto the United States … all right, title and claim" to the territory "northwest of the river Ohio." Since Virginia had promised land bounties to the soldiers of the state militia, and it was unclear that these claims could all be fulfilled in Kentucky (which until 1792 remained a part of Virginia), this cession exempted the land between the Little Miami and Scioto Rivers—which became known as the Virginia Military District.[7] As Archer Hulbert explains, this meant that "what is, perhaps, the richest portion of Ohio, the 4,209,800 acres of land lying between the Scioto and Little Miami Rivers, was, during the years when the Ohio Company of Associates came into existence, under Virginia option."[8] Furthermore, by the terms of the Land Ordinance of 1785, the territory from the western border of Pennsylvania to the Muskingum River—the so-called Seven Ranges—was to be surveyed and sold in small portions to the general public. Therefore, when the Ohio Company first proposed a purchase along the northern bank of the Ohio, the only land that was available as a large chunk lay between the Muskingum and Scioto Rivers.[9]

This entire waterfront territory, lying just across the Ohio from the Kentucky settlements, was a prize that many people wished to acquire. Despite its being occupied by the First Nations, it was seen by American settlers as empty territory—"some of the best land that was ever warmed by the sun"—

and by 1784 people were "already removing in thousands to live over the mountains."[10] Without a plan of government for the territory, Federal politicians feared that the value of the land as a saleable resource would be forever lost. As the Secretary of Congress, Charles Thomson, wrote his wife,

> To set off a [western] district and at once declare it to be a free, sovereign and independent state, would be to make a cession of it to the first stragglers who might settle there & would be a relinquishment of all the benefits expected to be derived from the sale of the lands.... [Therefore] it was proposed that Congress should prescribe the terms of purchase & settlement, & prepare for them a temporary form of government, under which they should live till their numbers and circumstances were such as might entitle them to a representation in Congress.[11]

Thus it was that in 1784, just as the Virginia cession was being finalized, a Congressional committee composed of Thomas Jefferson of Virginia, David Howell of Rhode Island, and Jeremiah Chase of Maryland was composing a plan for the future government of the western territory. As Howell wrote at the time, "There are at present many great objects before Congress: but none of more importance ... than that of the western Country," which "as a national fund ... is equal to our debt."[12] Though this has often been called Jefferson's plan—because the draft presented to Congress is in his handwriting—Howell's letter suggests that it was a joint accomplishment by the entire committee.

> It is proposed to divide the Country into fourteen new States.... The new States are each of them to contain two degrees of latitude and what lies above the 45th degree is to be added to the State adjoining South.

In the map that accompanied the committee's proposal, nine of these states were to be north of the Ohio River, a figure that Southerners would find to their distaste, as it could potentially throw control of Congress—each state having a single vote—into the hands of Northern interests; similarly, the Eastern states would also object to the large number of states west of the Appalachians. (In Article 5 of the Northwest Ordinance, the number of potential states north of the Ohio would be reduced to "not less than three nor more than five.") Howell's letter continues with a discussion of various other items that would find their way into the preliminary draft of the Resolve of 1784; perhaps the most important clause states that "after the year eighteen hundred there shall be no slavery in any of said States, nor involuntary servitude other than as punishment for crimes."[13] Notably, this is the first mention in the historical record that a Congressional committee has considered the exclusion of slavery from any part of the United States.

On March 1, 1784, the "United States in Congress assembled" voted to receive from Virginia all of the lands lying northwest of the Ohio River.[14] Other states having claims to this territory—New York, Massachusetts—had

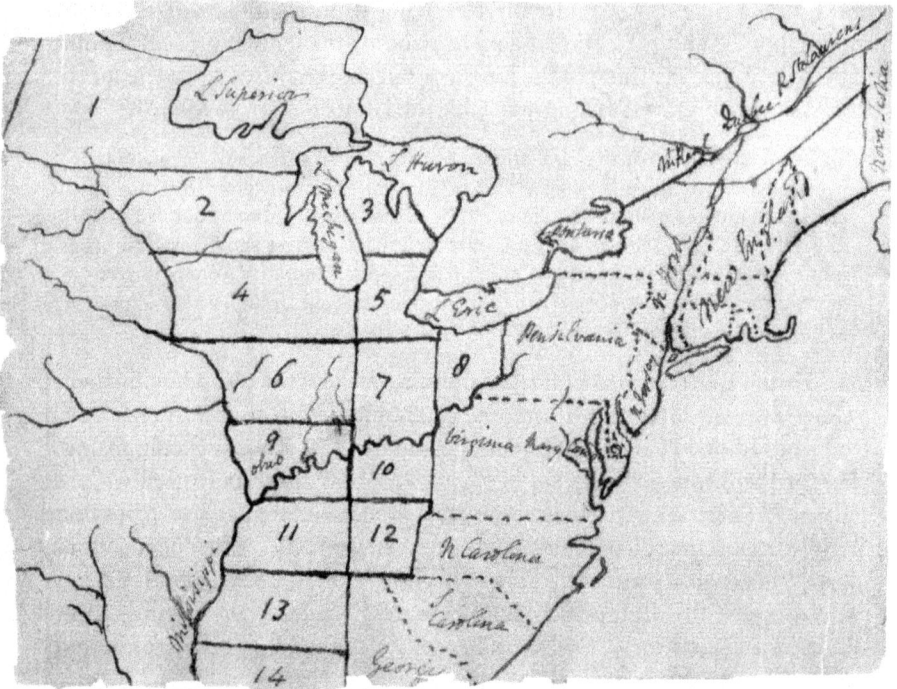

The Jefferson-Hartley Map, 1784. The area east of the Mississippi River ceded to the United States by the Treaty of Paris is divided by parallels of latitude and longitude into fourteen new states.

previously ceded their putative rights, all except for Connecticut, whose claim lay along the south shore of Lake Erie.[15] For the first time, the national government owned territory of its own, and policies set at this time would serve as a precedent for all future acquisitions. Immediately after Congress voted to accept the Virginia cession, the committee Jefferson chaired had ready a plan for the government for the western territory. It should be emphasized that this plan applied not only to the area northwest of the Ohio River, but to *all* territories that would in the future be ceded by the states, both north *and* south of the Ohio. This draft document, as Howell had indicated, included language that would establish a limit to the expansion of slavery:

> That after the year 1800 of the Christian era, there shall be neither slavery nor involuntary servitude in any of the said States, otherwise than in punishment of crimes, whereof the party shall have been duly convicted to have been personally guilty.[16]

Because the proposed ordinance was written to apply to all "territory ceded or to be ceded by individual states," this clause—if it passed a vote in Congress—meant that after 1800 there would be no slavery anywhere west of the existing states. Like a fruit fly, however, it had a lifetime measured only in days, though it would reappear, altered as to geographic coverage, in the Northwest Ordinance, and at the close of the Civil War it would become the law of the entire land in the Thirteenth Amendment to the Constitution.

On April 19, when Congress debated the proposed ordinance, a motion was made to eliminate the anti-slavery clause. Under the rules of Congress, when a motion was made to delete a part of a piece of legislation, there had to be a majority in favor of the contested language for it to stand—and in this case it failed that test by one vote—"so the question was lost, and the words were struck out."[17] As Jefferson wrote later,

> There were ten states present. Six voted unanimously for it, three against it, and one was divided: and seven votes being requisite to decide the proposition affirmatively, it was lost. The voice of a single individual of the state which was divided, or of one of those which were of the negative, would have prevented this abominable crime from spreading itself over the new country. Thus we see the fate of millions of unborn hanging on the tongue of one man, & heaven was silent in that awful moment![18]

Finally, on April 23, Congress approved the Resolve of 1784, which set out the form of government that would be applied to the new territories of the United States.[19] This couldn't have happened at a better time, as a fever for land was sweeping the young Republic:

> The American Lands and Funds open the most inviting and gainful Prospect that is now beheld under the Sun.—The extent of Territory, the Variety of Soil, the Lakes and Rivers, the Harbours for Ships, the Advantages for Building, for the Fisheries, and for universal Commerce, offer Accommodation and Employment for Millions. Here is ample Room for the Sons of America, and the Offspring of Europe to exert their Talents and build their Fortunes.—The American Funds, open a Field for Speculation and Profit, which cannot escape the Attention of enterprising Minds.
>
> Land-Office, in Boston
> April, 1784.[20]

Once a preliminary form of government was in place for the Northwest, it remained to be decided how the land would actually be sold—and, most important, how to acquire it from the nations who lived there. On April 30, 1784, another committee chaired by Thomas Jefferson proposed "An Ordinance for ascertaining the mode of locating and disposing of lands in the western territory ... when the same shall have been purchased of the Indian inhabitants, and laid off into States."[21] After some preliminary consideration, this Land Ordinance was postponed. It would engender much discussion, and not until April of 1785—Jefferson having long since departed on his diplomatic mission to France—would the Land Ordinance be passed in its final form. As William Grayson wrote a year later, "I think there has been as much said and wrote about it as would fill forty volumes ... so difficult is it to form any system ... where the interests of the component parts are suppos'd to be so different."[22]

Another roadblock to sale of the land lay in the fact that contrary to the terms of the Treaty of Peace, the British had yet to yield the forts which were scattered at strategic points across the region: Detroit and Niagara, to name two, as well as at the Miami Villages, the all-important portage along the Wabash valley waterway from Lake Erie to the Ohio River—or as the Americans would later call it, Fort Wayne.[23] As justification for this recalcitrance, the British cited the Americans' failure to live up to the terms of the Treaty, particularly as it applied to the collection of prewar American debts to British merchants. Several states had passed laws interfering with the collection of these debts, and the British pointed to these violations as reason for their retention of the strategic posts in the west. Though unstated by British diplomats, the value of the fur trade was also a motivating factor.[24]

As Congress dickered and bickered about the exact terms of the Land Ordinance, speculators and prospective settlers were growing impatient. Late in 1784, George Washington, now a private citizen—and for many years past an investor in western lands—took a fact-finding tour of the Ohio Country:

> Such is the rage for speculating in, and forestalling of Lands on the North West side of the Ohio, that scarce a valuable spot within any tolerable distance of it, is left without a claimant. Men in these times talk with as much facility of fifty, a hundred, and even 500,000 Acres as a Gentleman formerly would do of 1000 acres. In defiance of the proclamation of Congress, they roam over the Country on the Indian side of the Ohio, mark out Lands, Survey, and even settle them. This gives great discontent to the Indians, and will, unless measures are taken in time to prevent it, inevitably produce a war with the western Tribes.[25]

Of extreme importance to the potential sale of western land, therefore, were treaties with the Indian Nations who actually inhabited the region.

The first postwar conference took place in 1784 at Fort Stanwix in upstate New York—and it was there that the Six Nations ceded their claim to the Ohio Country. In the course of the proceedings, the American commissioners—Oliver Wolcott, Richard Butler, and Arthur Lee—stated unequivocally that "the King of Great Britain renounces, and yields to the United States all pretensions, and claims, whatsoever, of all the country South, and West of the Great Northern Rivers, and Lakes, as far as the Mississippi."[26] According to the great Native leader Joseph Brant, Richard Butler reminded the Indian negotiators that they had been left out of the terms of the peace treaty:

> The King did not choose to say a word about the Indians when he was settling the peace with the Americans; the King did as it were tread upon the Indians, and did not see where they were, so it was left entirely to the management of Congress to settle all the affairs within the limits which the King had given to them.[27]

Because most of the members of the Six Nations had allied themselves with the British in the late war, Butler continued, the Americans would only "receive them into their protection" if the Indians ceded to the Thirteen Fires all land west of a line drawn from the western end of Lake Ontario south to the Pennsylvania border, then further south and west to the Ohio River. This line, according to the treaty signed on October 22, 1784, "shall be the western boundary of the lands of the Six Nations ... and then they shall be secured in the peaceful possession of the lands they inhabit east and north of the same."[28] Thus the Six Nations ceded over to the Federal government their claim to the future state of Ohio.

After the Treaty of Fort Stanwix, the commissioners continued to Fort McIntosh, at the mouth of the Muskingum River, where they would attempt to quiet the claims of the various other nations who inhabited the Ohio Country. But there were storm clouds on the horizon. On October 29, Arthur Lee wrote Jacob Read, congressman from South Carolina, that despite having "secured everything we could with the Six Nations," it seemed they were not entirely satisfied with the arrangement. "The Indians have formed a Confederation," Lee stated, and "Brant has gone to try if he can engage the British Court to support the Confederates."[29] Lee's journal from this trip contains a vivid description of Pittsburgh—which, as the first American city west of the Allegheny Divide, was the setting-off point for many of the pioneers heading down the Ohio River after stocking their flatboats with supplies:

> Pittsburgh is inhabited almost entirely by Scots and Irish, who live in paltry loghouses, and are as dirty as in the north of Ireland, or even Scotland. There is a great deal of small trade carried on; the goods being brought at the vast expense of forty-five shillings per cwt., from Philadelphia and Baltimore. They take in the shops, money, wheat, flour and skins. There are in the town four attorneys, two doctors, and not a priest of any persuasion, nor church, nor chapel.... Batteaux pass daily, with whole families, stock, and furniture, for Kentucky.[30]

The Treaty of Fort McIntosh got underway in January 1785. The American commissioners this time around were Arthur Lee and Richard Butler, with the addition of George Rogers Clark. Colonel Josiah Harmar, commanding officer at the fort, explained to a correspondent that the Indians were not entirely complaisant:

> Their chiefs in their first speech held out an idea that they still conceived the lands as their own, & did not imagine that they had forfeited them by the part they took during the late war; but the answer of the Commissioners was in a very high style; that they were conquered people, & from their adherence to the King of Great Britain, had nothing to expect from the United States, but must throw themselves entirely upon their mercy and generosity; otherwise if this great force was provoked, it would fall upon and crush them like the vast oak upon the little shrub.[31]

This bullying stance by the Americans had its desired effect—and by the terms of the Treaty of Fort McIntosh, signed on January 21, 1785, a line was established by which "the Sachems and Warriors" of the Wyandot and Delaware nations yielded their claim to all of southern Ohio.[32]

No sooner was the treaty completed than the commissioners issued a proclamation forbidding any settlement on the newly acquired land.[33] The reason for this was purely pecuniary: the Federal government needed the proceeds from *buyers*, and until the Land Ordinance has provided a means of dividing and parceling out the land, it was extremely important to keep *squatters* from setting up shop. As David Howell wrote on February 9, "the Western lands are in great demand, & frequent applications are made for grants. It is expected that Congress, before they rise, will be enabled to open their Land-Office, & to establish some government in the Western wilderness."[34] As Richard Henry Lee noted in a letter to George Washington, however, there was at least one major problem with this plan: arguably the most important nation which inhabited southern Ohio at that time were the Shawnees, and they were absent from the talks both at Fort Stanwix and at Fort McIntosh. According to Lee, "it seems that persons, disaffected to us, prevented them from meeting the Commissioners"—which is to say, the British were keeping them alienated.[35] For the Shawnees, this land was sacred, where their fathers and grandfathers had laid their heads and their bones. The American hope was that one more treaty would complete the process, and the Shawnees would at that time fall into line.[36]

As Congress continued to debate the Land Ordinance, which would enable the surveying and sale of this enormous territory, an event occurred which underlined the urgency of the deliberations, and at the same time revealed the need for a governmental ordinance that gave more control over the territory to Congress. Taking seriously the Resolve of 1784, which allowed settlers to form a government of their own in the new territory, an individual named Emerson (or as it's sometimes spelled, Amberson) posted handbills on trees on the north side of the Ohio—flying in the face of the proclamation outlawing settlement that the commissioners had made a few weeks earlier at Fort McIntosh. For these Americans, the land north of the Ohio was "vacant country," and the Confederation had no power to stop them from settling there. Equally alarming from the Federal point of view, the pioneers denied the right of Congress to sell the land:

March 12th, 1785

Notice is hereby given to the inhabitants of the west side of the Ohio river that there is to be an election for the choosing of members of the Convention for the framing [of] a Constitution for the governing of the inhabitants, the election to be held on the 10th day of April next ensuing—one election to be held at the mouth of the Miami river, and one to be held at the mouth of the Scioto river, and one on the

Muskingum river, and one at the dwelling house of Jonas Menzons—the members to be chosen to meet at the mouth of the Scioto on the 20th day of the same month.

I do certify that all mankind, agreeably to every Constitution formed in America, have an undoubted right to pass into any vacant country, and there to form their Constitution, and that from the Confederation of the whole United States, Congress is not empowered to forbid them, neither is Congress empowered from that Confederation to make any sale of the uninhabited lands to pay the public debts; but the Confederation has prescribed a particular mode for the payment of all public debts, which is to be by a tax levied and lifted by the authority of the Legislature of each State.

(signed) John Emerson[37]

There can be a lot of discussion about numbers at this time, about how many settlers and how many indigenous people there were across the Ohio Country, however one chooses to define the region. For the Native Americans, perhaps, as a round number, fifty thousand is the best figure to use, which translates to somewhere in the neighborhood of ten thousand warriors, though perhaps only several thousand of them, or fewer, were available or willing to fight at any given time.[38] Likewise, at this time, the number of pioneers actually west of the Appalachians was probably in that same neighborhood—with several thousand militia, or fewer, available to join the fray in any given week or month.[39] Here is the important fact: at some point the numbers were approximately equal ... and then they were not. The tipping point was reached sometime toward the end of the eighteenth century, as the great mass of settlers, in small or large groups, or as individuals, kept crossing the mountains to seek a better life than was possible in the crowded cities of Europe or among the growing population of the seaboard states. But for a while, there was a balance of sorts, and neither one side nor the other was able to strike a final blow that would seal the fate of those they saw as enemies.

Responding to the handbills on the trees, Colonel Harmar ordered the U.S. Army, such as it was, to "dispossess the said settlers."[40] As George Washington wrote Hugh Williamson, settlement should be restricted to a compact area, which would "give strength to the Union"; otherwise, "sparse settlements ... will have the direct contrary effects, [opening] a large field to land jobbers and speculators, who are prowling about like wolves in every shape."[41] But in the spring of 1785, Congress was still debating how the Federal government would sell the land. At that time, there was a crucial distinction in the custom of laying out and selling land *north* or *south* of the Mason-Dixon line. The Southern method, as William Howell explained it, was to issue warrants from a land office: "The person taking the warrant has to look for unlocated lands to cover with his warrant.... In this way the good land is looked out & seized on first—and land of little value ... [is] left in the hands of the public."[42] In Kentucky, this system of so-called indiscriminate locations had created a legal house of cards caused by overlapping claims. Unintelligible legal descriptions created a situation where someone attempting to purchase a parcel would have no idea whether competing claims had already been laid out.

As one author explains the process, "surveys were made in all conceivable shapes, with no system whatever ... [causing] numerous interferences and encroachments of one land entry upon another." To make matters worse, "the surveys were made principally in the winter, there being then less danger from the Indians.... Surveying with deep snow on the ground and in the midst of heavy forests was not especially conducive to accuracy."[43]

Here's one example:

> Surveyed for Richard Clough Anderson and Mayo Carrington 2,000 acres of land, on part of a military warrant No. 856, on the waters of the Little Miami, beginning at a sugar tree, ash and black oak, running N. 45 W. 400 poles to three sugar trees; thence S. 45 E. 800 poles, crossing a small creek at 500 poles, to a black oak, sugar tree and sassafras; thence N. 45 E. 400 poles, crossing a creek at 38 and at 200 poles to two sugar trees and a sassafras; thence N. 45 W. 800 poles, crossing a branch at 70, and the creek at 300 poles, [and back] to the [point of] beginning.[44]

The problems caused by this system—or lack of system—would provide work for lawyers in Kentucky for many years to come (including Henry Clay, who cut his teeth in Kentucky courtrooms arguing about metes and bounds). This is one reason that the "empty" land across the Ohio River was so appealing to Kentucky residents.

In contrast to this system of "indiscriminate locations," as William Howell also explained, was the method used in "the Eastern states": to divide the land into measured parcels and sell it in a controlled fashion, "good & bad together, & to push out settlement in compact columns." In a prescient understatement, Howell concluded that "the measures to be finally adopted on this head must be the result of mutual concessions: & what they will be remains quite uncertain."[45] In fact, the compromise finally reached involves the grid system that is so familiar to anyone buying property west of the Appalachians—a pattern of sections and townships all neatly laid out in rectangular parcels. Sections comprise a square mile each—six hundred and forty acres—and thirty-six of these, laid out in a square, constitute a township.

On Friday, March 4, 1785, "An Ordinance for ascertaining the mode of locating and disposing of lands in the Western territory" had its first reading in Congress.[46] Just a few days later, Timothy Pickering wrote a letter to Rufus King, once again raising the question of slavery in the new western territory. The first attempt to exclude slavery had been defeated a year earlier—but now, Pickering suggested, with the Land Ordinance on the point of becoming the law of the land, it might be a good time to renew the discussion, since it would be easier to keep slavery out of territories not yet settled than it would be to bring emancipation to slave states already in existence:

To suffer the continuance of slaves until they can gradually be emancipated in States already overrun with them may be pardonable, because unavoidable without hazarding greater evils; but to introduce them into countries where none now exist, countries which have been talked of—which we have boasted of—as an asylum to the oppressed of the earth—can never be forgiven. For God's sake, then, let one more effort be made to prevent so terrible a calamity.[47]

A week and a half later, on March 15, Rufus King moved to commit a proposition that "there shall be neither Slavery nor involuntary servitude in any of the States, described in the Resolve of Congress of the 23 April, 1784, otherwise than in punishment of crimes, whereof the party shall have been personally guilty."[48] This motion passed—being unanimously approved by delegates from north of the Mason-Dixon line—and the proposal was sent to a committee.[49] William Grayson of Virginia voted in favor of the proposal, the only Congressman to do so from the states south of Maryland. On the same day this vote took place, the Land Ordinance received its second reading.

The committee to which King's proposal was referred soon issued a report. Significantly, there was now a clause attached which pertained to fugitive slaves. The three members of the committee—Rufus King, David Howell, and William Ellery—were all New Englanders, but they apparently had input from others. Although the Resolve of 1784 would have prohibited slavery in the territories after 1800, and King's original proposal would have eliminated it immediately, this revision offered a means of appeasement to the Southern representatives: it mandated the return of runaway slaves, adding the following language:

Provided always, that upon the escape of any person into any of the states described in the said Resolve of Congress of the 23d. Day of Apl. 1784, from whom labor or service is lawfully claimed in any one of the 13 original states, such fugitive may be lawfully reclaimed, and carried back to the person claiming his labor or service as aforesaid.[50]

This is the first appearance, so far as I know, of the fugitive slave language which later appeared in both the Northwest Ordinance and the Constitution. The report was scheduled to be considered a week later, on April 14—but there is no evidence that it was ever taken up by Congress.[51] Nonetheless, this clause echoes down through history, the same precise language appearing again in the Northwest Ordinance, and its substance in the Constitution— further developed in the Fugitive Slave Acts that haunt the antebellum period.

Throughout the spring of 1785, debate continued on the Land Ordinance. Meanwhile, the march of boots continued west, one traveler recording that

I kept an account of the number of souls I overtook in one day going to that country; and though I was the whole day in riding about thirty miles, but very little faster than a wagon could drive, I overtook two hundred and twenty one. They seem absolutely infatuated by something like the old crusading spirit to the holy land.[52]

Not surprisingly, the First Nations complained to Alexander McKee of the British Indian Agency that the Americans were encroaching on their territory: "You now see trouble is coming upon us fast.... The Virginians are settling our Country & building Cabins in every place."[53] Colonel Josiah Harmar, with his single regiment of Federal troops, attempted with little success "to dispossess sundry persons who have presumed to settle" north of the Ohio.[54] One report indicated that there were now thousands of squatters between Wheeling and the mouth of the Scioto.[55]

Finally, on May 20, the Land Ordinance received its third reading and passed into law.[56] This Ordinance established the grid system and defined the first region to be surveyed and sold to the general public—the Seven Ranges—which extended forty-two miles westward from the point where the Ohio River touches the boundary of Pennsylvania, with its northwestern corner—because the Ohio flows southwest—located about ninety miles north of the river. As John Jay wrote William Bingham, "A rage for emigrating to the western country prevails, and thousands have already fixed their habitations in that wilderness."[57] This enthusiasm isn't surprising, given the reports that trickled back east:

> I wish you were here to view the beauties of Fort McIntosh. What think you of pike of 25 lbs.—perch of 15 to 20 lbs.—cat-fish of 40 lbs.—bass, pickerel, sturgeon, etc.? You would certainly enjoy yourself.... This would be a glorious season for Colonel Wood, or any extravagant lover of strawberries. The earth is most luxuriantly covered with them. We have them in such plenty, that I am almost surfeited. The addition of fine rich cream is not lacking.[58]

At this same time, the Indian Nations were meeting in the Ohio Country with American emissaries, explaining their displeasure. Despite the treaties, there were many members of the First Nations who felt that in truth they hadn't ceded any land at all north of the river. A Shawnee chief named Captain Johnny told the Americans, "We people of one Colour are United, so that we make but one man, that has but one Heart and one Mind."

> But we see your intention—you are drawing close to us, and so near our bedsides, that we can almost hear the noise of your axes felling our trees and settling our Country. According to the lines settled by our forefathers, the boundary is the Ohio River, but you are coming upon the ground given to us by the Great Spirit ... [and] it is too clear to us your design is to take our Country from us—we remind you that you will find all the people of our Colour in this Island strong, unanimous, and determined to act as one man in defence of it, therefore be strong and keep your people within bounds, or we shall take up a rod and whip them back to your side of the Ohio.[59]

Meanwhile, British troops continued to occupy their western forts, putting a crimp in the Americans' plans to settle the area. Partly this policy served to protect the fur trade and ensure that it stayed in the hands of British merchants, and partly it arose from the fear that should the soldiers withdraw, it would provoke the First Nations—from feelings of betrayal—to fall upon the civilian population of Canada and wreak vengeance. As long as the red-coats remained in the Northwest, the Indians believed that their old friends would not abandon them to the Americans' mercies—and in this way the British, without taking any aggressive action, managed to stiffen the Nations' resistance[60]:

Arthur Lee to Col. Josiah Harmar
New York, 12 Sept 1785

Our good friends, the British, seem desirous of saving us the trouble of regulating the Indian trade, & the expense of garrisons in the western posts. I have long thought that this would be the case, unless we make it more convenient for them to evacuate than to keep those posts. It is probable, I think, Sir, that we shall yet be obliged to take measures for that purpose.[61]

CHAPTER 9

New York in July 1787

You know very well, when the white people came first here they were poor; but now they have got our lands, and are by them become rich, and we are now poor; what little we have had for the land goes soon away, but the land lasts for ever.

—Gachradodow[1]

At the prodding of Charles Thomson, Secretary of Congress, William Blount and Benjamin Hawkins of North Carolina left the Constitutional Convention after the July 2 session and headed for New York City, where since May Congress had lacked enough delegates for a quorum.[2] As we recall from the previous discussion of the key vote in the Convention on July 2, two delegates from Georgia, William Few and William Pierce, had also returned to New York. It's my contention, or perhaps suggestion would be a better word, that these Southern delegates brought with them to Congress information about a political arrangement agreed to in the Convention, involving the ordinance for the western territory that had been postponed the previous May. Despite the injunction of secrecy on the delegates to the Convention, these men who were members of both bodies could certainly share information—but over and above that, communication between the two bodies was confirmed by James Madison, according to a comment later reported by his personal secretary, Edward Coles, in a speech to the Historical Society of Pennsylvania:

> This brings to my recollection what I was told by Mr. Madison, and which I do not remember ever to have seen in print. The Old Congress held its session, in 1787, in New York, while at the same time the convention which framed the constitution of the United States held its sessions in Philadelphia. Many individuals were members of both bodies, and thus were enabled to know what was passing in each—both sitting with closed doors and in secret sessions. The distracting question of slavery was agitating and retarding the labors of both, and led to conferences and inter-communications of the members ... creating the great unanimity by which the [Northwest] Ordinance passed, and also in making the Constitution the more acceptable to the slaveholders.[3]

On July 3, Alexander Hamilton, who had also returned to New York from the Convention, wrote George Washington that he was "seriously and deeply distressed at the aspect of the Councils which prevailed when I left Philadelphia," and that he would remain in New York "ten or twelve days"— but then, "if I have reason to believe that my attendance at Philadelphia will not be mere waste of time, I shall after that period rejoin the Convention."[4] Though Hamilton was not at that time a member of Congress, the significance of this comment will become evident later in our discussion.

With more delegates present, Congress on July 4 was once again able to muster a quorum and return to doing the country's business. (Unlike the members of the Convention, Congress did not take a holiday to celebrate the eleventh anniversary of independence.) Since the President of Congress, Arthur St. Clair of Pennsylvania, was away on personal business, William Grayson was elected chairman.[5] Grayson was a Virginian, and as his biographer writes, "he played an important and even crucial role in the formation of American land policy." One of his foremost concerns was the free navigation of the Mississippi: "He viewed the whole land matter as subordinate to an issue he believed the keystone of American and especially Southern interests—Mississippi River navigation rights."[6]

On July 6, Manasseh Cutler, having just arrived from Massachusetts, delivered "introductory letters to the members of Congress." He submitted his petition for the Ohio Company, proposing "terms and conditions of purchase" for a parcel of land north of the Ohio River. That evening, according to his journal, Cutler visited with "several members of Congress." The next day, Saturday, July 7, he was introduced to Thomas Hutchins, Geographer of the United States, and "consulted him, where to make our location"; he also met with General Knox.[7] On Sunday he met with Arthur Lee, Congressman from Virginia—one of the original investors in the Ohio Company's lands— and also with Nathan Dane, Congressman from Cutler's home state of Massachusetts.[8] In the meantime, with a minimum quorum of seven states present, Congress had begun to consider a report on Indian affairs sent them by Beverly Randolph, who was acting governor of Virginian while his cousin Edmund attended the Constitutional Convention.[9]

On Monday, July 9, Richard Henry Lee took his seat in Congress, having just arrived in New York after a week in Philadelphia, "almost destroyed with heat and fatigue."[10] That same day, a new committee was appointed to deal with "the report on [the] temporary government of western territory," which had been postponed on May 10.[11] This committee included Richard Henry Lee and Edward Carrington, both from Virginia (Carrington was chairman), John Kean of South Carolina, Melancton Smith from New York, and Nathan Dane. Carrington and Smith were both among the early investors in the Ohio Company—as were Arthur Lee, Henry Knox, Alexander Hamilton, and

William Duer.[12] Just four days later, the Northwest Ordinance passed in a nearly unanimous vote, and Nathan Dane credited the arrival of Richard Henry Lee for its swift completion (after having been under consideration for well over a year): "There appears to be a disposition to do business, and the arrival of R. H. Lee is of considerable importance. I think his character serves, at least in some degree, to check the effects of the feeble habits and lax modes of thinking in some of his countrymen."[13]

Peter Force, one of the first historians to write on the Northwest Ordinance, asks and answers an important question:

> [W]hy was Mr. Carrington, a new member of the committee, placed at the head of it, to the exclusion of Mr. Dane and Mr. Smith, who had served previously? In the absence of positive evidence, there appears to be but one answer to this question. The opinions of all the members were known in Congress. In the course of debate, new views had been presented, which must have been received with general approbation. A majority of the committee were the advocates of these views, and the member by whom they were presented to the House was selected as the chairman.[14]

What exactly were these "new views" approved by the Southerners, who formed a majority of the committee? At its formation, on July 9, the committee was delegated to focus on the ordinance for the government of the *western* territory—not yet limited, as it will be in the final version, to the territory *northwest* of the Ohio River. There is a printed version of this draft of the ordinance in the Papers of the Continental Congress.[15] The title at the top of the first page is as follows: "An Ordinance for the government of the Western Territory." On this draft, the following emendations have been made (I have indicated insertions by bold type, and words blackened out are indicated by striking-through):

> An Ordinance for the **temporary** government of the ~~Western~~ Territory **of the US NW of the River Ohio,** ~~until the same shall be divided into different States~~

This geographical distinction was the most significant change introduced by the committee in its initial meeting. Interestingly, the final clause was added and then later struck out—perhaps because the single word *temporary* took its place. Roscoe Hill's notes in the *Journal of the Continental Congress* state that these handwritten changes were made either on May 10 or on July 9, but if we examine the Rough Journals of Congress, it becomes clear that no debate on the ordinance took place on May 10.[16] That day, the "Ordinance for the Government of the Western Territory" was scheduled to have its third and final reading—but the Massachusetts delegates requested a postponement. The record reads as follows:

> The order of the day was called by the State of Massachusetts, for the third reading of the Ordinance for a Temporary Government of the Western Territory, and being postponed,

temporary

95

An Ordinance for the government of the ~~Western~~ Territory *of the US NW of the River Ohio,* ~~~~

1 **T** is hereby ordained by the United States in Congress assembled, that there shall be appointed from time to time, a governor, whose commission shall continue in force for the term of three years, unless sooner revoked by Congress.

There shall be appointed by Congress, from time to time, a secretary, whose commission shall continue in force for four years, unless sooner revoked by Congress. It shall be his duty to keep and preserve the acts and laws passed by the general assembly, and public records ~~of the district~~, and ~~as~~ the proceedings of the governor in his executive department, and transmit authentic copies of such acts and proceedings every six months, to the secretary of Congress.

There shall also be appointed a court, to consist of three judges, any two of whom shall form a court, who shall have a common law jurisdiction, whose commissions shall continue in force during good behaviour.

And to secure the rights of personal liberty and property to the inhabitants and others, purchasers in the said ~~district~~, it is hereby ordained, that the inhabitants ~~of such districts~~ *thereof* shall always be entitled to the benefits of the act of *habeas corpus,* and of the trial by jury. *being duly aforsd.*

The governor and judges, or a majority of them shall adopt and publish in the ~~district~~, such laws of the original ~~states~~, criminal and civil, as may be necessary, and best suited to the circumstances of ~~~~ and report them to Congress from time to time, which *Laws* shall ~~~~ until the organization of the general assembly, unless disapproved of by Congress; but afterwards the general assembly shall have authority to alter them as they shall think fit; provided, however, that said assembly shall have no power to ~~create perpetuities.~~

The governor for the time being shall be commander in chief of the militia, and appoint and commission all officers in the same, below the rank of general officers; all officers of that rank shall be appointed and commissioned by Congress.

Excerpt from a draft of the Northwest Ordinance: note the marked-up title restricting its operation to the area north of the Ohio River.

A motion was made by Mr. Kearney seconded by Mr. Blount … that on the 16th of the present month, May, Congress will adjourn to meet on the second Monday in June next in the city of Philadelphia in the State of Pennsylvania for the dispatch of public business.[17]

After the third reading of the ordinance was postponed, Congress moved on to the business of where Congress would next meet, a subject which over the next few years took up many hours of debate before Congress settled on Washington as the nation's capital. These notes prove beyond a reasonable doubt that no debate on the Western ordinance took place on May 10. Further proof, if needed, is supplied by an endorsement on the second page of the printed broadside just referred to, which reads:

Transcribed agreeably to
order May 9th 1787—&
assigned for Thursday May 10th—
May 10th—postponed—
July 9, 1787
Referred to
   Mr Carrington

Mr Dane
Mr Lee
Mr Kean
Mr Smith

We can therefore conclude definitively that the handwritten changes on this printed draft—limiting the ordinance to the territory northwest of the Ohio River—were added no earlier than July 9. As we will see, this is what was crucial to the Southerners on the committee.

These changes were incorporated in the printed version of the new draft ordinance, which was reported to Congress on Wednesday, July 11, when it had its first reading.[18] At this time there was still no anti-slavery language included in it. There is a broadside of this version in the Library of Congress, and attached to this draft is a handwritten copy of the anti-slavery clause—in Nathan Dane's script—with a note that it is to be inserted after the end of Article 5. There is also an endorsement on the left margin of the first page of this document: "read 2nd time / third reading to be 13 July." As the editor states in a note in the *Journals of the Continental Congress*, this "corrected printed form represents the second reading on July 12."[19] In other words, the handwritten emendations to this draft, including the anti-slavery clause, were made before the second reading on July 12—which is to say, Article 6 was most likely added in the course of debate on Wednesday, July 11:

> There shall be neither Slavery nor involuntary Servitude in the said territory otherwise than in the punishment of crimes, whereof the party shall have been duly convicted; provided always that any person escaping into the same, from whom labor or service is lawfully claimed in any one of the original States, such fugitive may be lawfully reclaimed and conveyed to the person claiming his or her labor or service as aforesaid.[20]

On July 16, Dane wrote Rufus King in Philadelphia that he only introduced the anti-slavery clause when he found, to his surprise, that the Southerners were at that moment—as they had never been previously and would never be again—open to the restriction of slavery:

> When I drew the ordinance which passed (in a few words excepted) as I originally formed it, I had no idea the States would agree to the sixth Art. prohibiting Slavery—as only Massa. of the Eastern States was present—and therefore omitted it in the draft—but finding the House favourably disposed on this subject, after we had completed the other parts I moved the art.—which was agreed to without opposition.[21]

In other words, Dane was *encouraged* to submit the anti-slavery clause by the Southern members of the committee. Because of its geographical limitation, the exclusion of slavery in 1787 was far more palatable to Southerners than it had formerly been, both in the original draft of the Resolve of 1784—which was voted down in the full Congress—or in Rufus King's proposal a year later, which never made it out of committee. In these two previous cases, the exclusion of slavery would have applied to *all* western territory. By limiting its action to territory north of the Ohio only, the modified ordinance in 1787 effectively guaranteed that the slaveowners' system of plantation agriculture would be able to expand without restriction into the Southwest. From this point of view, the Northwest Ordinance is a pro-slavery document as much as it is a stepping-stone on the way to the Thirteenth Amendment—and the inclusion of a clause mandating the return of fugitive slaves, even before such a clause is included in the Constitution, makes that point abundantly clear.

My theory is that a political "arrangement" had originated among a small group in Philadelphia and was brought north by Southern Congressmen who were also delegates to the Constitutional Convention. This led, first, to a geographical restriction being introduced into the ordinance for the government of the western territory, so that it would apply only to land north of the Ohio River. When this new version of the ordinance was presented to Congress on July 11, the Southerners told Dane that they would be amenable to the anti-slavery language which Jefferson's committee had first proposed in 1784, so long as it also contained the provision about the return of fugitive slaves which had been added to Rufus King's revised proposal in 1785. Once the anti-slavery clause was added to the draft ordinance during the debate on July 11, the news could easily have been transmitted by express rider overnight to Philadelphia, so that Northern delegates to the Convention would learn of it before debate opened on Thursday. They in turn would approve the second part of the "arrangement"—giving Southerners a system of proportional representation which would take into account their slave population. (My discussion of events in Philadelphia follows in a later chapter.)

Meanwhile, coincident to the forming of the Northwest Ordinance, Manasseh Cutler was in New York negotiating the Ohio Company's purchase of land in that very same region. On Monday morning, July 9, Cutler met with Thomas Hutchins, the Geographer of the United States. Hutchins had long experience mapping the western country, and as Cutler wrote in his journal, Hutchins "gave me the fullest information of the western country, from Pennsylvania to the Illinois, and advised me, by all means, to make our location on the Muskingum, which was decidedly, in his opinion, the best part of the whole of the western country." Cutler then "attended the Committee before Congress opened"—a committee which had been appointed back in May to report on the original petition of Samuel Parsons, consisting of Rufus King, Edward Carrington, Nathan Dane, James Madison, and Egbert Benson of New York. Of these men, King and Madison were absent in Philadelphia, and Carrington and Dane were also members of the committee redrawing the territorial ordinance. When Cutler met with this committee on July 9, they "debated on terms, but were so wide apart that there appears little prospect of closing a contract." After Congress adjourned, Cutler "called again on Mr. Hutchins and consulted him farther on the place of location." After that, he continued his lobbying—"spent the evening with Dr. Holten [a delegate from Massachusetts] and several other members of Congress."[22]

On the morning of July 10, Cutler had another conference with the committee, and then later in the day "dined with Colonel Duer, and several other gentlemen." William Duer, a New York speculator with many national and international connections, was Secretary of the Board of Treasury—and an investor in the Ohio Company. As Cutler recorded, Duer "lives in the style of a nobleman. I presume he had not less than fifteen different sorts of wine at dinner, and after the cloth was removed, besides most excellent bottled cider, porter, and several other kinds of strong beer."[23] Also on July 10, the committee with which Cutler had been meeting reported back to Congress concerning the Ohio Company proposal. Apparently Cutler's lobbying efforts had been successful, as the committee submitted the following resolution:

> That the Treasury Board be authorised and empowered to contract with Samuel Holden Parsons, Esqr., or any other Agent or Agents, duly authorised by the Company styled and known by the name of the Association for the purchase of Lands on the N. West side of Ohio River.[24]

In fact, this was just the beginning of bargaining about the precise terms of the sale, which wouldn't be finalized until July 27.

After dinner with Duer that evening, July 10, Cutler departed for Philadelphia:

> As Congress was now engaged in settling the form of government for the Federal Territory, for which a bill had been prepared, and a copy sent to me, with leave to make remarks and propose amendments, and which I had taken the liberty to remark upon, and to propose several amendments, I thought this the most favorable opportunity to go on to Philadelphia.[25]

Without doubt, it is in the service of his lobbying effort for the Ohio Company that Cutler went to Philadelphia, just as he had already come to New York to press the Company's proposal in Congress. This point cannot be overstressed, as indeed Archer Hulbert has pointed out:

> One thing should be kept in mind in all discussions of Cutler's relations with Congress and the New York financiers. He came to make a purchase of land for the soldiers and others who were to make up the Ohio Company of Associates. He did not come to New York to frame an Ordinance for the western country—whatever influence he may have exerted to that end....
>
> Had his business been ordinance-making (and who could doubt that he glimpsed the consequences of the matter) his diary would have been filled with this subject and his own part in the transaction been put clearly on record. Yet he passes the matter with the single nonchalant statement that he was given *carte blanche* to revise the final draft![26]

As we examine Cutler's itinerary, this single-mindedness will become evident. According to his journal, Cutler left New York the evening of July 10 and arrived in Philadelphia the evening of July 12, having stopped along the way in Princeton to visit George Morgan. Since he left New York *before* the first reading of the newly formed Northwest Ordinance on July 11—and therefore before the debate during which the anti-slavery clause was added— he could not have brought the crucial news to Philadelphia of the addition of Article 6. (Furthermore, he arrived in Philadelphia on Thursday evening, after the crucial vote in the Convention had already taken place.) On the other hand, it is clear that his goal was to build support for the Ohio Company land purchase.

So much attention has been paid over the years to his possible involvement, or lack of it, in the anti-slavery aspect of the Northwest Ordinance, that it seems to have escaped many people's attention that the men he visited in Philadelphia, or on the way there, were those most connected with the various land companies that had been of such importance during the previous decades. George Mason, Ben Franklin, and George Morgan, for example, had each been a principal manager—Mason of the Ohio Company of Virginia, Franklin of the Vandalia venture, and Morgan of the Indiana Company— and all of them still had significant interests in western land. George Mason and his son owned tens of thousands of acres in Kentucky, George Morgan would later be the key investor in a scheme to start a colony, New Madrid, west of the Mississippi, and Ben Franklin was a close colleague and client of James Wilson, one of the largest speculators in western land. We will never know exactly what Cutler spoke with these men about, but we can assume it had something to do with what he terms his "business with Congress [which] required so speedy a return to New York."[27] As Archer Hulbert reminds us, "He came as an agent of the Ohio Company [and] all he did was in the capacity of an agent."[28]

Nevertheless, Cutler has often been given credit for the anti-slavery clause in the Northwest Ordinance. As one of his many biographers writes, "It was distinctly understood in Dr. Cutler's family that this anti-slavery provision was due to his influence," but there is no evidence of that beyond later statements he made, and facts point to a somewhat different inference.[29] When Cutler returned to New York the following week, he was presented with the Northwest Ordinance as passed by Congress on July 13, and wrote in his journal that "it is in a degree new-modeled," and "the amendments I proposed have all been made except one."[30] This was the first time he'd seen the anti-slavery provision—which had not yet been added to the draft he saw on July 10, before he departed for Philadelphia—and in his journal he makes no specific mention of that clause. Cutler may well have requested this addition before he left for Philadelphia, in line with the conditions for a western settlement originally proposed by Massachusetts officers in 1783—but as we've seen, Nathan Dane didn't include the anti-slavery provision until he was encouraged to do so by the Southerners in Congress. Cutler, however, most likely being unaware of the machinations taking place behind the scenes, might well have thought himself the sole agent responsible for Article 6.

On Tuesday, July 10, the same day Cutler left for Philadelphia, Congress received a report from Henry Knox, Secretary at War, detailing conditions along "the frontiers of Virginia bordering on the Ohio," a region which had been subject to "the greatest distress, by parties of hostile Indians who plunder and murder the inhabitants." Moreover, Knox continued,

> the deep rooted prejudices, and malignity of heart, and conduct reciprocally entertained and practised on all occasions by the Whites and Savages will ever prevent their being good neighbours. The one side anxiously defend their lands which the other avariciously claim. With minds previously inflamed, the slightest offence occasions death, revenge follows which knows no bounds. The flames of a merciless war are thus lighted up which involve the innocent and helpless with the guilty.[31]

Unfortunately, "the small corps of troops on the Ohio" had been unable "to prevent intrusions on the public lands, to cover the surveyors and to protect the inhabitants of the frontiers." Consequently, as Knox concluded, "the whole western territory is liable to be wrested out of the hands of the Union," but "in the present embarrassed state of public affairs … an Indian war of any considerable extent and duration would most exceedingly distress the United States." This is not what Secretary Knox had hoped for, at the beginning of 1786, when a treaty had been signed with the Shawnees at the mouth of the Great Miami River.

CHAPTER 10

Treaty at the Mouth
of the Great Miami

On the 6th of October [1785] I arrived at the mouth of the great Miami
on the Ohio—fully impressed with an opinion the Indian nations who
were invited to attend at the treaty to be held there were unfavourably
and generally disposed to refuse the protection and friendship of the
United States.

—Samuel Montgomery[1]

In January 1786, the third treaty concerning the Ohio Country took
place, this one with the Shawnees. Their agreement to the conditions imposed
by the United States left the way open—or so the Americans wanted to
believe—to sale and settlement of the territory. Richard Butler and George
Rogers Clark were joined as Indian Commissioners by Samuel Parsons, one
of the charter members of the Ohio Company, and his biographer provides
an excellent summary:

The task before the Commissioners was to persuade the Shawanese to surrender
peaceably the lands occupied by them in that part of the Northwest Territory, and
accept the protection of the United States.... But the Shawanese proved far less pli-
able than the other tribes. They objected most strenuously to the advance of the
white man beyond the Ohio, and were reluctant to enter into any treaty surrendering
their lands and acknowledging the supremacy of the United States.[2]

The clearest contemporary description of the proceedings at the mouth
of the Great Miami River comes from the combined efforts of Richard Butler
and Major Ebenezer Denny, second in command to Josiah Harmar at the
hastily built Fort Finney. As will become evident, the Americans had not
come to negotiate but rather to bluster and dictate a settlement by which the
Shawnees would be shoved westward onto land that had been owned by the
Miami Nation for an untold number of years. After months of preparation,
everything was in place. Hundreds of women and young men had arrived

95

along with the Native diplomats, so it was a spectacle for the commissioners and the seventy-some soldiers present at the post.[3] Though we can examine the different reports by white men, it's unfortunate that no Indian account is available of the proceedings.

We start with Denny, who as a military man sticks to the facts of the matter:

> Jan. 26th—Business opened this day by an excellent speech from our commissioners to all the Indians—about four hundred present. The boundary lines, designating the lands allotted the several nations, were particularly described and pointed out on the map. They were told that as they had joined the English and taken up the hatchet against the United States, and the war having terminated in favor of the latter, and that the English, also, to obtain peace, had ceded the whole of the country on this side of the lakes to the Americans; that they, the Indians, must now look up to the Americans, and ought to be thankful if allowed to occupy any part of the country, which by the war they had forfeited; nevertheless, more perhaps than they expected would be done for them, but they must leave hostages for their good behavior, etc.
>
> 27th.—Shawanees met in council house. Their head warrior, Kekewepellethe, replied to the speech of yesterday; denied the power and right which the United States assumed; asked if the Great Spirit had given it to them to cut and portion the country in the manner proposed. The Ohio River they would agree to, nothing short; and offered a mixed belt [of wampum], indicating peace or war. None touched the belt—it was laid on the table; General Clark, with his cane, pushed it off and set his foot on it. Indians very sullen. Commissioners told them it was well, that the United States did not wish war, that two days yet would be allowed to consider of the terms proposed, and six days more with provisions to return home; but after that to take care, for they would certainly feel the force of the United States. Council broke up hastily. Some commotion among the Shawanees. Returned same afternoon and begged another meeting, when their old king, Molunthy, rose and made a short speech, presented a white string [of wampum], doing away all that their chief warrior had said, prayed that we would have pity on women and children, etc.[4]

Kekewepellethe, also known as Captain Johnny, was the principal war chief of the Shawnee Nation present at the treaty. The other chief mentioned, Molunthy (also spelled Moluntha or sometimes Malunthy), was responsible for peacemaking.[5]

The other account of the treaty comes from Richard Butler:

> The Commissioners met and examined the articles, which being approved the chiefs of the Shawnese were sent for, and the whole explained fully to them; also the boundary line which we first proposed. This not pleasing, they complained that we were putting them to live on ponds, and leaving them no land to live or raise corn on. This being found to be the case, on inquiry, we agreed to enlarge the boundary from a branch to the main of the Miami river, and joining on the southwest corner of the lands of the Wyandots and Delawares. This did not seem fully to satisfy, but we would go no further.[6]

Beside the Shawnees, there were also Wyandots and Delawares attending the treaty, though individuals from both those nations had previously signed the Treaty of Fort McIntosh. Butler summarizes the main points that the commissioners wished to accomplish:

> The Shawnese acknowledge the United States have the sole and absolute sovereignty of the whole country ceded by the King of Great Britain, etc.
>
> The U.S. grant to the Shawnese lands on the west of the main branch of the Miami, etc., as described [522].

His account continues:

> The chiefs and people being collected—the Commissioners, Officers, civil and military, the chiefs and warriors of the Shawnese, the chiefs of the Wyandots and Delawares—the business was opened by a head captain of the Shawnese, Kekewepellethe; he recapitulated the speech and articles of treaty, and explained them to the whole. He then addressed the Commissioners:
>
> "Brothers: By what you have said to us yesterday, we expected every thing past would be forgotten; that our proposals for collecting the prisoners were satisfactory, and that we would have been placed on the same footing as before the war. Today you demand hostages till your prisoners are returned. You next say you will divide the lands. I now tell you it is not the custom of the Shawnese to give hostages—our words are to be believed, when we say a thing we stand to it, we are Shawnese—and as to the lands, God gave us this country, we do not understand measuring out the land; it is all ours. You say you have goods for our women and children; you may keep your goods, and give them to the other nations, we will have none of them.
>
> "Brothers, you seem to grow proud, because you have thrown down the King of England; and as we feel sorry for our past faults, you rise in your demands on us. This we think hard. You need not doubt our words; what we have promised we will perform. We told you we had appointed three good men of our nation to go to the towns and collect your flesh and blood; they shall be brought in. We have never given hostages, and we will not comply with this demand."

The problem of returning white captives ("your flesh and blood") came up at every treaty. It was a tradition of the First Nations to take captives in their raids; partly this was punitive, and certain of the individuals, particularly warriors, would be put to death—but part of this was also a means to replenish losses due to war and disease, and many captives would be adopted into the Nation. When these were children or young adults, often they grew up, after a period of difficult readjustment, feeling like part of the family into which they were absorbed, and they had no wish to return to the communities from which they had been taken. This created a difficult situation for the Native communities faced with the demand to return them to white society, and many times the "captives" themselves would attempt to run back to their new homes when brought to the place where the treaty took place.[7]

After responding to the demands of the Americans, Kekewepellethe laid a black string of wampum on the table. As Butler recorded it, "The

Commissioners conferred a short time on this answer, and resolved they would not recede from any of the articles, considering them just and as liberal as the interests of the U.S. would admit of." Butler then responded to the Indians' challenge:

> Shawnese—You have addressed us with great warmth. We think the answer unwise and ungrateful; and in return for just and generous proposals, you have not only given us improper language, but asserted the greatest falsehoods. You say you cannot give hostages for the performances of your promises, as it is contrary to your usages, and that you never break your word. Have you forgotten your breach of treaties in the beginning of the late war with Britain? ... Do you think we have forgotten the burning of our towns, the murder and captivity of our people in consequence of your perfidy—or have you forgotten them? [523]

Butler continued in this vein, citing the "barbarous murders" that were carried out while the Nations were "barbarously ravaging our frontier"—and accusing the Shawnees of "repeated violations of treaties of the most sacred nature." Under these circumstances, Butler told them, the Indians couldn't expect to be "enjoying the blessings of peace in common with us."

> You joined the British King against us, and followed his fortunes; we have overcome him; he has cast you off, and given us your country; and Congress, in bounty and mercy, offer you country and peace. We have told you the terms on which you shall have it; these terms we will not alter—they are liberal, they are just, and we will not depart from them. We now tell you, if you have been so unfortunate and unwise as to determine and adhere to what you have said, and to refuse the terms we have offered to give to your nation—peace, friendship, and protection—you may depart in peace; you shall have provisions to take you to your towns, and no man shall touch you for eight days after this day; but after that time is expired, be assured that we shall consider ourselves freed from all the ties of protection to you, and you may depend the U.S. will take the most effectual measures to protect their citizens, and to distress your obstinate nation [523–524].

After making these threats, Butler asserted American sovereignty: "We plainly tell you that this country belongs to the United States—their blood hath defended it, and will forever protect it." And he concluded with another warning:

> It rests now with you: the destruction of your women and children, or their future happiness, depends on your present choice. Peace or war is in your power; make your choice like men, and judge for yourselves.

In regard to the black string of wampum, Butler told the Shawnees that the Americans reject it: "We shall not receive it or any other from you in any such way." At that point, according to his journal, Butler "took it up and dashed it on the table." Following that startling act, "We then left them and threw down a black and white string"—indicating that the Shawnees could choose war or peace.[8]

It didn't take long, according to Butler, for the Shawnees to give in. The First Nations had suffered many losses in the recent war, and perhaps the Shawnees saw their only chance of survival in acceding at this point to American demands, and then waiting for a better chance to resist. Or they may have felt they had no choice, since the neighboring Midwest Nations had already signed off on cessions of the Ohio Country, and they figured they would have had to bear the brunt of an American attack by themselves. Little did they realize how weak the American army was, and how much the bluster of the commissioners was just that, empty threats backed up by a mere five hundred troops.

In the afternoon, the Shawnese sent a message requesting we would attend in the Council-house; on which we went in. Kekewepellethe then arose and spoke as follows:

"Brothers, the Thirteen Fires—We feel sorry that a mistake has caused you to be displeased at us this morning. You must have misunderstood us.... Brethren, our people are sensible of the truths you have told them. You have every thing in your power—you are great, and we see you own all the country; we therefore hope, as you have everything in your power, that you will take pity on our women and children. Brothers, everything shall be as you wish; we came here to do that which is good, and we agree to all you have proposed, and hope, in future, we shall both enjoy peace, and be secure." (A white string.)

We can doubt here the accuracy of Butler's reporting. It seems unlikely that the Shawnees were as cowering as they are represented, particularly as this picture differs so much in tone from the previous account by Ebenezer Denny. In particular, Denny states that Molunthy, the peace chief, made the speech of reconciliation, whereas Butler insists that it was the war chief, Kekewepellethe, who was so abject. Butler then concludes his account:

These ceremonies being over, all parties shook hands, the Wyandots, Delawares, Shawnese, Commissioners, etc., mutually congratulating each other. Some tobacco, drink, provisions, etc., being ordered, the Commissioners drank with the Nations and retired to dinner, and took with them some of the chiefs. Liquor was given to the Indians and they got drunk [531].

According to the final treaty document, "The Shawanoe nation do acknowledge the United States to be the sole and absolute sovereigns of all the territory ceded to them by treaty of peace." As for the boundaries set forth,

The United States do allot to the Shawanoe nation, lands within their territory to live and hunt upon, beginning at the south line of the lands allotted to the Wiandots and Delaware Nations, at the place where the main branch of the Great Miami, which falls into the Ohio, intersects said line; then down the river Miami, to the fork of that river, next below the old fort which was taken by the French in one thousand seven hundred and fifty-two; thence due west to the river de la Panse; then down that river to the river Wabash ... and the Shawanoes do relinquish to the United States, all title, or presence of title, they ever had to the lands east, west and south, of the east, west and south lines before described.[9]

It's particularly interesting that this legal description of the lands ceded by the Shawnees makes no real sense, as "the lands east, west and south, of the east, west and south lines before described," taken literally, could be said to apply to all land whatsoever north of the Ohio River. It could of course have read, "west of the east line, east of the west line, and south of the north line"—but it doesn't. And the Shawnees, being no fools, would certainly have picked this up if they had been able to decipher the terms of the treaty. One must assume from this fact that the treaty *as read* to the Shawnees said something very different from what was written in English on the piece of parchment presented to them for their marks of assent. In fact, we have proof of this in a message that the Shawnees sent to the British Indian Agency several months later, in which we learn the real reason for their acceptance of the terms offered them by the American commissioners at Fort Finney:

> Last fall the Americans our Brethren call'd us to Big Miami, when we arrived they told us they had something to communicate for our future welfare and that of our children after us. But alas we heard nothing good from them; they told us that our Father [the King] had given us to them with our lands likewise. The commissioners assur'd us, that every thing in the Articles we now send you, were agreeable to our best wishes and more generous than we cou'd have expected from them; this induced us to sign their proposals, but we find we have been ignorant of the real purport of them till we returned here.... We were not sensible of the error we committed, till our friend [Matthew] Elliott explained it to us.[10]

The note concludes by asking for help:

> We request that you'll be strong and give us the best advice you are capable of, in our present situation; you see we never have been in more need of your friendship and good offices, we have been cheated by the Americans, who are still striving to work our destruction, and without your assistance they may be able to accomplish their ends. You have too much wisdom not to be convinced of this truth as well as we are.

This message was signed by Maluntha, Shade, and Painted Pole, "Principal Chiefs of the Shawanese"—who had signed the Treaty of Fort Finney.

Even before the successful conclusion of this treaty—that is, from the American point of view—the Ohio Company's plans for western settlement were proceeding apace. On January 25, 1786, there appeared in the Boston *Public Prints* a piece titled "Information":

> The Subscribers take this method to inform all officers and soldiers who have served in the late war, and who are by an Ordinance of the Honourable Congress to receive certain tracts of land in the Ohio Country; and also all other good citizens who wish to become adventurers in that delightful region; that from personal inspection, together with other incontested evidences, they are fully satisfied that the lands in that quarter are of a much better quality than any other known to New England

people; that the climate, seasons, produce etc. are in fact equal to the most flattering accounts which have ever been published of them.[11]

The article goes on to propose the establishment of "an association by the name of the Ohio Company" to "prosecute a settlement in this Country"— and sets up a means whereby interested persons can elect delegates who will meet at the Bunch of Grapes Tavern in Boston, on Wednesday, March 1, "to consider and determine upon a general plan of association for said Company." As Manasseh Cutler wrote Winthrop Sargent later that month, if people were "made sensible of the fertility and temperature of the climate in the Ohio country, they would turn their faces to the southward."[12]

On March 27, three days after Cutler wrote this letter, a Speaker of the Six Nations explained to the Western Indians that they had "calmly considered our present situation, & in particular the state of our affairs with the Americans." They intended "to demand from them with the voice of the Six Nations, the deeds given them at the Treaty of Fort Stanwix for lands given away by some of our people who had no authority to grant or dispose of them." The treaty, they said, was "entirely void."[13]

David Duncan to Colonel Harmar
Pittsburgh, 28 March 1786

I shall now point out the disposition of the Indians. While I was among them, the Wyandotts, Delawares & Shawnees seemed to be tolerable peaceable, & rather inclined for peace than to have any more war. Notwithstanding their good inclinations, the warrior chiefs in conversation, both drunk & sober, say their old Counselors & Kings have given up the land to the Big Knife; but we the chiefs of the warriors have not given our consent—that if the surveyors come to survey the land, or if any of the white people come to sit down on it, we will then put our old men & chiefs behind us & fight for our land while we have a man.[14]

At that same time, far to the east, Congress formed another committee, under the direction of James Monroe, "To consider and report forms of government to be instituted in the Western territory of the United States by Congress prior to the institution of temporary government there [according] to the resolve of April 23, 1784."[15] We should note the wording here: the future ordinance is not to *replace* the Resolve of 1784, but rather to fill in the gap that exists "prior to" that law taking effect. In other words, it is to forestall expressions of democracy such as the handbills that Mr. Emerson had posted on trees north of the Ohio River, and to ensure executive control by Congress from the earliest days of settlement. Meanwhile, there were rumors about the intentions of the First Nations, such as a story in the *Pennsylvania Packet and Advertiser*, datelined London, April 1, 1786:

We hear from Philadelphia that there never were known so many different Indian Nations to be confederated, as have now entered into an union against the United

States of America ... and there is every reason to suppose that they will commence the bloodiest hostilities in the spring.[16]

As usual under the Articles of Confederation, there was a lack of money in the public coffers. On April 1, the Board of Treasury sent the bad news to the Secretary at War, who had complained about his inability to pay the troops along the frontier. The amount of taxes coming in from the states was not even enough "for the payment of the officers on the civil list, and the discharge of the foreign interest. If the former is withheld the general government can no longer exist, if the latter is not punctually paid the most fatal consequences will inevitably ensue."[17] After receiving this letter, Henry Knox reported to Congress that "the propensity of lawless men to establish themselves on the public lands ... rises to a great height and is even spreading itself among men who have been supposed to be under the influence of reason and law."[18] Consequently, once spring arrived, the attention of Congress turned to the surveying of the western country, revealing a desperate need to sell the land for ready cash.[19]

In the meantime, James Monroe's committee had been considering an ordinance for government in the western territory—a necessary prerequisite for land sales to begin—and on May 10 they presented a draft plan to Congress.[20] Though the original mandate of the committee was to consider legislation to precede the Resolve of 1784, in this draft it was stated that "the resolutions of the 23d. of April, 1784 ... are hereby repeal'd." That previous document apparently provided for too much democracy on the part of the settlers and not enough control by Congress; in this draft, the territorial officials from the very start were to be appointed by Congress, not elected by the people's assembly. Meanwhile, out west, in the very region the ordinance presumed to control, the British were continuing to refuse to evacuate the western posts, and on June 21 the Secretary at War shared his concerns with Congress:

[T]he troops now in service may be adequate to prevent intrusions on the public lands and to cover the surveying of that district of country ... [but] they are utterly incompetent to protect a frontier, from Fort Pitt to the Mississippi, from the incursions and depredations of the numerous tribes of savages who inhabit that extensive country between the Ohio and the Lakes.[21]

The next day, Congress ordered Knox to send two companies of troops to the Falls of the Ohio—to control the settlers as much as the Indians—and Knox relayed the orders to Colonel Harmar, with a proviso that, if at all possible, he shouldn't involve the country in an Indian war, as "in the present moment [it] would exceedingly embarrass the United States."[22] Despite all this, there was a growing fervor for western land. One overseas investor, for example, reported that "grants of American lands are becoming merchantable commodities on the Exchange of London."[23]

On July 7, Monroe's committee on the government of the western territory introduced the idea of limiting the number of western states north of the Ohio, which had been set at nine on Jefferson's proposed map in 1784, and Congress resolved that in the future such states be restricted to "not more than five nor less than three"—numbers that would later be included in the Northwest Ordinance.[24] This would reduce the power of the west in a legislative body which allocated a single vote per state, and was also the first indication that a future territorial ordinance might apply only to the region north of the Ohio. On July 13, Monroe's committee presented a new draft of the territorial ordinance.[25] In this version, to impose executive control, Congress "will appoint a governor ... [and also] a Court, to consist of five judges."

South of the Ohio, meanwhile, Native warriors were inflicting great damage on the Kentucky settlements. As Colonel Levi Todd of the militia wrote Virginia Governor Patrick Henry, "Much mischief has been done in different parts of the District this summer, and much property lost.... Much Kentucky blood I fear will be spilt."[26] In September, Colonel Harmar received information that a gathering of warriors was taking place somewhere in the Ohio country—though it wasn't clear to what end.[27] Shedding some light on the situation, a letter dated September 13 appeared in the *Maryland Journal*, reporting that "there are 700 warriors collected at the Shawanoe Towns, and more are expected." The writer then added, "I had almost forgot to tell you, that the Indians say they will not disturb the whites, if they will confine themselves within the bounds of Pennsylvania, and on this side [of] the Ohio."[28] Despite what the Indians wished for, Congress at this point received yet another draft of the ordinance for the government of the new territories.[29] This version of September 19 contained the same components of centralized control as previously—a governor and court to be appointed by Congress—but the population required for admission as a state had increased, from that of "the least numerous of the thirteen original states" (as it had been in the Resolve of 1784, and also in the previous draft of July 13) to "one thirteenth part of the citizens of the Original States." This increase would tend to delay the addition of future states and prolong the political dominance of the original thirteen.[30]

At this very time, affairs were beginning to unravel in Massachusetts with the beginnings of Shays' Rebellion. As Nathan Dane wrote Rufus King in August, "Friends to government appear to be very much alarmed at these appearances of disorder."[31] Henry Knox, whose responsibility it was, as Secretary at War, to respond to such events, was powerless to act since the few troops he had available were tied down along the frontier—and finances forbade the hiring of more.[32] As a result, by packing the courthouses and shutting down legal proceedings, the rebels prevailed in their attempt to put at least a temporary stop to the foreclosure of small farms, and began to force open the doors of prisons for those who had been locked up for bad debts.[33] It seemed as though the possibility of outright civil war was hanging over the young Republic, and on October 18 Henry Knox wrote the President of Congress, "It is my firm conviction ... that unless the present commotions are checked with a strong hand ... an armed tyranny may be established on the ruins of the present constitutions."[34] Yet in spite of these commotions, land speculation was still a popular topic of conversation.

> James Monroe to Thomas Jefferson
> New York, 12 October 1786
>
> Mr. Madison and myself have been desirous if possible of forming an engagement for land in this State which would hereafter put us at ease. He promis'd me to advise you of it, and to tell you of our little plan ... in my estimation a better opportunity cannot present itself.[35]

Such is the state of affairs when General Benjamin Logan and the Kentucky militia set out northward across the Ohio River one fall day in 1786.

CHAPTER 11

Back to Philadelphia

Mr. Gouverneur Morris is one of those Geniuses in whom every species of talents combine to render him conspicuous and nourishing in public debate:—He winds through all the mazes of rhetoric, and throws around him such a glare that he charms, captivates, and leads away the senses of all who hear him. With an infinite stretch of fancy he brings to view things when he is engaged in deep argumentation, that render all the labor of reasoning easy and pleasing. But with all these powers he is fickle and inconstant,—never pursuing one train of thinking,—nor ever regular. He has gone through a very extensive course of reading, and is acquainted with all the sciences. No Man has more wit,—nor can any one engage the attention more than Mr. Morris. He was bred to the Law, but I am told he disliked the profession, and turned merchant. He is engaged in some great mercantile matters with his namesake Mr. Robt. Morris. This Gentleman is about 38 years old, he has been unfortunate in losing one of his Legs, and getting all the flesh taken off his right arm by a scald, when a youth.

—William Pierce[1]

We turn now to a discussion of the events in Philadelphia the crucial week of July 9–13, when the delegates were tackling the knotty problem of how to apportion seats in the "first branch" of Congress.

July 9

On Monday, July 9, Gouverneur Morris, delegate from Pennsylvania (though his home is in New York), reports back from the Committee of Five, which had been selected to suggest an agreeable solution to the problem of how to allocate seats in the initial session of the House of Representatives. The clause referred to this committee states that "in the first branch of the Legislature each of the States now in the Union be allowed one Member for every forty thousand inhabitants of the description reported in the seventh resolution of the Committee of the whole House" [Farrand, 1:524]. First off, we should note that this clause refers *only* to states currently in the Union. As for *which* inhabitants will be counted, the resolution of June 13—to which this sentence refers—states that "the rights of suffrage in the 1st. branch of the National Legislature" should be "in proportion to the whole number of white & other free citizens & inhabitants, of every age sex and condition, including those bound to servitude for a term of years, & three fifths of all other persons" [236]. The rubric concerning "three-fifths of all other persons," it will be recalled, dates back to the Congressional Resolution of April 18, 1783, which first utilized this so-called Federal ratio—though in that case it was meant to apply to the counting of slave and free population for the apportionment of Congressional "requisitions" among the several states.[2]

The Committee of Five, as they report on July 9, has decided that at the first meeting of the new national legislature there will be fifty-six members in the House of Representatives—thirty from north of the Mason-Dixon line, twenty-six from the South:

> But as the present situation of the States may probably alter as well in point of wealth as in the number of their inhabitants ... the Legislature [shall] be authorised from time to time to augment the number of representatives: and in case ... any new State[s] [be] created within the limits of the United States[,] the Legislature shall possess authority to regulate the number of Representatives ... upon the principles of their wealth and number of inhabitants [557–558].

Notably, wealth is proposed along with numbers as a determining factor in future apportionment—and at the same time, the scheme of representation is extended to any new states yet to be formed, presumably in the western territory. This inclusion of wealth will give the richer, existing thirteen states a means to protect their influence in the new government.

Immediately, Roger Sherman of Connecticut questions the number fifty-six, wondering how the committee came up with it, as "it did not appear to correspond with any rule of numbers ... hitherto adopted by Congress" [559]. Nathaniel Gorham of Massachusetts, who was a member of the Committee of Five, explains that "some provision of this sort was necessary in the outset. The number of blacks & whites with some regard to supposed wealth was the general guide." Gouverneur Morris and John Rutledge then move to postpone consideration of the initial numbers in the legislature and to vote on the second paragraph alone—which passes, 9–2. So now wealth will officially be included, along with numbers of inhabitants, in any scheme of apportionment for both existing and new states.

Sherman then moves to refer back to a committee the first part of the report, allocating numbers in the first meeting of a new Congress, and Morris seconds the motion, "observing that this was the only case in which such Committees were useful." In fact, he continues, "The report is little more than a guess.... The Committee meant little more than to bring the matter to a point for the consideration of the House" [560–561]. Before this motion passes, debate turns to the specifics of what is meant by the phrase "according to wealth and numbers." This is the crucial matter, of course: *who* and/or *what* will be counted? William Paterson, delegate from New Jersey, immediately questions the language as being "too vague":

> He could regard negroes slaves [*sic*] in no light but as property. They are no free agents, have no personal liberty, no faculty of acquiring property, but on the contrary are themselves property.... Has a man in Virginia a number of votes in proportion to the number of his slaves? and if Negroes are not represented in the States to which they belong, why should they be represented in the Genl. Government?

This is an old debate, as we've seen, going back to the early days of the rebellion, when the Continental Congress was first trying to figure out how to apportion the expenses of war and the distribution of power in the new Republic.

Paterson continues with his argument:

> What is the true principle of Representation? It is an expedient by which an assembly of certain individuals chosen by the people is substituted in place of the inconvenient meeting of the people themselves. If such a meeting of the people was actually to take place, would the slaves vote? they would not. Why then should they be represented?

The future governor of New Jersey has gone straight to the heart of the matter. A Congressional district in Virginia, as he says, includes a certain number of residents, including slaves, all of whom will be counted for Federal apportionment, albeit at a reduced "value." That same slice of countryside, however, sends delegates to the House of Burgesses in Richmond proportioned according only to the number of free white folks in the neighborhood. (In the *Federalist* 54, Madison will attempt to justify this discrepancy.) Paterson further notes in his speech that even in 1783, Congress "had been ashamed to use the term 'Slaves' & had substituted a description." Likewise in 1787, the delegates are avoiding the use of the word *slaves* in proposals and counterproposals (though not in the debate itself)—perhaps hoping that circumlocution will facilitate the process of ratification. That process has yet to be defined, and at this time the men are probably assuming that the new Constitution will need the approval of the various state legislatures. (In fact, as we've seen, the Convention has been authorized to meet only "for the sole and express purpose of revising the Articles of Confederation," and according to that document, any change would require ratification by *all* the state legislatures.)[3]

Most delegates to the Convention probably realize that slavery is a crime against humanity of singular proportions—and these are politicians who perhaps more than any other cohort in any other generation see themselves as actors on the great stage of history. They know they will be held up to scrutiny in the future, to say nothing of the newspapers and pulpits of their contemporary constituents. They are therefore loath to use the word *slavery* in the document that they hope will go down in history as the founding cornerstone of a successful Republic.

Madison, changing the subject somewhat, immediately points out to Paterson—a small-state delegate who has been demanding equal state representation in the Senate—that the argument he just raised about proportional representation is in direct contradiction to his previous position [562]. Rufus King, from the commercial state of Massachusetts, supports the inclusion of slaves in the formula of apportionment in return for the Southern states allowing the Northerners some sort of preferential treatment in their shipping interests. (This important bargaining chip, later in the summer, will be used by Southerners to guarantee the survival of the international slave trade for another twenty years.) King reminds the Convention that when the three-fifths ratio was first proposed in 1783, "eleven out of thirteen of the States had agreed to consider Slaves in the apportionment of taxation; and taxation and Representation ought to go together."[4] Several days later, this connection between representation and taxation will be of utmost importance in passage of the final compromise.

July 10

On Tuesday, July 10, the session opens with a report from the committee given the task of establishing numbers for the initial meeting of the legislature. Now the seats total sixty-five, and the balance between North and South is somewhat different—but the Northern states will still be in the majority, thirty-five vs. thirty [563]. There is some bickering about the justice of the allocation, but finally "the apportionment of Representatives as amended by the last committee ... passed in the affirmative" [570]. This is crucial, as the Southerners are now certain that, in the short term at least, they will be outnumbered by Northerners.

After approval of these initial numbers, debate returns to the part of the report of the Committee of Five about modifying the states' representation in the future "upon the principles of their wealth and number of inhabitants" [558]. Edmund Randolph, governor of Virginia, suggests an amendment:

> That in order to ascertain the alterations in the population & wealth of the several States the Legislature should be required to cause a census, and estimate to be taken within one year after its first meeting; and every _____ years thereafter—and that the Legislature arrange the Representation accordingly [570–571].

Gouverneur Morris, concerned about the relative power of new states to the west, opposes this language "as fettering the Legislature too much." Despite the fact that an assessment of wealth will be part of the formula, he objects to the notion that the same scheme of apportionment will apply both to existing and new states:

> He dwelt much on the danger of throwing such a preponderancy into the Western Scale, suggesting that in time the Western people would outnumber the Atlantic States. He wished therefore to put it in the power of the latter to keep a majority of votes in their own hands.

George Washington, presiding over the debate, is beginning to doubt his wisdom in coming out of retirement to serve as a delegate from Virginia. His fame as victor in the Revolution is secure, but if this Convention fails to yield a positive result he fears his reputation might suffer. He is alarmed at all the jockeying over the mechanics of power. He describes these concerns in a letter to Alexander Hamilton, who has left Philadelphia for private business in New York: "In a word, I *almost* despair of seeing a favourable issue to the proceedings of the Convention, and do therefore repent having had any agency in the business.... I am sorry you went away—I wish you were back."[5]

July 11

On Wednesday, July 11, the Convention resumes discussion of Randolph's motion "requiring the Legislature to take a periodical census for the purpose of redressing inequalities in the Representation" [578]. For a while, the discussion revolves around the wisdom, or lack thereof, in putting "shackles" on the legislature, as Morris refers to it. George Mason of Virginia voices the fear that since Northerners will have numerical domination in the first legislature, they will act to ensure the continuation of their power if no "proper rule of representation" is fixed from the outset. He is also concerned by Morris's desire to limit the power of the West, fearing that future states "will speedily revolt from the Union, if they are not in all respects placed on an equal footing with their brethren." He thinks that "numbers of inhabitants, though not always a precise standard of wealth, was sufficiently so for every substantial purpose" [578–579].

Hugh Williamson of North Carolina moves that Randolph's proposition be postponed, and instead submits the following language:

> That in order to ascertain the alterations that may happen in the population and wealth of the several States, a census shall be taken of the free white inhabitants and ⅗ths of those of other descriptions ... and that the representation be regulated accordingly [579].

Williamson has specifically introduced the three-fifths ratio into the discussion, which was previously only alluded to by reference to the seventh resolution reported on June 13. Moreover, Williamson's language, unlike Randolph's, no longer prescribes an estimate of wealth to be taken along with the census. The only "property" that will be considered will be slaves.

Now that the debate over slave representation has started in earnest, Pierce Butler of South Carolina, seconded by his colleague General Charles Cotesworth Pinckney, insists that "blacks be included in the rule of Representation, equally with the Whites: and for that purpose moved that the words 'three fifths' be struck out" [580]. Elbridge Gerry objects to any ratio greater than three-fifths, and Nathaniel Gorham, his fellow delegate from Massachusetts, recurs to the former debate in 1783, when the ratio was being discussed in Congress as a "as a rule of taxation."

> Then it was urged by the Delegates representing the States having slaves that the blacks were still more inferior to freemen. At present when the ratio of representation is to be established, we are assured that they are equal to freemen. The arguments on the former occasion had convinced him that three-fifths was pretty near the just proportion and he should vote according to the same opinion now [580].

Hugh Williamson, responding to Gorham, reminds the Convention that "the Eastern States on the same occasion contended for their equality" [581]. Abjuring such "extreme" positions for himself, however, he says that he, like Gorham, would now approve of the three-fifths ratio as a compromise. Butler's motion for including slaves equally in the apportionment fails to pass, only Georgia and the Carolinas voting aye.

Gouverneur Morris now raises the point that Williamson's proposal, with no specific mention of wealth, is inconsistent with the resolution passed on Monday, regulating the number of representatives according to *both* "wealth and number of inhabitants." He asks, "why is no other wealth but slaves included?" [582]. On Monday, as we've seen, it was decided to apply the scheme of apportionment to new states as well as old—and if a population count alone is used for apportionment, Morris fears that western states will have undue influence in the government: "The Busy haunts of men not the remote wilderness, [is] the proper School of political Talents. If the Western people get the power into their hands they will ruin the Atlantic interests" [583]. He has another objection as well: he doesn't want slaves counted at all, since "the people of Pennsylvania would revolt at the idea of being put on a footing with slaves. They would reject any plan that was to have such an effect." The best course, he says, "would be to leave the interests of the people to the Representatives of the people"—that is, let future legislators set their own rules [584].

George Mason objects to Morris's proposal, fearing that if the means of apportionment in the future isn't set by law, equitable representation will be short-lived: "It would continue so no longer than the States now containing a majority of the people should retain that majority." In other words, the

Northern states will maintain their hegemony over "the Southern & Western population" which will "predominate … in a few years," and their power "would never be yielded to the majority, unless provided for by the Constitution" [586]. Like most people at the time, as we've noted previously, Mason expects that the bulk of migration will be to the Southwest. Few people at the time anticipate the great population shift to the Old Northwest which will occur over the next seventy years.

When the voting turns to Williamson's proposal, the first clause passes— "That in order to ascertain the alterations that may happen in the population and wealth of the several States a census shall be taken of the free inhabitants of each State"—and then attention turns to the phrase, "⅗ of the negroes" [586].

Rufus King objects "to fixing numbers as the rule of representation, [and] particularly so on account of the blacks." Like Gouverneur Morris a few minutes previously, "He thought the admission of them along with Whites at all, would excite great discontents among the States having no slaves" [586]. Nathaniel Gorham, King's colleague from Massachusetts, agrees that "there might be some weight in what had fallen from his colleague, as to the umbrage which might be taken by the people of the Eastern States" [587]. James Wilson "had some apprehensions also from the tendency of the blending of the blacks with the whites, to give disgust to the people of Pennsylvania as had been intimated by his colleague (Gouverneur Morris)." Wilson wonders

> on what principle the admission of blacks in the proportion of three-fifths could be explained. Are they admitted as Citizens? Then why are they not admitted on an equality with White Citizens? Are they admitted as property? Then why is not other property admitted into the computation?

These men may honestly fear that public reaction to the inclusion of non-whites in the population count will affect the passage of the Constitution through an as-yet-undefined ratifying process—or they may just be using this inferred racism as a means to argue against the expansion of Southern representation. Given my supposition that James Wilson has very likely agreed with John Rutledge to support the inclusion of slaves in the scheme of apportionment in return for the Southerners' support of proportional representation, I think we must take at face value his worries about the ratifying process. As for the other men, I'm not so sure. It would depend upon their knowledge and support of the political arrangement concocted by Wilson and Rutledge, and that is a topic for further investigation.

Morris then makes one of the more significant speeches in this process. He is, he says, "reduced to the dilemma of doing injustice to the Southern States, or to human nature" [588]. He must do the former, he says, despite the probability that the Southern states will not agree to it. He is adamant here, saying in essence that he would never vote for a compromise, three-fifths or otherwise, that would include slaves in the apportionment of representation—and we can conclude that Morris, so far at least, is not a party to any sort of political arrangement:

> For he could never agree to give such encouragement to the slave trade as would be given by allowing them a representation for their negroes, and he did not believe those States would ever confederate on terms that would deprive them of that trade.

The question is then called "for agreeing to include ⅗ of the blacks." It fails, 4–6, with Pennsylvania voting no. Presumably Morris has voted against the proposal, as he just said he would.

July 12

Thursday, July 12, opens with Gouverneur Morris moving to add a proviso to the clause which allows the legislature to vary future representation "according to the principles of wealth and number of inhabitants" [591–592]. What he wishes to add are the words "that taxation shall be in proportion to Representation." Twelve days later, after the Great Compromise has been approved, Morris states that he only meant this clause as a "bridge to assist us over a certain gulf" [Farrand, 2:106]. As Madison explains in a footnote, "The object was to lessen the eagerness on one side, & the opposition on the other, to the share of Representation claimed by the Southern States on account of the Negroes." As we examine the debate on July 12, we will see that Morris's phrase does in fact facilitate acceptance of the three-fifths ratio. Moreover, in the final voting on this clause, later in the day, Pennsylvania now votes aye—so it seems that Gouverneur Morris, despite his adamant refusal on the previous day, has switched his position to support the compromise.

Pierce Butler begins the debate by "admitting the justice of Mr. Gouverneur Morris's motion," but he also argues that "Representation should be according to the full number of inhabitants, including all the blacks" [592]. General C. C. Pinckney adds to this, stating that though he also likes the idea of Morris's motion, he is "alarmed at what was said yesterday concerning the Negroes." He is worried that South Carolina's peculiar institution is being attacked.

At this point the fireworks start. William Davie of North Carolina rises to address the delegates:

> Mr. Davie said it was high time now to speak out. He saw that it was meant by some gentlemen to deprive the Southern States of any share of Representation for their blacks. He was sure that North Carolina would never confederate on any terms that

did not rate them at least as ⅗. If the Eastern States meant therefore to exclude them altogether the business was at an end [593].

William Johnson, delegate from Connecticut, offers a conciliatory note; despite being a Northerner, he accepts the Southern proposal that slaves be counted equally with free whites, perhaps hoping by this to get the Deep South to agree to equal state representation in the second branch of the national legislature:

> Dr. Johnson thought that wealth and population were the true, equitable rule of representation; but he conceived that these two principles resolved themselves into one; population being the best measure of wealth. He concluded therefore that the number of people ought to be established as the rule, and that all descriptions including blacks equally with the whites, ought to fall within the computation.

Despite his desire to "bridge a gulf," this whole line of reasoning annoys Morris:

> It has been said that it is high time to speak out. As one member, he would candidly do so. He came here to form a compact for the good of America. He was ready to do so with all the States … [but] it is in vain for the Eastern States to insist on what the Southern States will never agree to … and he verily believed the people of Pennsylvania will never agree to a representation of Negroes.

Frustrated, Morris falls back on his original argument: "What can be desired by these States more than has been already proposed; that the Legislature shall from time to time regulate Representation according to population & wealth." At this point, General Pinckney repeats the concern of the Southerners, "that property in slaves should not be exposed to danger under a Government instituted for the protection of property" [594].

Oliver Ellsworth, Johnson's colleague from Connecticut, attempts to move things along, bringing in the three-fifths ratio by the back door, so to speak—that is, in reference only to taxation. He proposes, seconded by Pierce Butler, to add to Morris's clause (about taxation being in proportion to representation) additional language:

> and that the rule of contribution by direct taxation for the support of the Government of the United States shall be the number of white inhabitants, and three fifths of every other description in the several States, until some other rule that shall more accurately ascertain the wealth of the several States can be devised and adopted by the Legislature.

This, of course, is pretty much the same rubric as was used in the proposed amendment to the Articles of Confederation that Congress passed on April 18, 1783. But Edmund Randolph, the Virginian, is still unsatisfied. He wants to make sure that the Legislature is forced to alter representation as population shifts, lest the North continue to maintain their control over the government. He also slips back into allusion, not even wanting to mention the three-fifths ratio by name. He proposes, in lieu of Ellsworth's motion,

> that in order to ascertain the alterations in Representation that may be required from time to time by changes in the relative circumstances of the States ... a census shall be taken ... of all the inhabitants of the United States in the manner and according to the ratio recommended by Congress in their resolution of the 18th day of Apl. 1783 ... and that the Legislature of the United States shall arrange the Representation accordingly.

Though Randolph is careful to ensure that the word *slaves*—or even the phrase "three-fifths of all other persons"—won't be in the final document sent to the states for approval (and thereafter inscribed on parchment for future generations to read), he isn't shy about using the word in debate, urging "strenuously" that "express security ... be provided for including slaves in the ratio of Representation," since "it was perceived that the design was entertained by some of excluding slaves altogether." Ellsworth withdraws his motion and seconds Randolph's.

James Wilson then adds a further obfuscation, also looking toward the ratifying process, observing "that less umbrage would perhaps be taken against an admission of the slaves into the Rule of representation, if it should be so expressed as to make them indirectly only an ingredient in the rule" [595]. To the clause that the legislature has the power to vary future representation according to "wealth and number of inhabitants," Wilson adds a proviso that "representation ought to be proportioned according to direct taxation," which will be assessed "according to the ratio recommended by Congress in their resolution of April 18, 1783." What Wilson does here, cleverly, is to switch the position of taxation and representation as it appears in Morris's original language ("that taxation shall be in proportion to representation") so as to make Randolph's circumlocution appear even more innocuous.

Rufus King, delegate from Massachusetts, still objects to "tying down the Legislature to the rule of numbers," warning presciently about the growing power of the Southern states, and how they will threaten secession:

> He must be short sighted indeed who does not foresee that whenever the Southern States shall be more numerous than the Northern, they can & will hold a language that will awe them into justice. If they threaten to separate now in case injury shall be done them, will their threats be less urgent or effectual, when force shall back their demands. Even in the intervening period there will no point of time at which they will not be able to say, do us justice or we will separate [595–596].

Here King foreshadows the next seventy-plus years of Congressional argument. Indeed, King himself participates, several decades later, in the controversy surrounding the admission of Missouri as a slave state, when threats of civil war first echo throughout Congress. At that point, he states that the three-fifths compromise was intended (by Northerners, at any rate) to apply only to the existing states in 1787, and not to new states in the west—but that is thirty-two years after the fact.[6]

Charles Pinckney, still beating a dead horse, moves "to amend Mr. Randolph's motion so as to make 'blacks equal to the whites in the ratio of representation.' " He holds out the notion that this will also benefit the Northern states, "as taxation is to keep pace with Representation." After some debate about how often to hold a census—every ten years is soon agreed upon—Pinckney's motion goes down to defeat, 8–2, with only South Carolina and Georgia supporting it. This is one of the rare cases in which James Madison, in his notes, records the breakdown of a state's voting—and Pennsylvania is listed as being 3–2 against the motion.

Finally, the question is called on "Mr. Randolph's proposition (as varied by Mr. Wilson)" [597]: that is, adding to the original language that the legislature has the power to vary future representation "according to the principles of wealth and number of inhabitants"—which was approved on July 9—a proviso "proportioning representation to direct taxation & both to the white & ⅗ of black inhabitants." In the specific language of the proposition, this time around, the three-fifths ratio, and the slaves to whom it applies, are only mentioned by allusion: "according to the ratio recommended by Congress in their Resolution of April 18, 1783" [591].[7] This paragraph is approved, 6–2, with two states divided [597]. At least one Pennsylvania delegate has altered his stance, since Pennsylvania now reverses its negative vote of the previous afternoon. It seems quite likely that Gouverneur Morris voted against Pinckney's motion to include slaves in their entirety in the formula for apportionment, which was just defeated—but that he switched his vote to support the three-fifths ratio. The Convention now adjourns for the day—and, according to my theory, an express rider departs northward to New York with news of this important vote.

It would appear that sometime between Wednesday evening and Thursday morning, Morris has changed his mind—and that he is responsible for Pennsylvania's swing vote. At the close of business on Wednesday, Morris has committed himself to "never" accepting black people into the apportionment of representation. On the very next morning, he starts the day off with a proposal whose purpose is to "build a bridge" between the two sides and hence effect a compromise. This abrupt about-face is, I believe, a key to the whole business.

On Wednesday, July 11, Congress in New York had a first reading of the draft of the Northwest Ordinance—which, for the first time, is limited to the territory northwest of the Ohio River—and during debate that day, Article 6 is added with its prohibition of slavery. The news of this significant development could have been carried overnight to Philadelphia and shared with the Pennsylvania delegation in plenty of time for Gouverneur Morris, on Thursday morning, to propose a "bridge over a certain gulf." Subsequently, on Thursday afternoon, he switched his vote to support the three-fifths compromise. At George Washington's urging, Alexander Hamilton had returned to Philadelphia around this time, and he may have been the one to bring the news of Article 6, or at least—as a longtime friend of Morris—he could well have helped convince Morris to change his position.[8]

As an investor in the Ohio Company, Hamilton shared Morris's interest in western land. If indeed there was a political arrangement that tied the three-fifths compromise to a slave-free Northwest Territory (one of the conditions presumably requested by Manasseh Cutler), passage of the compromise would go a long way to raise the value of these investments. It may well be that James Wilson had been trying all along to enlist Morris's support in his arrangement with the Southerners. Learning on Thursday morning that the Southerners in Congress were willing to accept Article 6, and that his vote in favor of the three-fifths ratio was the final price to pay for their agreement, Morris might have decided to go along with the plan—freeing the Northwest from the curse of slavery while at the same time enhancing the value of his financial assets. This is, at least, consistent with his otherwise puzzling change of sentiment between Wednesday afternoon and Thursday morning.

July 13–16

The next day it becomes even more apparent that Gouverneur Morris in all likelihood switched his vote on July 12. On Friday, Edmund Randolph makes a motion to remove "wealth" from the formula for "periodical revisions" of apportionment, so that "the Legislature of U. S. shall possess authority to regulate the number of Representatives … [solely] upon the principle of their number of inhabitants," which now includes three-fifths of the slaves [603]. However, *wealth* was the term that—in Morris's mind, at least—would protect the power of the richer Eastern states from the growing West, and in particular from the Southwest, a section of the country (most people believed at the time) which would receive the bulk of immigration. With no wealth other than slaves being counted, as Randolph now proposes, the Northern states like Pennsylvania and Massachusetts would be at a serious disadvantage.

Foremost in opposition to Randolph's motion is Gouverneur Morris. He was willing to vote for the three-fifths ratio as long as Northern property was also taken into account in legislative apportionment; now he realizes that without the counterbalance other forms of wealth would have brought to the equation, this will only serve to increase the political power of the slaveholders. He questions the whole basis of the compromise that, the day before, he had helped bring to fruition. He opposes Randolph's "alteration" because of what he calls its "incoherence." "If Negroes [are] to be viewed as inhabitants," he says, "they ought to be added in their entire number, and not in the proportion of ⅗"—but if they are to be viewed as property, the removal of other forms of wealth "would produce [an] inconsistency." He is outraged:

> The train of business & the late turn which it had taken, had led him he said, into deep meditation on it, and he would candidly state the result. A distinction had been set up & urged, between the Northern & Southern States. He had hitherto considered this doctrine as heretical. He still thought the distinction groundless. He sees however that it is persisted in; and that the Southern Gentleman will not be satisfied unless they see the way open to their gaining a majority in the public Councils [603–604].

Butler now steps right in, blustering: "The security the Southern States want is that their negroes may not be taken from them which some gentlemen within or without doors, have a very good mind to do" [605]. In the end, Randolph's motion passes unopposed, and *wealth* is removed from the equation. Whatever the reasons for Morris's outburst, he is not so concerned that he speaks up again that day. In fact, his name does not reappear in Madison's notes of the Convention until the following Tuesday.[9]

Probably because wealth has been removed from the language regarding future representation, Elbridge Gerry starts the debate on Saturday, July 14, with a final request "that the attention of the House might be turned to the dangers apprehended from Western States" [Farrand, 2:2]. He wants to revisit the decision made the previous Monday to apply the same scheme of apportionment to all states, and moves, "that in order to secure the liberties of the States already confederated, the number of Representatives in the 1st. branch of the States which shall hereafter be established shall never exceed in number, the Representatives from such of the States as shall accede to this confederation" [3]. This proposal, seconded by Rufus King, is defeated 4–5, with Pennsylvania divided. Morris's fear has been realized, and the new states of the Southwest will share equally with other Southern states an advantage provided by their slave population.

Following this decision, Luther Martin calls for a vote on the whole report of the Committee of Five, as amended, including the clause about the equality of votes in the second branch. As this is still a very sticky point, there is a lot of debate, a lot of bitter language about equal state representation in the second branch, and no resolution that day; but on Monday morning, when it comes up again (after the Sunday recess), the entire Great Compromise passes—though by one vote only—probably because there is no other option than to dissolve the Convention [15]. In fact, the delegates almost vote to adjourn *sine die*—which would have killed any hope of a new Constitution indefinitely—but they step back from the brink. On Tuesday, July 17, back in the Convention, Gouverneur Morris tries unsuccessfully to reopen the can of worms, moving to "reconsider the whole Resolution … concerning the constitution of the two branches of the legislature" [25]. At that time, no one seconds his motion; it is, by then, a fait accompli. After this, the three-fifths ratio—alluded to only as "the ratio recommended by Congress in their Resolution of April 18, 1783"—is part of the draft Constitution. Never again during the remaining eight weeks of the Convention, despite the many issues still to be resolved and the many votes still to be taken, will the three-fifths compromise be seriously threatened.[10]

On July 17, William Davie writes his colleague James Iredell in North Carolina a letter which hints, obliquely, at a deal worked out by two members of the Convention: "The two great characters you inquire after move with inconceivable circumspection. This hint will satisfy you. Their situations, though dissimilar, are both peculiar and delicate."[11] Unfortunately, the original inquiry to which William Davie was responding has disappeared from the pages of history, so we have no way of knowing who he was referring to. It is tempting to see the "two great characters" as James Wilson and John Rutledge, working behind the scenes to achieve a complex arrangement by which the three-fifths clause in the Constitution was the price for a slave-free Northwest Territory.

In examining the events of the entire week, we can imagine an interlocking process of quid pro quo, which I suggest had been worked out in advance. On Monday, July 9, a committee in Congress was appointed to reconsider the ordinance for government of the western territories that had been postponed the previous May. That day (or the next), the ordinance became limited in geographical extent to apply only to the area north of the Ohio River. Because of this modification, on Wednesday, July 11, Southerners in Congress agreed to the addition in the ordinance of an anti-slavery clause. This news was transmitted by express rider overnight to Philadelphia, and on Thursday, July 12, in return for the promise of a slave-free Northwest Territory, Gouverneur Morris switched his negative vote and a resulting majority of the Convention accepted a three-fifths ratio in the Constitutional formula for Congressional apportionment. That evening, news of the acceptance of this compromise was carried back to New York, arriving the next morning—and on Friday, July 13, Southerners in Congress voted their unanimous and final approval of the anti-slavery Sixth Article in the Northwest Ordinance. Had the three-fifths language *not* been accepted by the Convention on July 12, the Southerners in Congress, on July 13, could have reneged on their preliminary agreement, and insisted on the removal of the anti-slavery clause before they would approve the Ordinance at its third reading.[12]

　　Some historians have objected to the possibility of this sort of collusion by arguing that overnight communication between New York and Philadelphia was impossible in 1787. But this is a specious argument, since overnight mail between the two cities was an established fact long before the Revolution. As advertised a few years later, even a stagecoach could reach New York from Philadelphia in one day:

PHILADELPHIA AND NEW YORK STAGES
The New Line Dispatch

　　Starts from Mr James Thompsons, at the Indian Queen, in Fourth-street, between Market and Chesnut Streets, every morning precisely at 3 o'clock, Sundays excepted, and arrives at Powles-Hook so as to be the same evening in New-York, at their usual price of 3 dollars each seat, and three pence per mile for way passengers. In order to accommodate select companies of ladies and gentlemen who will engage eight seats, a genteel carriage and four good horses will be started any hour in the day most suitable to the company, and proceed whatever distance they may please the same day, and the next arrive at New York.

　　　　　　　　　　　　　　　　　—Page, Ward and Co.[13]

CHAPTER 12

Logan's Raid

The Indian towns on the Mad River would have been completely surprised, had not one of Logan's men deserted to the enemy. As it was, eight of the Machacheek villages were burned—numerous cornfields destroyed—70 or 80 warriors taken prisoners, and about twenty others killed, among them a distinguished chief, Moluntha, by a treacherous act of one of the officers. Logan was accompanied by Daniel Boone, Simon Kenton, Robert Patterson, and other familiar names of border history.

—James W. Taylor[1]

Tom Corwin has well described this valley. "If there is a line," said he, "Where Mac-o-chee ends and Heaven begins, it is imperceptible—the easiest place to live and die in, I ever saw."

—Keren Jane Gaumer[2]

On a bright fall day in 1786 the troops crossed the Ohio River. It was, perhaps, a sunny afternoon, and a cool northerly breeze was blowing that dispelled the heat and humidity of the past week. The river was low, and if you had been there you would have felt the breeze on your face and seen the spectacle of eight hundred Kentucky militiamen under the command of General Benjamin Logan swimming their horses across the river at Limestone (now Maysville, Kentucky). Having gathered from across the District, they were launching an expedition against the Shawnee towns on the Mad River. Above all, it was the horse stealing that had gotten out of control. This was a punitive attack, and the larger plan was to burn the hundreds of acres of corn the Shawnees had grown that summer, to force them northward for the winter.

This was the first such foray since the end of the Revolutionary War. Four years previously, during the last year of the war, a similar group of horsemen with revenge on their minds had headed northward. Many of the same men, in fact: Daniel Boone, Simon Kenton, and a man named Hugh McGary,

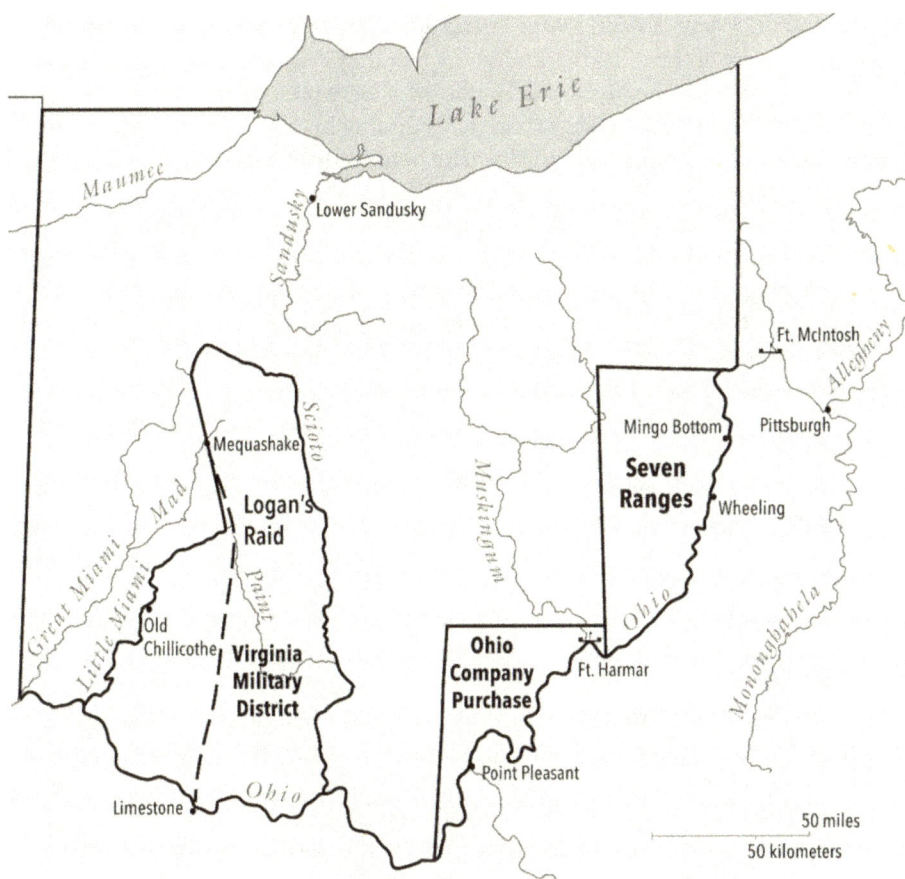

The Ohio Country, 1787.

to name just three. Boone had advised against an advance, seeing a landscape where the Shawnees and their allies (including a British officer or two) might be waiting. But McGary challenged the men, saying that only cowards would stay behind, and rushed from cover, followed by others. The Shawnees were in fact waiting just where Boone suspected they were, and the day ended with the death of seventy-two militiamen and officers, the cream of Kentucky manhood, including one of Boone's sons. This was the Battle of Blue Licks, and it pretty much marked the end of organized warfare in the west. But in the minds of all those men who crossed the Ohio in 1786, it was a fresh wound, and four years later it still rankled.[3]

The Shawnees had their own wounds. Six months before the Battle of Blue Licks, a similar group of militiamen had headed out from Fort Pitt toward the Indian towns in northern Ohio, but the Native Americans had for the most part eluded them. Frustrated, they were returning to Pennsylvania by way of the Muskingum River when they came upon a group of Praying Indians from the Moravian Towns, who were returning to their fields on the Muskingum to harvest the corn left standing in their fields months earlier when they had been forced to evacuate behind British lines. They had been relocated because the British suspected them of spying for the Americans. Members of the Delaware or Lenape Nation who had converted to Christianity, they had originally settled with their pastors in towns along the Muskingum River to lead lives of farming and meditation—though in fact, unknown to most of the congregation, one of their religious leaders, David Zeisberger, was in fact aiding the Americans by passing them messages with information about British troop movements.[4]

The returning militia came upon these Indians and at first were friendly and jovial. They accompanied them back to their town, Gnadenhutten. Once there, they saw all the trappings of "civilization" which the so-called Praying Indians had accumulated—pieces of farm equipment, china for afternoon tea—and accused them of plundering American communities. Suddenly they seized the men and bound them, and over the course of the next night they took them all, more than ninety men and women and children, to the chapel, where—one by one—they bludgeoned them to death, while the remaining members of the congregation sang hymns and prayed for forgiveness for their murderers.[5] Warriors from the Delaware Nation had taken out their anger on William Crawford, whom they captured somewhat later while on a similar punitive expedition to the Indian towns. Colonel Crawford, who had been George Washington's agent for land purchases before the war, paid with his life for the murders at Gnadenhutten, though he was not personally responsible. Throughout a long afternoon and evening, he was tortured at the stake, forced at the end to lie dying on burning coals, with more coals heaped upon him.[6]

Such was warfare in the west.

That, however, was before the Peace of Paris. For three years since then, there had been an uneasy peace along the frontiers. There were continuing "depredations"—horse stealing and murders on both sides. The U.S. Army, such as it was, had the task of keeping peace between the Indian Nations north of the Ohio River, most notably the Shawnees, and the settlers—some of whom who hoped to move across the river from Kentucky to build homes and farms, and some of whom had already done so. As far as the pioneers were concerned, land north of the Ohio was uninhabited, ripe for settlement. Now they were riding north from the Ohio, eight hundred of them, to prove their point:

Col. Benjamin Logan to Governor Randolph
17 December 1786

On Sept. 17, 1786, I received orders to collect a sufficient number of men in the District of Kentucky to march against the Shawnee's Towns. Agreeable to said orders I collected 790 men, and on the 6th of October I attacked the above mentioned Towns, killed ten of the chiefs of that nation, captured thirty-two prisoners, burnt upwards of two hundred dwelling houses and supposed to have burnt fifteen thousand bushels of corn, took some horses and cattle, killed a number of hogs, and took near one thousand pounds value of Indian furniture, and the quantity of furniture we burnt I cannot account for.[7]

Among the Shawnees these men were attacking was a fourteen-year-old American boy, Jonathan Alder, who had been captured years earlier and then adopted by a Native family:

The spring of 1786 opened finely, and the Indians raised a good crop and harvested it nicely; but great havoc was made of it before we had time to enjoy the fruits of our labor.... Logan, with a large force of men, made a raid on us; they burned all the Mack-a-chack towns, with all our corn and beans; and made a complete destruction of everything we had; and it would have been a total surprise on our part, and many more Indians been killed, had not one of Logan's men deserted and given the Indians notice of his approach a few hours before.[8]

The town of Mequashake was notable in being composed for the most part of members of the peacemaking division of the Shawnee Nation, including Chief Moluntha.[9] As the trader Obidiah Robins had informed General Richard Butler, on September 29, "There is one town of the Shawanoes called Meckachuck, that has done all in their power to keep the Shawanoes from going to war, & all to no purpose."[10]

William Lytle, who was sixteen when he accompanied General Logan, wrote a concise account of the skirmish. (He later served in the War of 1812 and went on to found the University of Cincinnati.) With the exception of Lytle's use of the word *savages*, his is a fairly evenhanded account:

We came in view of the two first towns, one of which stood on the west bank of Mad river, and the other on the northeast of it. They were separated by a prairie, half a mile in extent. The town on the northeast was situated on a high, commanding point of land, that projected a small distance into the prairie, at the foot of which eminence broke out several fine springs, This was the residence of the famous chief of the nation....

I heard the commander give his orders, and caution the colonels against allowing their men to kill any among the enemy, that they might suppose to be prisoners. He then ordered them to advance, and as soon as they should discover the enemy, to charge upon them.... As we approached within half a mile of the town on the left, and about three fourths from that on the right, we saw the savages retreating in all directions, making for the thickets, swamps, and high prairie grass....

I had not advanced more than a mile, before I discovered some of the enemy, running along the edge of a thicket of hazel and plum bushes.... The warrior I was about to shoot held up his hand in token of surrender, and I heard him order the other Indians to stop. By this time, the men behind had arrived, and were in the act of firing upon the Indians. I called to them not to fire, for the enemy had surrendered.

The warrior that had surrendered to me, came walking towards me, calling his women and children to follow him. I advanced to meet him, with my right hand extended; but before I could reach him, the men of the right wing of our force had surrounded him. I rushed in among their horses. While he was giving me his hand, several of our men wished to tomahawk him. I informed them that they would have to tomahawk me first. We led him back to the place where his flag had been....

When we arrived at the town, a crowd of our men pressed around to see the Chief.... Gen. Logan's eye caught that of M'Gary. "Col. M'Gary," said he, "you must not molest these prisoners." "I will see to that," said M'Gary in reply.... He came up to the Chief, and the first salutation was in the question, "Were you at the defeat of the Blue Licks?" The Indian, not knowing the meaning of the words, or not understanding the purport of the question, answered, "Yes." M'Gary instantly seized an axe ... and raised it to make a blow at the chief. I threw up my arm, to ward off the blow. The handle of the axe struck me across the left wrist, and came near breaking it. The axe sank in the head of the chief to the eyes, and he fell dead at my feet.[11]

McGary was the individual who had led the charge into disaster at the Battle of Blue Licks. A fellow Kentuckian described him as "a fractious, ill tempered man, hated by the people & constantly engaged in fights and affrays."[12] By killing Moluntha, he has in fact murdered one of the Shawnee leaders who is most inclined toward peace. Not for the first time, the Americans have set themselves up for war by killing a peacemaker.[13] Thankless is a polite way of describing how they treated their friends among the nations.

Once the raid was over, the news began to spread outward. Simon Girty sent a report of the incident to his superior Alexander McKee, who was married to a Shawnee woman and had a home in one of the Shawnee Towns that had been destroyed:

The number of Indians that were kill'd I do not know, but in the Town where Capt Elliott lived there were 10 Indians found lying in the Town dead, and among them the Chief of the Town was dead slain and an Indian named Shade and another one Messquaughenacke, the Indians there do say the Yankeys tyed him up and burned him, and Mr. Coon's Brother is likewise kill'd.[14]

After hearing of the raid, two Wyandot chiefs wrote Richard Butler, Superintendent of Indian Affairs, saying that it had been "quiet and peaceable" until the Americans destroyed "the Shawanoes' Villages ... & likewise killed ten of the Shawanoes." At that very time, the chiefs continued, they were "gathering together from every quarter in order to have a council concerning of settling affairs in the best manner, & the peaceablest between you & us both." The chiefs then asked the Americans "to halt & not to survey anymore at present, as we are going to have a Great Council with all nations at the Wyandott Town."[15] One of the men who signed this letter was Abraham Coon, whose brother was killed in the raid. His equanimity as expressed in the letter, despite this loss, reflects in my opinion his deep desire for peace.

As it turns out, an inquest was held into the death of Moluntha. While such an inquest was highly unusual, this particular incident also involved charges of insubordination on the part of a militia officer. This inversion of the normal social order—insubordination being more serious than murder— is a reflection of the racist state of affairs along the frontier. The following account is taken from the *Calendar of Virginia State Papers* for 1786:

Proceedings of a General Court Martial
Wednesday, 21 March 1787

Held by order of the Council for the trial of Colonel Hugh McGary, of Mercer county, who was charged with murdering with a tomahawk or small ax one of the Chiefs or King of the Shawnese Indians, named Malunthy, after the said Chief had surrendered himself a Prisoner of war, and was received as such and brought back to the Town of Mcocheek.

Secondly, With acting in disobedience of orders, which was to spare all prisoners, which orders were never countermanded.

Thirdly, With behaving in a disorderly manner in insulting and abusing Lieutenant-Col. Trotter, of Fayette County, for taking measures to prevent the Prisoners being murdered, and swore, by God, he would chop him down, or any other man who should attempt to hinder him from killing them at any time.

Fourthly, With abusing several Field Officers in a public manner, but who were absent at Limestone on the return of the Expedition; and his Conduct in general was unbecoming the character of a Gentleman and an Officer.

[Oddly, the transcript of the trial itself is missing here.]

Finding of the Court:

The Court, on maturely considering the Evidence, together with the circumstances of the case, are of opinion that Col. Hugh McGary is guilty of the first charge, viz.: of murdering Molunthy, the Indian King, after he had surrendered himself a prisoner. Not guilty of the second charge, viz.: Disobedience of Orders.

Guilty of the third charge, viz.: of abusing Col. Trotter, etc. In part guilty of the fourth charge, viz.: That his conduct in general was unbecoming the character of an officer and a Gentleman. And Sentence him to be suspended [from rank] for one year.[16]

Murder of an Indian, then, was punishable only by loss of rank for one year. We are fortunate that the *Calendar of Virginia State Papers* is not our sole source of information on the inquest, for pages have apparently been removed from the historical record. We can only speculate about the motives of the person or persons involved—or perhaps the missing pages were burned when fires consumed downtown Richmond on April 2, 1865, after the Confederate forces abandoned the capital city.[17] Fortunately, Lyman Coleman Draper, a lifelong collector of material about the early frontier, traveled to Richmond during the summer of 1860 and copied a good deal of material he found in the Virginia state archives. It is because of Draper's manuscript copy that we have the missing pages of the trial transcript:

Bardstown, March 21, 1787

Capt. James McDowell testifies, that when the action in the vicinity of the town of Macocheek was nearly over, he was told the Indian King was taken prisoner, upon which he rode immediately to see him—when he came near, he perceived him surrounded by a number of people, & Col. Hugh McGary talking to him, who asked him if he was at the battle of the Blue Licks? The Indian seemed to reply that he was: upon which Col. McGary struck him with the poll of a small ax, which brought him to the ground, & with a second blow, turning the edge, struck it into the side of his head, & then scalped him.

[General Benjamin's order is entered into evidence:]

October 5, 1786

Ordered that the field officers of the different counties direct their militia under their commands to march as silent as possible, and in case any person, under any description or any color, attempt to come to the army, all persons are forewarned to receive them in a friendly manner; it is further ordered, that no officer or soldier shall leave his post to take in custody and plunder without further orders, and upon disobedience of this order, be he officer or soldier, he may depend on being tried under the articles of war, by a court martial, and forfeit his part of any plunder that may fall into our hands.

Adjutant Jesse Yocum testified that he was present when Col. McGary knocked down the Indian King Molunthy with a squaw ax, & then stuck it into his head & scalped him. Capt. Rout was the only person wounded before the death of Molunthy.[18]

The memories of Logan's Raid would live on into the nineteenth century, and not only among the Shawnees. The soldiers impressed into service, and the farmers and merchants who had provided supplies—and had received only promissory notes in return—demanded payment. More fortunate than the Native Americans, they would receive some recompense, though it could be used only for payments due the state of Kentucky. For example:

An Act making provision for William Hadden
Approved December 9, 1806.

Whereas it is represented to the general assembly, that William Hadden served as a soldier under the command of Gen. Benjamin Logan, against the Shawanee Indians, in the year 1786, and that he, the said Hadden, never received any compensation for the same:

Sec. 1. Be it therefore enacted by the general assembly, That the auditor of public accounts shall issue a warrant to the said William Hadden for the sum of four dollars and twenty-one cents, and that six per centum per annum interest shall be allowed thereon from the 21st day of December 1799; and the warrant for said services shall specify the consideration, and be payable only in discharge of installments due for lands granted to settlers south of Green river.[19]

As the Wyandot chiefs had informed Richard Butler, a council of representatives from various nations was interrupted by Logan's raid on the Shawnee Villages. These men reconvened toward the end of 1786 at the Huron Town just south of Detroit, to determine a unified strategy opposing American encroachment on their lands north of the Ohio River. The British government offered no promise of support. As Lord Dorchester, governor general of Canada, wrote to the British superintendent of Indian affairs,

> You will take proper means to make them clearly understand, that this country is a small part of the King's Dominions, that with us in Canada no power is lodged to begin a war, nor ought we to have such a power, which might involve half the globe with all the seas in blood & destruction.[20]

For the Native Americans, therefore, it was crucial that they speak with one voice to the Americans. As Joseph Brant told the assembled council, "Whilst we remain disunited, every inconvenience attends us. The interests of any one nation should be the interests of us all, the welfare of the one should be the welfare of all the others."[21]

On December 18, the Confederated Tribes sent a message to Congress—the result of all their consultations and discussions—asking for peace based upon the Americans respecting the border agreed to by the Haudenosaunee and the British nearly twenty years earlier, at the first Treaty of Fort Stanwix in 1768. This document was directed first to Richard Butler, along with a cover letter from Joseph Brant to Henry Knox. This Christmastime message, I would suggest, is one of the most important documents in the long history of Indian affairs. More than six months later, however, when Congress voted unanimously by states to pass the Northwest Ordinance, it was still in transit.[22]

> *To the Congress of the United States of America:*
>
> BRETHREN OF THE UNITED STATES OF AMERICA: It is now more than three years since peace was made between the King of Great Britain and you ... [and] we thought that its conclusion would have promoted a friendship between the United States and Indians....
>
> BROTHERS: We still are of the same opinion as to the means which may tend to reconcile us to each other ... all treaties carried on with the United States, on our parts, should be with the general voice of the whole confederacy, and carried on in the most open manner ... [and] any cession of our lands should be made in the most public manner, and by the united voice of the confederacy; holding all partial treaties as void and of no effect.
>
> BROTHERS: We think it is owing to you that the tranquility which, since the peace between us, has not lasted....
>
> BROTHERS: We say let us meet half way, and let us pursue such steps as become upright and honest men. We beg that you will prevent your surveyors and other people from coming upon our side [of] the Ohio river.[23]

CHAPTER 13

Back in New York

The substantial yeomanry of America, the most valuable part of the community, will give place to lawyers and statesmen, who, in time, will engross all property, and thus the inhabitants of America will consist of two classes, the very rich and the very poor.

—"Agrarius"[1]

On Thursday, July 12, 1787, "the Ordinance for the government of the territory of the United States North-west of the river Ohio was read a second time," and the next day assigned for its third and final reading.[2] Congress also received a letter from Henry Knox, Secretary at War, transmitting a message from Colonel Josiah Harmar, ranking officer in the Continental Army, informing Knox that he was moving troops down the Ohio "in consequence of the orders of Congress respecting the intruders at St. Vincents on the Wabash." The next day, Friday the 13th, the Northwest Ordinance was read a third time and passed. Article 6, outlawing slavery north of the Ohio River, became the law of the land, and the "previous Resolution of the 23rd of April 1784" was "hereby repealed and declared null and void."[3] The only dissenting vote, in a Congress largely filled by Southerners, was that of Abraham Yates of New York, a vote which he never afterward explained and which has always puzzled historians. In fact, however, I believe that Yates did leave a record stating precisely why he voted against the Ordinance. A series of four articles, opposing the expropriation of Indian land, had previously appeared in the *New-York Packet* pseudonymously—and has never been noted by historians. There are various reasons to believe that Abraham Yates wrote these pieces, in which the author argued that the United States was involved in an extensive landgrab from the First Nations—both immoral and illegal according to international law—and he presciently warned that the citizens of the nation would face financial burdens due to the cost of the resulting Indian war. These articles were written just weeks after General Logan's incursion into Indian Country but more than six months before the passage of the Ordinance, which may explain why historians have overlooked them in seeking to explain Yates's negative vote.[4]

Though attempts would be made to circumvent the anti-slavery clause in the Ordinance, the states formed out of the Northwest Territory would all be free states: Ohio, Indiana, Illinois, Michigan, and Wisconsin (and a sliver in the northwest corner of the Territory would become part of Minnesota). In the Civil War, these five states together would send a million men to the Union army, tipping the balance of power and facilitating a Federal victory— culminating in the passage of the Thirteenth Amendment, which outlawed slavery everywhere in the country and rid the Constitution of the three-fifths ratio. At that point, the anti-slavery language that began with the first draft of the Resolve of 1784 came full circle.[5] But in July 1787 there were still no legal settlements north of the Ohio—except the villages of the First Nations and the few communities left over from Nouvelle France—and Josiah Harmar was sent with his troops to clear out the "intruders" in Vincennes. It was essential to remove the squatters before the land could be sold to help pay off the national debt:

Richard Henry Lee to George Washington
New York, 15 July 1787

I have the honor to enclose to you an Ordinance that we have just passed in Congress for establishing a temporary government beyond the Ohio, as a measure preparatory to the sale of the lands. It seemed necessary, for the security of property among uninformed, and perhaps licentious people, as the greater part of those who go there are, that a strong toned government should exist, and the rights of property be clearly defined. Our next object, is to consider of a proposition made for the purchase of 5 or 6 millions of acres, in order to lessen the domestic debt.[6]

On July 16, Nathan Dane, who had drafted the Northwest Ordinance, wrote Rufus King at the Constitutional Convention, enclosing a copy of the Ordinance and predicting that "the Ohio purchase ... will probably be completed tomorrow."[7] This is the same letter I've discussed previously, in which Dane expresses surprise that the Southerners agreed to the anti-slavery clause, and in which he also makes a reference to Yates's negative vote: "All agreed finally to the inclosed except A. Yates—he appeared in this case, as in most others, not to understand the subject at all." In my opinion, however, Yates understood well enough that the underlying purpose of the Ordinance was to dispossess the First Nations. As if to prove this point, Dane concluded his letter by expressing his vision—or hope—that the first state to be formed in the Northwest Territory "will no doubt be settled chiefly by Eastern people, and there is, I think, full an equal chance of its adopting Eastern politics." As Dane foresaw, Ohio throughout the antebellum period remained a strongly anti-slavery state.

On Wednesday, July 18, Henry Knox delivered to Congress a long report concerning Indian affairs. This included, long overdue, the "Speech of the United Indians, December 18, 1786," along with the cover letter from Joseph Brant; it had taken seven months to the day for this message to reach Congress.[8] The Northwest Ordinance had been law for five days—and negotiations were already underway for the sale of millions of acres that the Indians' speech declared off-limits!

> William Blount to Richard Caswell
> New York, 19 July 1787
>
> Congress yesterday received a Letter from Mr. Brandt [sic] written in the Indian language informing that all the nations of Indians of the North West of the Ohio had formed a Confederacy offensive & defensive; it was couched in hostile language and contained a request in the terms of a demand that our surveyors should desist from surveying the lands west of the Ohio.[9]

The message from the First Nations to Congress laid out their desire to live in peace with the "Thirteen Fires," so long as the Americans would abide by the Ohio River boundary that had been promised to them by the British Crown.[10] Because the message took so long to arrive in New York, the Indian Confederacy had every reason to believe that it had long since been delivered to Congress. If they were to consider the Northwest Ordinance a response to their request that the United States keep to the south side of the Ohio, it would no doubt seem to them like a declaration of war.

Also on Wednesday, July 18, Manasseh Cutler arrived back in New York from Philadelphia: "Paid my respects this morning to the President of Congress, General St. Clair; called on a number of my friends; attended at the City Hall on Members of Congress and their committee. We renewed our negotiations" [Cutler,1:292]. The next day, he again called on various members of Congress. He was at that time given a copy of the Northwest Ordinance passed six days earlier. "It is," he wrote in his journal, "in a degree new-modeled" [293]. With no mention of the anti-slavery clause, he immediately turns in his journal to discussion of the land deal, and sets out a plan for his lobbying efforts:

> As there are a number in Congress decidedly opposed to my terms of negotiation, and some to any contract, I wish now to ascertain the number for and against, and who they are, and must then, if possible, bring the opponents over.

On Friday, July 20, Congress resumed "consideration of the report on the Memorial of Samuel Holden Parsons."[11] This report included contractual language, as Cutler says in his journal, "to which I shall by no means accede" [294]. In response, Cutler informed the Committee that he "could not contract on the terms proposed," and he had therefore decided "to leave the City immediately," since he "saw no prospect of a contract, and wished to spend no more time and money on a business so unpromising" [295].

They appeared to be very sorry no better terms were offered, and insisted on my not thinking of leaving Congress until another attempt was made ... they would take the matter up that day on different ground, and did not doubt they should still obtain terms agreeably to my wishes.

At this point the deus ex machina entered the picture that would make all things possible. After an early oyster dinner at the Stone House Tavern in Brooklyn—"oysters were cooked in every possible form, but the fried were most delicious"—Cutler spent the evening "closeted" with William Duer, Secretary of the Board of Treasury:

Colonel Duer came to me with proposals from a number of the principal characters in the city, to extend our contract, and take in another Company, but that it should be kept a profound secret. He explained the plan they had concerted, and offered me generous conditions, if I would accomplish the business for them. The plan struck me agreeably.

It is this oyster dinner that has been credited with solidifying the entire speculation, with the so-called Scioto Group entering into the picture with an offer to purchase 3.5 million acres on top of the 1.5 million that the Ohio Company had already committed to. (This land was to be located immediately north and west of the Ohio Company purchase, and would extend westward to the Scioto River.)[12] This shadowy group of speculators included a number of very wealthy Americans and Europeans—without whom, as Cutler later indicated, the land deal would probably have failed to materialize.[13] Early on Saturday morning, July 21, Cutler was visited by "several members of Congress" [296]. They seemed anxious about a contract, and assured Cutler that they "had discovered a much more favorable disposition, and believed if I renewed my request I might obtain conditions as reasonable as I desired."

That same day, Congress resumed consideration of a report from Henry Knox "relative to incursions and depredations on the frontiers of Virginia"— finally resolving that either Richard Butler or Josiah Harmar proceed to hold a conference with those nations, "to hear their complaints ... [and to] make strict enquiry into the causes of their uneasiness and hostile proceedings."[14] It seems clear that if the members of Congress had actually paid attention to the Christmastime message from the Confederated Indians, they would have known precisely "the causes of their uneasiness," which was, simply put, that American settlers had been for many years encroaching on Indian lands. Though Congress had been issuing edicts ordering that squatters stay off land north of the Ohio River, and had attempted ineffectually to enforce those proclamations, their intention was not to ensure that the territory remain a homeland for the First Peoples who lived there, but rather that it remain unsettled for the sole purpose of serving as a bank account to pay off the national debt. The first step in that process, a sale to the Ohio Company and its shadowy business partners, was already nearing completion.

On Monday, July 23, the committee dealing with the Ohio Company proposal made a report to Congress:

> That the Board of Treasury be authorised and empowered to contract with any person or persons for a grant of a tract of land which shall be bounded by the Ohio from the Mouth of Scioto to the intersection of the western boundary of the seventh range of townships now surveying.... [t]he price to be not less than one dollar per acre for the contents of the said tract.[15]

The specific terms of the contract were not to Cutler's liking, however, since it required "not less than 500,000 dollars of the purchase money to be paid down upon closing of the contract."[16] Nonetheless, it was clear that Cutler's friends in Congress had been working to make the plan a reality. As Edward Carrington wrote James Madison, "we are trying to do something with our Western Territory to make it useful.... Col. Lee joins Grayson & myself with great zeal, but what will be the issue of our efforts I know not."[17]

On Friday, July 27, after further unsuccessful lobbying, Cutler was again ready to leave New York, making one last pitch to Congress and threatening, for the last time, to walk out the door:

> I rose very early this morning, and, after adjusting my baggage for my return, for I was determined to leave New York this day, I set out on a general morning visit, and paid my respects to all the members of Congress in the city, and informed them of my intention to leave the city that day. My expectations of obtaining a contract, I told them, were nearly at an end [304].

Cutler explained once again why a sale of several million acres would be beneficial for the young Republic:

> The uneasiness of the Kentucky people with respect to the Mississippi was notorious. A revolt of that country from the Union, if a war with Spain took place, was universally acknowledged to be highly probable. And most certainly a systematic settlement in that country, conducted by men strongly attached to the federal government, and composed of young, robust, and hardy laborers, who had no idea of any other than the federal government, I conceived to be objects worthy of some attention.... These and such like were the arguments I urged.

When Cutler told the Congressmen he'd reached the end of his tether, "all urged me not to leave the city so soon; but I assumed the air of perfect indifference, and persisted in my determination, which had apparently the effect I wished." After eating lunch, Cutler "was informed that an Ordinance had passed Congress on the terms stated in our letter" [305]. He had requested a delay of three months "for collecting the first half-million dollars and for executing the instruments of Contract, which was acceded to." Cutler had started the day with uncertainty—and he ended it exulting in the coup he had just pulled off:

By this Ordinance, we obtained the grant of near 5,000,000 of acres of land, amounting to three millions and a half of dollars, one million and a half of acres for the Ohio Company, and the remainder for a private speculation, in which many of the principal characters in America are concerned. Without connecting this speculation, similar terms and advantages could not have been obtained for the Ohio Company.

His job now done, Cutler left the city to return to his position of pastor in the seacoast town of Ipswich, Massachusetts.[18] From his point of view this was all a spectacular success—though not for the First Nations. Concluded just two weeks after passage of the Northwest Ordinance, this contract was the de facto reply to their request that the Americans stay to the south of the Ohio River. Taken together, the Ohio Company purchase, along with the Seven Ranges (still being surveyed) and the Virginia Military District (reserved for veterans from the Old Dominion)—these three parcels comprised much of the southern tier of Ohio, which had now been preempted from the Nations who still called it their home.

On July 30, Congressman William Blount wrote his brother Thomas, who was overseas in London. Now that the Ohio Purchase had been finalized, the letter suggests, it may be a good time for the brothers to jump into western land themselves:

As when you were last here you [expressed] an inclination to make a purchase of a large body of land from the United States on the northwest of the River Ohio, I presume it will not be unacceptable to you to be informed that the door is now open to such a speculation—that is, Congress have within these few days sold ... five millions of acres of land situated between the Muskingum and the Scioto at two thirds of a dollar per acre. Thus the precedent is established of selling the back lands in large quantities so that should you still wish to purchase and will come forward with proposals I have no doubt but they will be equally attended to.[19]

A week later, on August 7, Edward Carrington sent his fellow Virginian, James Monroe, a similar message:

We have at last made a break into the Western Lands—the Ohio Company have adjusted with Congress a Contract for 4 or 5 Million of Acres in a body on the east side of Scioto.... I am about to join them with a few shares—what think you of such an adventure.[20]

Just one day after that, William Grayson also asked James Monroe if he might be interested in investing some money in western land—"a speculation of about eight or ten thousand acres apiece"—which would "immediately become valuable" due to the Ohio Company purchase.[21] In this same letter, Grayson refers to "political reasons" which have induced the Southern Congressmen to approve the anti-slavery clause in the Northwest Ordinance.

Clearly, the money to be made in western land was very much on the minds of these men when they passed the Ordinance, and was an added inducement for investors on both sides of the Mason-Dixon line to support a political deal that would lead to a stronger Federal government. As Charles Beard explains, "Every leading capitalist of the time thoroughly understood the relation of a new constitution to the rise in land values beyond the Alleghanies."[22] A fever of speculative energy—which led to the first financial bubble in American history—set the context in which the "Compromise of 1787," as Staughton Lynd has called it, makes complete sense. It's almost as if the three-fifths ratio was an afterthought, a figure Congress had already agreed upon, in 1783, which four years later would serve the purpose of bringing Northerners and Southerners together to plunder the lands of the Western Indian Confederacy and divide the country between themselves. The North would take the land northwest of the Ohio, free of slavery, and the South, with its system of plantation agriculture, would expand into the Southwest— for there was money to be made, and quickly, by all and sundry. This agreement to split the country would be threatened when the Louisiana Purchase, and after that the Mexican War, opened huge territories west of the Mississippi River. A subsequent series of disputes and hard-fought agreements (the Missouri Compromise, the Compromise of 1850, and finally, the Kansas-Nebraska Act) would ensure that the country remained, in Abraham Lincoln's words, half slave and half free—until in 1861 the house divided against itself could no longer stand.

This is not to say that money was at the heart of Manasseh Cutler's mission. True enough, it was only by tying his purpose to the interests of an international group of speculators that he was able to pull off the Ohio Company purchase—but his endeavor was primarily designed to promote the settlement of western lands. The Massachusetts men who came together at the Bunch of Grapes Tavern in Boston were strongly anti-slavery, and their goal from 1783 onward was to establish a toehold in the west for a slave-free community. Finally, in 1787, the Southerners in Congress decided to go along with the plan, or were convinced to do so by a political agreement worked out in Philadelphia. Though Nathan Dane might not have been aware of this when he wrote Rufus King on July 16, expressing surprise that the Southern delegates had agreed to Article 6, by the middle of August he might well have known of it. On August 12, he wrote King that the Eastern states "gave up as much as could be reasonably expected" for the sake of "establishing some order in that Country."[23] Though we have no proof of what precisely Dane meant, he was clearly referring to some sort of quid pro quo. The additional Congressional representation guaranteed to the South by the three-fifths compromise, in my considered opinion, was without doubt a contributing factor in the passage of the Northwest Ordinance, complete with Article 6.

Like thieves in the night, Congress acted, and the First Peoples woke one day to find themselves dispossessed of their ancient homelands. Like thieves too, the South and North would end up fighting over the spoils—but not for another seven decades. The summer of 1787 is the moment when the two original sins of the United States intersect: the theft of Native land and the enshrinement of slavery in the Constitution. And for what?—a quick profit in real estate, an abiding American dream. Like locusts, the buyers would come, spreading over the great American west:

Josiah Harmar to Henry Knox
Fort Harmar, 9 December 1787

I have continued to order the officer of the day to take an account of the people emigrating down the river. From the 1st of June to this day there passed this garrison, bound for Kentucky, 146 boats, 3,196 souls, 1,371 horses, 165 wagons, 191 cattle, 245 sheep, and 24 hogs.[24]

Appendix A:
Abraham Yates's
Solitary Vote Against
the Northwest Ordinance

It has often been said that Abraham Yates was silent as to the reasoning behind his solitary negative vote against the Northwest Ordinance. That is not quite true. Perhaps he never indicated *afterward* why he opposed the Ordinance, simply because he had already explained himself in print—and anyone who cared already knew that. As I've noted previously, Logan's Raid in the fall of 1786 was one of the first significant conflicts between settlers and Shawnees since the late war, and it attracted a good deal of attention in the American press. One columnist who discussed its significance in the *New-York Packet* under a pseudonym—a common practice in those days— was probably Abraham Yates. His reaction to the battle, as expressed in his writing, sheds light on his negative vote.

From November 24 until December 19, 1786, four opinion pieces ran in the *New-York Packet*, all written by a person who gave his name as "Cato." This pseudonym would later appear in this same paper as the byline on a number of articles about the Constitution, during the period of debate before its ratification in New York, and these have generally been attributed to the Antifederalist governor, George Clinton. There is a minority opinion, however, that these essays could well have been written by Abraham Yates. Linda Grant De Pauw, in an appendix to her book *The Eleventh Pillar: New York State and the Federal Constitution*, argues that Yates was at least as likely as Clinton, and perhaps more so, to have been the author of these pieces.[1] If so, it is likely that he was also the author of the four articles that are reprinted in the following pages. This is an interesting supposition, given Yates's opposition to the Northwest Ordinance, since these pieces demonstrate quite

137

clearly that their author had become disaffected by the presumption that the Indian Nations had no right to determine the future of their land—a presumption that underlies the Ordinance. One comment Yates made elsewhere concerning Native Americans also tends to support his authorship of the articles in question. In an undated manuscript—which Staughton Lynd concludes was completed in June 1789—Yates says, "I have no doubt that by considering the Natives as human beings and not as wolves and bears, and acting agreeable to the laws of nature and good conscience and purchasing the lands from them, more may be done with one dollar than with ten thousand by extinguishing the Indian right by war."[2]

One point in particular made by the author of these four newspaper articles was borne out during Anthony Wayne's final assault in 1794 against the Miami Villages at the all-important Wabash portage. "Cato"—or Yates— argued against what he called the "celebrated notion" that "a nation may lawfully take possession of a vast country, in which there are found none but erratic nations, incapable, by the smallness of their numbers, to people the whole." According to Yates's reading of Vattel, because the Native Americans were nomadic hunter-gatherers, constantly "removing their habitations through these immense regions, [this] cannot be taken for a true and legal possession." Yates opposed this characterization: "One certain undeniable fact is, that these nations or tribes dwell in fixed and settled villages and towns." Proving this point, when Wayne and his soldiers approached the Miami Villages, just a few years later, they were amazed by what they saw:

> The very extensive and highly cultivated fields and gardens show the work of many hands. The margins of those beautiful rivers, the Miamies of the lake, and Au Glaize, appear like one continued village for a number of miles, both above and below this place; nor have I ever before beheld such immense fields of corn, in any part of America, from Canada to Florida.[3]

A week after the Northwest Ordinance became law, and the future of the Northwest Territory was established, Congress resolved that the Secretary at War send troops to "afford the most effectual protection to the frontier inhabitants ... from the incursions and depredations of the Indians." The troops were also to be deployed "for preventing intrusions on the federal lands."[4] When this resolution came to a vote, once again there was only one person in opposition—Abraham Yates.

The essays reproduced here were written in response to the recent raid on the Shawnee Villages by the Kentucky Militia in the fall of 1786—yet appear to us Cassandra-like when seen against the fever of land speculation, and its attendant policies, which led to passage of the Northwest Ordinance.

For the *New-York Packet* [Friday, 17 November 1786, no. 646, p. 2, col. 1]

To the Considerate Citizens of the State of New-York:

In democratical governments every man has a right to offer his sentiments publicly to his fellow citizens, upon any measure that may be pursued by those whom they have appointed their rulers; provided it be done with decency and discretion; under this impression, the following sentiments are offered to your serious consideration:—You may have observed by the late publications of Congress, that in all probability an Indian war will shortly take place;—the news papers are filled with accounts of the hostile intentions of the Indians—with their preparations for war—the quantity of horses they have plundered—and the number of scalps they have taken; and all which are calculated to shew the irresistible necessity there is for going to war:—Some of you possibly may have seriously asked yourselves the question from whence this necessity originated, and why the Indians should causelessly take up the hatchet against the States.—This is a question nowhere answered, and you are still left in the dark; it seems strange and opposite to the principles of human nature, that so many nations should collect themselves together for no other but predatory purposes, or sacrificing the lives of a few scattered unresisting families:—It is evident from the talks that have been had with them, that they are not deficient in mental powers, however untutored they may be by art. It is clear that they have ideas of honor and of honesty; that they have parental affections for their offspring; that they possess many of the exquisite feelings of sensibility, although they are not so highly refined as in more cultivated societies, or polished States;—whence then can it arise, that these people should so numerously, and almost universally collect themselves together for the horrid purposes of warfare?

If you should be certainly informed that any power whatever had sent into your State, a number of Surveyors, and others, who were to apportion out lands, in order to settle them—if thousands of the subjects of such power, without your consent, were to seize on your pleasant places, and fertile vallies—if your rich pastures were to be at the mercy of the unprincipled invaders—if your children were to be driven from their wonted places of habitation—and you with your families obliged at a distance from your accustomed dwellings, to seek a precarious subsistence in the wilderness, I can scarcely doubt, but that you would feel all your passions roused with resentment;—that however peaceably you may be inclined, you would unhesitatingly resist the violence. And that the din of *war* would once more echo through your streets, should you moreover be informed, that unless you surrendered every thing most dear and precious to you, and from freemen become the slaves of your oppressors; you would be the deliberate sacrifice of unrelenting cruelty: I am conscious you would put your life into your hands, and appealing to Heaven, try the event of battles. Should this, however, be the case of the Indians, a war with them on these principles would be unjust; and every life taken will be murder. I am aware that it will be said that their lands were fairly purchased; and that therefore the States have a right to the possession of them—whether fairly purchased or finessed from them is a question that may be put; and which has been by many answered in the latter way. It has been said they have been misled and deceived in their grant—It has at other times been said that they could not dispose of the land, but that being in common, and every individual, or tribe at least, entitled to it, the grant, if any, required the concurrent unanimous consent of all, in order to its complete ratification—Has this consent been had?—It is evident that the Indians are much dissatisfied with the intrusion—that they complain of the States. That these complaints are not silent our newspapers evidence. Why, with deference, it may be asked are not these complaints answered? And the people of the northern States made acquainted with the real grounds of the controversy? Unless our right is unequivocal, it is presumptuous to appeal to the God of Battles for success—Besides, in a political point of view let each of you, my Fellow-Citizens, turn your attention to our own State, and to the Southern States in particular: How many millions of acres of rich land lie uncultivated, unimproved, and uninhabited? Are your numbers sufficiently great that you can spare for colonization? And are your labourers sufficiently numerous that you can employ them in manufactures? I fancy the man of observation will answer these things in the negative.

In wars, carried on at this day, money is the most essential article—the Federal treasury I fear does not overflow with it. But if we go to war, it must be had, and from whence? The people of this and the other States must raise it. Your quota will be required; and this requisition necessarily brings on an increase of taxes, and new impositions—It is thought that these at present are sufficiently heavy, if we have a retrospect of our late situation—Are the ravages of war as yet done away—Are your dwellings repaired, or new ones erected since the destruction of the former:—Do you find yourselves in nearly the same easy situation you were generally in before the enemy invaded your gates?—I believe this not to be the case; and therefore, you cannot bear other burthens.

There is a very serious important political question yet remains to be decided before war is resolved on—And that is, whether from the remote situation of the new States (as they are commonly termed) it will be in the power of Congress to govern them, or draw any resources from thence? But this is a question I have at present neither leisure nor ability to discuss.

CATO

For the *New-York Packet* [Friday, 24 November 1786, no. 648, p. 2, cols. 3–4]

To the Considerate Citizens of the State of New-York:

In my last address to you, I asked a serious question from those in power; it was, Why we were going to war with the Indians? This is a question that has not, or, possibly cannot, be answered satisfactorily to your feelings or understanding—the veil of impenetrable darkness is often necessary to conceal certain political measures. As it is not in my power to shew why we ought, I will endeavour to shew why we ought not to go to war with them— In every undertaking, it is necessary the effect should be considered before the attempt is made, that the benefit intended to result from the war, should be proportionably greater than the risque incurred, and the means made use of—suppose (and yet this may be doubted) the war should terminate successfully in favor of the States—suppose you should make their families and children your captives and slaves; I would then ask what benefit is to flow from these measures? Will you be benefited by having your counties depopulated, and your strength impaired in settling these lands? Will you receive advantage from the monies you must necessarily expend in securing the new States from invasions? and above all, will you ever be repaid in any way for your labours and services?

You are unacquainted with the nature of the governments intended for the new States—You, erroneously[,] suppose them to be intended for republican democratical governments—nothing less! I shall take the liberty of transcribing a part of the proceedings of the Honorable the Congress, relative to this subject, and attempt to make a few remarks thereon:—"Friday, September 29, 1786. Congress proceeded in the consideration of an ordinance for the government of the Western territory, reported by Mr. Johnson, Mr. Pinckney, Mr. Smith, Mr. Dane and Mr. Henry, and the following clause being under debate, to wit: The Governor, Judges, Legislative-Council, Secretary, and such other officers as Congress shall at any time think proper to appoint in such district, shall take an oath of office, prescribed on the 27th day of January, 1785, to the Secretary at War[,] *mutatis mutandis*, was carried in the affirmative." Here you may observe that Congress have the appointment of all the principal officers, and bodies of men in the State; by which means they are virtually in possession of the legislative, executive and judicial branches of government—Surely this is not a democracy. When the body of the people in a republic are possessed of the supreme power, this is called a democracy—Here, however, the people are not possessed of the supreme power; they have not, even the shadow of it—Besides it is a fundamental maxim in this government, that the people should chuse their ministers, that is, their magistrates. It is idle, after reading the above extract from the proceedings of Congress, to say that the people in these new States are invested with any power of election whatever—What government are they then to have? it may be asked. I answer an arbitrary despotic government. The form of a republic may perhaps farcically be held up to common view, but the real strength and direction of it, are vested in Congress; they appoint the Governor, the Judges, the Legislative-Council, the Secretary, and such other officers as they shall at any time think proper—Will these officers, thus appointable, have virtue enough to resist a compliance with the requisitions of those who have appointed and may recall them? It is true, there is a possibility they may have that virtue; but the common course of human events, and the greatness of a temptation of this kind, almost prelude the hope—These States are not to possess such a kind of government, as can, with any propriety, be called a free government. They are to be regulated, controuled, and governed according to the will of Congress; and not by Magistrates elected from out of, and by themselves:—Persons whom they never saw, who know nothing of their internal police, and who are unacquainted with the temper of the people, may be appointed to the first offices in the State, without the knowledge, and contrary to the consent of its inhabitants. Now, my Fellow-Citizens, what necessity is there for us to go to war, when success itself will lead us into the dilemma of giving our consent to the formation of governments which are diametrically opposite to our principles. In this point of view, however, it may, for some time, be in the power of Congress to govern them, and draw some resources from thence; but not such resources as will be generally beneficial, or advantageous to the United States.

There is another motive, however, that may possibly have some influence upon your minds, and probably may lead you to adopt a stronger bias against the settlement of the western territory than any that has been offered—You may have observed, that by the latter part of the eleventh article of confederation and perpetual union of the United States, any colony may be admitted into the confederation, if such admission is agreed to by nine States: Should it ever happen[,] therefore, that nine of the United Sates should agree in sentiment, that the new States, now forming in the western territory, should be admitted respectively to a seat in the Congress of the United States of America, what will your situation be? You have observed Congress have the right of appointment of all the officers of every kind in each of the new States: These new States must be represented by Delegates in Congress—Who are to appoint these Delegates? Either the Governor of the respective States, or the Legislative Body, or perhaps, for form sake, the concurrence of both—or Congress—If the Governor, or the Legislative Body should have the power of appointment, is it to be supposed they will send persons who are obnoxious to their masters? Should they appoint such as are obnoxious, their places, power and preferment are possible gone forever. If they do not appoint such as are obnoxious, we may reasonably conclude that they understand what they are about, and Congress eventually becomes the electors of its own members; if Congress themselves should elect (a measure their wisdom will always induce them to avoid) the consequences are (if our freedom is preserved) too obvious to need any comment thereon—what then will be the necessary consequences of this power with which they already are, or in all probability, will soon be invested; the confederation, all the United States have solemnly approved of and ratified—the State of New-York in particular, has done it by a very solemn act. Not doubting, therefore, but the considerate citizens, to whom I have addressed myself, will obey the laws of their country; at a future day they will find themselves in a strange predicament, they will be either under the necessity of seeing the loss of their liberty, or of resisting a law of the State solemnly and perpetually confirming and approving the articles of confederation: Whenever any congregated body of men can appoint part of its own members, or whenever the members can appoint themselves, as may be the case under the intended regulation of the new States, it is easy to see that a hateful aristocracy will be the unavoidable consequence; but, this is not all, from the resources in favor of themselves, that they may draw for a time from these States, they may arm themselves with such a power that resistance on your parts must and will be impracticable; besides what weight will the delegates of the Northern States have in the councils of the Honorable Body? Forever out-numbered, and continually out-voted, a revolution, possible a calamitous civil war must take place, and once more deluge your country with blood—This, however, it is still in your power to prevent by attending to the internal regulation of the respective States at present in the Union— You may prevent it without wandering from home in countries where you want a guide; where you may be misled, and must be deceived

CATO

For the *New-York Packet* [Friday, 8 December 1786, no. 652, p. 2, cols. 1–2]

To the Considerate Citizens of the State of New-York:

The management of Indian Affairs, so far as they respect this state, both internally and externally, have been dissatisfactory: This management has been attended with many circumstances that have excited reasonable cause of suspicions, and induced inquiries, the result of which have changed the suspicions into disagreeable certainties. This must always be the unavoidable consequence of undertakings not founded upon the basis of public justice; and public integrity must mark proceedings that are attended with a want of candor, and a criminal disingenuity. The human mind in the investigation of a question of this kind, naturally and unavoidably fixes its opinion on the side which is supported by reason and principle. In examining the situation

of the controversy now subsisting between the United States of America and
the Indians possessing the Western Territory, it may be well to enquire what
right the United States have to go to war with them? The answer to this question is attended with some difficulty. Vattel, one of the best writers upon the
law of mations, has taken up the celebrated question, Whether a nation may
lawfully take possession of a vast country, in which there are found none but
erratic nations, incapable, by the smallness of their numbers, to people the
whole? The solution given by him to this question, is as curious as it is dissatisfactory—He replies, their removing their habitations through these
immense regions, cannot be taken for a true and legal possession: And the
people of Europe, too closely pent up, finding land, of which these nations
are in no particular want, and of which they make no actual and constant
use, may lawfully possess it, and establish colonies there. This question takes
for granted what is not proved. It supposes all the Indian Nations to be erratic,
eluding the great dispute, and circumscribing himself within limits almost
too narrow for a philosophical investigation of the principle. When the
Spaniards by Cortez, took possession of the Mexican empire, had the Mexi-
cans no permanent habitations? Where was Montezuma taken? In the wilderness! Had he elegant palaces, sumptuous edifices and populous cities? Did
his empire consist merely of erratic nations? Were they continually removing
their habitations through these immense regions? Turn to the page of history,
and you will find the reverse to be the case. It is, for the purposes of humanity,
[such] a hard case that even the finest writers on this question have not given
it a candid discussion: They have never attended to the millions murdered
by the cruel instruments of their more cruel oppressors. While they have
shrinked at the torture and torment inflicted on the innocent and guiltless
inhabitants, they have stifled the voice of philanthropy, and shut their ears
against the cries of the distressed. The governments of Mexico and Peru, did
not consist of erratic nations; and therefore did not come within the reply
given by this writer: But if this would be a full and satisfactory answer, I
would then inquire, whether, upon the same principle, the Indian tribes might
not lawfully take possession of all such lands in our state as we do not make
use of. We will go, say they, and settle in the state of New-York, our ancient
hunting grounds—the citizens cannot rightfully dispossess us, because nature
has imposed an obligation on mankind to cultivate the soil. Every nation
then is obliged, by the law of nature, to cultivate the ground that has fallen
to its share; and it has not right to expect or require assistance from others,
any farther than the land in its possession is incapable of furnishing it with
necessaries. But the state of New-York does not cultivate a large part of their
soil; therefore, not fulfilling the duty imposed on them by the law of nature,
we may rightfully take possession of the uncultivated soil; and we shall be
justified in our consciences under the great law of nature imposed upon all

mankind. Should this be the case, and such their reasoning, upon what principle could we oppose them? Upon no other principle could you take up arms against them, than that which you are now about calling to your aid, that is violence. The advocates for the dispossessing the Indians of their country, will not, I trust, pretend to say that the same arguments shall not be made use of, and the same means pursued by the Indians as well as the states; by the red as well as the white man. If it is admitted that the measure of justice should govern each, upon the forgoing deductions, I shall draw this necessary inference with regard to the first part of the question, that is, the reply is not only dissatisfactory, but the offspring of ignorance and puerility. "The people of Europe," it is said, "too closely pent up, finding land of which these nations are in no particular want, and of which they make no effectual and constant use, may lawfully possess it, and establish colonies there." If we take a view of Europe at large, we shall find the writer has taken for granted, a fact that does not exist. We cannot particularise any one nation, as his observation is general, and as such is untrue. But taking for granted what cannot be admitted as fact, it becomes necessary for us seriously to enquire whether this is our case: Are we so closely pent up that we are under the necessity of finding land of which these nations "are in no particular want?" Are our manufactories so well supplied with artificers and labourers that we can afford to people new countries? Not only afford to do this, but under a necessity of forming colonies in order to provide for our redundant citizens. The argument, drawn from necessity, it is true is supreme; but until this is our situation, we ought not to be unjust—we ought not to be dishonest. We may, by this means, it has been said, leave a fair possession to descend to posterity: By making war with the Indians, or in other words, cruelly scalping them, their wives and helpless offspring, we shall transmit to our descendents a noble inheritance— an inheritance basely tarnished with the blood of the oppressed—gained by dishonest practices—and desolated by the instruments of violence and injustice.

Some have held that a nation is never punished by the great and benevolent Author of our being for its political sins. If we should confine ourselves solely to the language of the holy scriptures, we shall easily be able to show that punishment hath been and always will be the consequence of national injustice. But this is not all—Inferences within our own consideration tend to evidence, that political injustice is accompanied with political destruction; previous to the Spaniards discovering South America they were flourishing, rich and war-like, famed for their honesty, and sacred to their word; as soon[,] however, as the riches of Mexico and Peru were discovered—as soon as the glittering metals were transported into their country, their national character began to decay; they grew listless, and indolent, and at this time their strength and respectability, in a great measure[,] depend upon the arrivals of their

American galleons. The great political features which marked the country at that time are done away; and the noble and elevated virtues that in general characterized the nation are only to be found among the more respectable people. They therefore may, with propriety, be said to suffer political punishment for their political dishonesty; that they are punished according to their own measure of injustice and consonant to the exact scale which they have made use of towards others.

I shall in my next, proceed to discuss the remaining part of this great question. I shall endeavor to answer some objections that I apprehend, may remain in the minds of my readers, with candor and without passion, submitting these rude outlines to the serious reflections of my considerate fellow citizens.

CATO

For the *New-York Packet* [Tuesday, 19 December 1786, no. 655, p. 2, cols. 1–2]

To the Considerate Citizens of the State of New-York:

In my last address to you, I apprehended some objections would rest in your minds, whether it might not be lawful for the Honorable the Congress to possess themselves of the Western Country, on the principle, that the numerous tribes of Indians inhabiting that territory, were comprehended within the denomination of erratic nations, and therefore, according to Vattel, might be dispossessed; their country taken from them, and on resistance the utter extirpation of them must be ranked among those laudable actions that render the glory of nations immortal; this question brings us nearer home in its investigations—we need not recur to history because facts are present with us. One certain undeniable fact is, that these nations or tribes dwell in fixed and settled villages and towns; now no nation that has a fixed place of residence can, with any propriety, be said to be an erratic nation—the term itself, in its definition, meaning a nation whose habitations are continually removing, who intend not to return to the place they have formerly left, and who leave no possessory marks behind them, by which they declare their intention of returning; or, in other words, a nation that to the spot it has left, surrenders up its occupancy to the next comer. But this is by no means the case with the inhabitants of the Western Territory, for they have fixed places of residence; places they have immemorially occupied, and which lawfully belong to them: should it be denied that they maintain such continual possession, and occupy such fixed habitations, it might be possibly proved by the numerous publications that are industriously circulated in the daily newspapers of the State; you find it proclaimed to you, that in a late incursion six of the Shawanese villages were utterly destroyed, a number of the Shawanese men, among whom were several Chiefs, tomahawked and scalped, and their women and children after the distressing scene of beholding the massacre of their tenderest connections, reduced to the more distressing condition of slavery—this one publication selected from many others, clearly proves that their habitations are fixed; and if so, they are not erratic nations. Yet it may be objected, they are not entitled to the extent of territory they possess because they cannot cultivate it; I would ask who is to be the judge of this possibility? not the United States; for they have no right to interfere in the decision of the question—indeed, according to the laws of nations, no nation has a right to interfere in this possession of theirs, unless they are under the necessity of finding new countries in order to support a number of their citizens, who cannot procure the means of subsistence in their native country; it is a clear position, that no nation has a right to expect or require assistance from other any farther than as the land in its possession is incapable of furnishing it with necessaries. It is not pretended that any such necessity exists in the United States, in any manner or way whatever, and if it did, these tribes no being erratic, the laws of nations will tell you, that in order to proceed lawfully, you must gain the territory you wish to occupy either by treaty or purchase. The law of necessity is nearly the same in political as in private life—if I am starving for want of food, and reduced to that situation not by any fault of mine, I may of right take a sufficiency of provision for my present immediate sustenance, from my neighbor, and that even by violence: This principle is recognized by all the laws of all civilized nations. It is incumbent however upon the person committing this act to how that the necessity did exist, that he could not supply himself in any other manner: And that therefore, by the operation of this great principle, he ought to stand at least excusable—similar should be the conduct of political societies: If the land in its possession is incapable of subsisting its inhabitants, let them apply to those nations whose territories are more widely extended, and infinitely superior to all their wants; let them endeavour to gain a residence either by persuasion or purchase! If this reasonable request should be denied, force becomes justifiable, and resistance on the part of the occupiers unlawful; but are we in want of any real necessities that the Western Territory can supply us with? Were this the case, fellow citizens, would there be any difficulty to raise armies to procure what was actually required for our subsistence? Would not the natural stimulus of necessity soon arm legions of men, ready to undertake the daring task? But this is all idle argumentation in the discussion of the present point—the truth is, when divested of the tinsel that glitters around it, that other than equitable principles sway the opinions and determinations of the leaders of the present measure—principles neither founded in justice, policy, nor reason—not founded in justice, because there is no necessity for the war, and without the necessity, the attempt is criminal—it is not politic, for we want, if I may be allowed the expression, even to colonize our own

State—not politic, for it may possibly involve us in wars that may be attended with the most dismal consequence—in fine, not politic, because a state of peace is at present the only means by which we can recruit and increase our strength; I hold it not to be reasonable, that any new burthens should be imposed upon the citizens of the States to make acquisitions of countries which they at present have no need of; and from whence the resources, if any, will be inadequate and precarious; and the settlement of which must ultimately tend to the political destruction of this and the other northern States.

It is remarked in common, and probably may be true in political life, that the voluntary confession of the party against himself, is the best evidence you can possibly gain of the truth of any fact. Should this hold true, from a late publication it may be gathered that no principle of necessity has any effect upon the business; the reason given why this extensive and valuable tract of country ought to be possessed by the United States, is, that this territory has been *justly* considered as a fund capable of going far towards discharging the foederal domestic debts—here at once is given up all pretence to equity, honesty, or justice; it is actually an excuse for substituting mean and mercenary motives instead of those grand and elevated principles that should guide all States in all their transactions—it is in fact, with the strong arm of violence declaring, we have no right either by the law of God or man, to take away your territories, but our interest is our matter, and we implicitly obey its impulses.—Possibly some expressions in this address may appear too harsh—possibly to many they may appear singular; permit me therefore in order to convince the Considerate Citizens of this State of the propriety of the arguments offered, to transcribe a passage from the great Judge Blackstone's commentaries: "When the multitude of men and cattle had consumed every convenience on one spot of ground, it was deemed a natural right to seize upon and occupy such other lands as would more easily supply their necessities." "Upon the same principle," says he, "was founded the right of migration, or sending colonies to find out new habitations, when the mother country was over-charged with inhabitants; which was practiced as well by the Phoenicians and Greeks, as the Germans, Scythians, and other northern people: And so long as it was confined to the stocking and cultivation of desart uninhabited countries, it kept strictly within the limits of the law of nature. But how far the seizing on countries already peopled, and driving out or massacring the innocent and defenceless natives, merely because they differed from their invaders in language, religion, in customs, in government or in colour; how far such a conduct was consonant to nature, to reason, or to christianity, deserved well to be considered by those who have rendered their names immortal by thus civilizing mankind."

CATO

Appendix B:
Johnson v. M'Intosh

It was then the middle of winter, and the cold was unusually severe; the snow had frozen hard upon the ground, and the river was drifting huge masses of ice. The Indians had their families with them, and they brought in their train the wounded and the sick, with children newly born and old men upon the verge of death. They possessed neither tents nor wagons, but only their arms and some provisions.

I saw them embark to pass the mighty river, and never will that solemn spectacle fade from my remembrance. No cry, no sob, was heard among the assembled crowd; all were silent. Their calamities were of ancient date, and they knew them to be irremediable. The Indians had all stepped into the bark that was to carry them across, but their dogs remained upon the bank. As soon as these animals perceived that their masters were finally leaving the shore, they set up a dismal howl and, plunging all together into the icy waters of the Mississippi, swam after the boat.

—Alexis de Tocqueville[1]

Not until 1823 did the Illinois and Wabash Land Company get its day in court. By then a succession of Congressional committees had responded to petitions by the Company to grant them land or money based upon the purchases of 1773 and 1775, and the response was consistently negative: "*Resolved*, That the prayer of the of the petition ought not to be granted."[2] By 1823, James Wilson had long since died, and the case involving his company's claims had worked its way up to the Supreme Court. By his ruling in *Johnson v. M'Intosh*, Chief Justice James Marshall determined once and for all the fate of this long-ago investment in the Old Northwest. The immediate result of the judgment was to deny the claim of James Wilson's company. But Marshall would go further: embodied in his ruling was the so-called Discovery Doctrine, stating that whatever relationship the Indians might have had to the land they lived upon in ancient times, the nature of that tenure mysteriously changed once Europeans claimed the continent as their own. From that point on, according to Marshall, it was only the "right of occupancy" which the Native people could sell—and only to the "lawful" conquerors. Lawful in whose eyes? Well, in their own, of course—but John Marshall wasn't about to argue with several hundred years of history. It was a only short step from Marshall's opinion—that the Native Americans hadn't owned the land since the first European sailor, high up in his crow's nest, spotted a vague shape on the horizon—to the whole sad policy of "Indian Removal."[3]

Not until 2010 did President Barack Obama announce that the United States would sign the United Nations Declaration on the Rights of Indigenous Peoples, affirming "the right to the lands, territories and resources which they have traditionally owned, occupied, or otherwise used or acquired."[4]

Johnson & Graham's Lessee v. M'Intosh[5]

March 10, 1823
Mr. Chief Justice Marshall delivered the opinion of the Court.

The plaintiffs in this cause claim the land, in their declaration mentioned, under two grants, purporting to be made, the first in 1773, and the last in 1775, by the chiefs of certain Indian tribes constituting the Illinois and the Piankeshaw nations, and the question is whether this title can be recognized in the courts of the United States?

The facts, as stated in the case agreed, show the authority of the chiefs who executed this conveyance so far as it could be given by their own people, and likewise show that the particular tribes for whom these chiefs acted were in rightful possession of the land they sold. The inquiry, therefore, is in a great measure confined to the power of Indians to give, and of private individuals to receive, a title which can be sustained in the courts of this country.

As the right of society to prescribe those rules by which property may be acquired and preserved is not and cannot be drawn into question, as the title to lands especially is and must be admitted to depend entirely on the law of the nation in which they lie, it will be necessary in pursuing this inquiry to examine not singly those principles of abstract justice which the Creator of all things has impressed on the mind of his creature man and which are admitted to regulate in a great degree the rights of civilized nations, whose perfect independence is acknowledged, but those principles also which our own government has adopted in the particular case and given us as the rule for our decision.

On the discovery of this immense continent, the great nations of Europe were eager to appropriate to themselves so much of it as they could respectively acquire. Its vast extent offered an ample field to the ambition and enterprise of all, and the character and religion of its inhabitants afforded an apology for considering them as a people over whom the superior genius of Europe might claim an ascendency. The potentates of the old world found no difficulty in convincing themselves that they made ample compensation to the inhabitants of the new by bestowing on them civilization and Christianity in exchange for unlimited independence. But as they were all in pursuit of nearly the same object, it was necessary, in order to avoid conflicting settlements and consequent war with each other, to establish a principle which all should acknowledge as the law by which the right of acquisition, which they all asserted should be regulated as between themselves. This principle was that discovery gave title to the government by whose subjects or by whose authority it was made against all other European governments, which title might be consummated by possession.

The exclusion of all other Europeans necessarily gave to the nation making the discovery the sole right of acquiring the soil from the natives and establishing settlements upon it. It was a right with which no Europeans could interfere. It was a right which all asserted for themselves, and to the assertion of which by others all assented.

Those relations which were to exist between the discoverer and the natives were to be regulated by themselves. The rights thus acquired being exclusive, no other power could interpose between them.

In the establishment of these relations, the rights of the original inhabitants were in no instance entirely disregarded, but were necessarily to a considerable extent impaired. They were admitted to be the rightful occupants of the soil, with a legal as well as just claim to retain possession of it, and to use it according to their own discretion; but their rights to complete sovereignty as independent nations were necessarily diminished, and their power to dispose of the soil at their own will to whomsoever they pleased was denied by the original fundamental principle that discovery gave exclusive title to those who made it.

While the different nations of Europe respected the right of the natives as occupants, they asserted the ultimate dominion to be in themselves, and claimed and exercised, as a consequence of this ultimate dominion, a power to grant the soil while yet in possession of the natives. These grants have been understood by all to convey a title to the grantees, subject only to the Indian right of occupancy.

The history of America from its discovery to the present day proves, we think, the universal recognition of these principles....

[Marshall proceeds here to outline the history of the European conquest of America.—RA]

Thus all the nations of Europe who have acquired territory on this continent have asserted in themselves and have recognized in others the exclusive right of the discoverer to appropriate the lands occupied by the Indians. Have the American states rejected or adopted this principle?

By the treaty which concluded the war of our revolution, Great Britain relinquished all claim not only to the government, but to the "propriety and territorial rights of the United States" whose boundaries were fixed in the second article. By this treaty the powers of government and the right to soil which had previously been in Great Britain passed definitively to these states. We had before taken possession of them by declaring independence, but neither the declaration of independence nor the treaty confirming it could give us more than that which we before possessed or to which Great Britain was before entitled. It has never been doubted that either the United States or the several states had a clear title to all the lands within the boundary lines described in the treaty, subject only to the Indian right of occupancy, and that the exclusive power to extinguish that right was vested in that government which might constitutionally exercise it.

Virginia, particularly, within whose chartered limits the land in controversy lay, passed an act in the year 1779 declaring her "exclusive right of preemption from the Indians of all the lands within the limits of her own chartered territory, and that no person or persons whatsoever have or ever had a right to purchase any lands within the same from any Indian nation except only persons duly authorized to make such purchase, formerly for the use and benefit of the colony and lately for the Commonwealth." The act then proceeds to annul all deeds made by Indians to individuals for the private use of the purchasers....

In pursuance of the same idea, Virginia proceeded at the same session to open her land office for the sale of that country which now constitutes Kentucky, a country every acre of which was then claimed and possessed by Indians, who maintained their title with as much persevering courage as was ever manifested by any people.

The states, having within their chartered limits different portions of territory covered by Indians, ceded that territory generally to the United States on conditions expressed in their deeds of cession, which demonstrate the opinion that they ceded the soil as well as jurisdiction, and that in doing so they granted a productive fund to the government of the Union. The lands in controversy lay within the chartered limits of Virginia, and were ceded with the whole country northwest of the River Ohio. This grant contained reservations and stipulations which could only be made by the owners of the soil, and concluded with a stipulation that "all the lands in the ceded territory not reserved should be considered as a common fund for the use and benefit of such of the United States as have become or shall become members of the confederation ... according to their usual respective proportions in the general charge and expenditure, and shall be faithfully and bona fide disposed of for that purpose, and for no other use or purpose whatsoever."

The ceded territory was occupied by numerous and warlike tribes of Indians, but the exclusive right of the United States to extinguish their title and to grant the soil has never, we believe, been doubted....

We will not enter into the controversy whether agriculturists, merchants, and manufacturers have a right on abstract principles to expel hunters from the territory they possess or to contract their limits. Conquest gives a title which the courts of the conqueror cannot deny, whatever the private and speculative opinions of individuals may be, respecting the original justice of the claim which has been successfully asserted. The British government, which was then our government and whose rights have passed to the United States, asserted title to all the lands occupied by Indians within the chartered limits of the British colonies. It asserted also a limited sovereignty over them and the exclusive right of extinguishing the title which occupancy gave to them. These claims have been maintained and established as far west as the River Mississippi by the sword. The title to a vast portion of the lands we now hold originates in them. It is not for the courts of this country to question the validity of this title or to sustain one which is incompatible with it....

However extravagant the pretension of converting the discovery of an inhabited country into conquest may appear; if the principle has been asserted in the first instance, and afterwards sustained; if a country has been acquired and held under it; if the property of the great mass of the community originates in it, it becomes the law of the land and cannot be questioned. So, too, with respect to the concomitant principle that the Indian inhabitants are to be considered merely as occupants, to be protected, indeed, while in peace, in the possession of their lands, but to be deemed incapable of transferring the absolute title to others. However this restriction may be opposed to natural right, and to the usages of civilized nations, yet if it be indispensable to that system under which the country has been settled, and be adapted to the actual condition of the two people, it may perhaps be supported by reason, and certainly cannot be rejected by courts of justice....

This opinion conforms precisely to the principle which has been supposed to be recognised by all European governments, from the first settlement of America. The absolute ultimate title has been considered as acquired by discovery, subject only to the Indian title of occupancy, which title the discoverers possessed the exclusive right of acquiring.

Appendix C:
Speech of the
United Indian Nations

Speech of the United Indian Nations, at their Confederate Council, held near the mouth of the Detroit river, the 28th November and 18th December 1786.[1]

PRESENT—The Five Nations, the Hurons, Delawares, Shawanese, Ottawas, Chippewas, Powtewattimies, Twichtwees, Cherokees, and the Wabash Confederates.

To the Congress of the United States of America:
BRETHREN OF THE UNITED STATES OF AMERICA: It is now more than three years since peace was made between the King of Great Britain and you, but we, the Indians, were disappointed, finding ourselves not included in that peace, according to our expectations: for we thought that its conclusion would have promoted a friendship between the United States and Indians, and that we might enjoy that happiness that formerly subsisted between us and our elder brethren. We have received two very agreeable messages from the thirteen United States. We also received a message from the King, whose war we were engaged in, desiring us to remain quiet, which we accordingly complied with. During the time of this tranquility, we were deliberating the best method we could to form a lasting reconciliation with the thirteen United Sates. Pleased at the same time, we thought we were entering upon a reconciliation and friendship with a set of people born on the same continent with ourselves, certain that the quarrel between us was not of our own making. In the course of our councils, we imagined we hit upon an expedient that would promote a lasting peace between us.

BROTHERS: We still are of the same opinion as to the means which may tend to reconcile us to each other; and we are sorry to find, although we had the best thoughts in our minds, during the beforementioned period, mischief has, nevertheless, happened between you and us. We are still anxious of putting our plan of accommodation into execution, and we shall briefly inform you of the means that seem most probable to us of effecting a firm and lasting peace and reconciliation: the first step towards which should, in our opinion, be, that all treaties carried on with the United States, on our parts, should be with the general voice of the whole confederacy, and carried on in the most open manner, without any restraint on either side; and especially as landed matters are often the subject of our councils with you, a matter of the greatest importance and of general concern to us, in this case we hold it indispensably necessary that any cession of our lands should be made in the most public manner, and by the united voice of the confederacy; holding all partial treaties as void and of no effect.

BROTHERS: We think it is owing to you that the tranquility which, since the peace between us, has not lasted, and that the essential good has been followed by mischief and confusion, having managed every thing respecting us your own way. You kindled your council fires where you thought proper, without consulting us, at which you held separate treaties, and have entirely neglected our plan of having a general conference with the different Nations of the confederacy. Had this happened, we have reason to believe every thing would now have been settled between us in a most friendly manner. We did every thing in our power, at the treaty of Fort Stanwix, to induce you to follow this plan, as our real intentions were, at that very time, to promote peace and concord between us, and that we might look upon each other as friends, having given you no cause or provocation to be otherwise.

BROTHERS: Notwithstanding the mischief that has happened, we are still sincere in our wishes to have peace and tranquility established between us, earnestly hoping to find the same inclination in you. We wish, therefore, you would take it into serious consideration, and let us speak to you in the manner we proposed. Let us have a treaty with you early in the spring; let us pursue reasonable steps; let us meet half ways, for our mutual convenience; we shall then bring in oblivion the misfortunes that have happened, and meet each other on a footing of friendship.

BROTHERS: We say let us meet half way, and let us pursue such steps as become upright and honest men. We beg that you will prevent your surveyors and other people from coming upon our side [of] the Ohio river. We have told you before, we wished to pursue just steps, and we are determined they shall appear just and reasonable in the eyes of the world. This is the determination of all the chiefs of our confederacy now assembled here, notwithstanding the accidents that have happened in our villages, even when in council, where several innocent chiefs were killed when absolutely engaged in promoting a peace with you, the thirteen United States.

Although then interrupted, the chiefs here present still wish to meet you in the spring, for the beforementioned good purpose, when we hope to speak to each other without either haughtiness or menaces.

BROTHERS: We again request of you, in the most earnest manner, to order your surveyors and others, that mark out lands, to cease from crossing the Ohio, until we shall have spoken to you, because the mischief that has recently happened has originated in that quarter; we shall likewise prevent our people from going over until that time

BROTHERS: It shall not be our faults if the plans which we have suggested to you should not be carried into execution; in that case the event will be very precarious, and if fresh ruptures ensue, we hope to be able to exculpate ourselves, and shall most assuredly, with our united force, be obliged to defend those rights and privileges which have been transmitted to us by our ancestors; and if we should be thereby reduced to misfortunes, the world will pity us when they think of the amicable proposals we now make to prevent the unnecessary effusion of blood. These are our thoughts and firm resolves, and we earnestly desire that you will transmit to us, as soon as possible, you answer, be it what it may.

Done at our Confederated Council Fire, at the Huron village, near the mouth of the Detroit river, December 18th, 1786.

> The Five Nations,
> Hurons,
> Ottawas,
> Twichtwees,
> Shawanese,
> Chippewas,
> Cherokees,
> Delawares,
> Powtewatimies,
> The Wabash Confederates.

Appendix D:
Complete Text
of the Northwest Ordinance
and the Resolve of 1784

AN ORDINANCE FOR THE GOVERNMENT
OF THE TERRITORY OF THE UNITED STATES
NORTH WEST OF THE RIVER OHIO[1]

Be it ordained by the United States in Congress Assembled that the said territory for the purposes of temporary government be one district, subject however to be divided into two districts as future circumstances may in the Opinion of Congress make it expedient.

Be it ordained by the authority aforesaid, that the estates both of resident and non resident proprietors in the said territory dying intestate shall descend to and be distributed among their children and the descendants of a deceased child in equal parts; the descendants of a deceased child or grand child to take the share of their deceased parent in equal parts among them; and where there shall be no children or descendants then in equal parts to the next of kin in equal degree and among collaterals the children of a deceased brother or sister of the intestate shall have in equal parts among them their deceased parent's share and there shall in no case be a distinction between kindred of the whole and half blood; saving in all cases to the widow of the intestate her third part of the real estate for life, and one third part of the personal estate; and this law relative to descents and dower shall remain in full force until altered by the legislature of the district. And until the governor and judges shall adopt laws as hereinafter mentioned estates in the said territory may be devised or bequeathed by wills in writing signed and sealed by him or her in whom the estate may be, being of full age, and attested by three witnesses, and real estates may be conveyed by lease and release or bargain and sale signed, sealed and delivered by the person being of full age in whom the estate may be and attested by two witnesses provided such wills be duly proved and such conveyances be acknowledged or the execution thereof duly proved and be recorded within one year after proper magistrates, courts and registers shall be appointed for that purpose and personal property may be transferred by delivery saving however to the French and Canadian inhabitants and other settlers of the Kaskaskies, Saint Vincents and the neighbouring villages who have heretofore professed themselves citizens of Virginia, their laws and customs now in force among them relative to the descent and conveyance of property.

Be it ordained by the authority aforesaid that there shall be appointed from time to time by Congress a governor, whose commission shall continue in force for the term of three years, unless sooner revoked by Congress; he shall reside in the district and have a freehold estate therein, in one thousand acres of land while in the exercise of his office. There shall be appointed from time to time by Congress a secretary, whose commission shall continue in force for four years, unless sooner revoked; he shall reside in the district and have a freehold estate therein in five hundred acres of land while in the exercise of his office; It shall be his duty to keep and preserve the acts and laws passed by the legislature and the public records of the district and the proceedings of the governor in his executive department and transmit authentic copies of such acts and proceedings every six months to the Secretary of Congress. There shall also be appointed a Court to consist of three judges any two of whom to form a court, who shall have a common law jurisdiction and reside in the district and have each therein a freehold estate in five hundred acres of land while in the exercise of their offices, and their commissions shall continue in force during good behaviour.

The governor, and judges or a majority of them shall adopt and publish in the district such laws of the original states criminal and civil as may be necessary and best suited to the circumstances of the district and report them to Congress from time to time, which laws shall be in force in the district until the organization of the general assembly therein, unless disapproved of by Congress; but afterwards the legislature shall have authority to alter them as they shall think fit.

The governor for the time being shall be Commander in chief of the militia, appoint and commission all officers in the same below the rank of general Officers; All general Officers shall be appointed and commissioned by Congress.

Previous to the Organization of the general Assembly the governor shall appoint such magistrates and other civil officers in each county or township, as he shall find necessary for the preservation of the peace and good order in the same. After the general Assembly shall be organized, the powers and duties of magistrates and other civil officers shall be regulated and defined by the said Assembly; but all magistrates and other civil officers, not herein otherwise directed shall during the continuance of this temporary government be appointed by the governor.

For the prevention of crimes and injuries the laws to be adopted or made shall have force in all parts of the district and for the execution of process criminal and civil, the governor shall make proper divisions thereof, and he shall proceed from time to time as circumstances may require to lay out the parts of the district in which the Indian titles shall have been extinguished into counties and townships subject however to such alterations as may thereafter be made by the legislature.

So soon as there shall be five thousand free male inhabitants of full age in the district upon giving proof thereof to the governor, they shall receive authority with time and place to elect representatives from their counties or townships to represent them in the general assembly, provided that for every five hundred free male inhabitants there shall be one representative and so on progressively with the number of free male inhabitants shall the right of representation encrease until the number of representatives shall amount to twenty five after which the number and proportion of representatives shall be regulated by the legislature; provided that no person be eligible or qualified to act as a representative unless he shall have been a citizen of one of the United States three years and be a resident in the district or unless he shall have resided in the district three years and in either case shall likewise hold in his own right in fee simple two hundred acres of land within the same; provided also that a freehold in fifty acres of land in the district having been a citizen of one of the states and being resident in the district; or the like freehold and two years residence in the district shall be necessary to qualify a man as an elector of a representative.

The representatives thus elected shall serve for the term of two years and in case of the death of a representative or removal from office, the governor shall issue a writ to the county or township for which he was a member, to elect another in his stead to serve for the residue of the term.

The general assembly or legislature shall consist of the governor, legislative council and a house of representatives. The legislative council shall consist of five members to continue in Office five years unless sooner removed by Congress any three of whom to be a quorum and the members of the council shall be nominated and appointed in the following manner, to wit; As soon as representatives shall be elected, the governor shall appoint a time and place for them to meet together, and when met they shall nominate ten persons residents in the district and each possessed of a freehold in five hundred acres of Land and return their names to Congress; five of whom Congress shall appoint and commission to serve as aforesaid; and whenever a vacancy shall happen in the council by death or removal from office, the house of representatives shall nominate two persons qualified as aforesaid, for each vacancy, and return their names to Congress, one of whom Congress shall appoint and commission for the residue of the term, and every five years, four months at least before the expiration of the time of service of the Members of Council, the said house shall nominate ten persons qualified as aforesaid, and return their names to Congress, five of whom Congress shall appoint and commission to serve as Members of the council five years, unless sooner removed. And the Governor, legislative council, and house of representatives, shall have authority to make laws in all cases for the good government of the district, not repugnant to the principles and Articles in this Ordinance established and declared. And all bills having passed by a majority in the house, and by a majority in the council, shall be referred to the Governor for his assent; but no bill or legislative Act whatever, shall be of any force without his assent. The Governor shall have power to convene, prorogue and dissolve the General Assembly, when in his opinion it shall be expedient.

The Governor, Judges, legislative Council, Secretary, and such other Officers as Congress shall appoint in the district shall take an Oath or Affirmation of fidelity, and of Office, the Governor before the president of Congress, and all other Officers before the Governor. As soon as a legislature shall be formed in the district, the Council and house assembled in one room, shall have authority by joint ballot to elect a Delegate to Congress, who shall have a seat in Congress, with a right of debating, but not of voting, during this temporary Government.

And for extending the fundamental principles of civil and religious liberty, which form the basis whereon these republics, their laws and constitutions are erected; to fix and establish those principles as the basis of all laws, constitutions and governments, which forever hereafter shall be formed in the said territory; to provide also for the establishment of States and permanent government therein, and for their admission to a share in the federal Councils on an equal footing with the original States, at as early periods as may be consistent with the general interest,

It is hereby Ordained and declared by the authority aforesaid, That the following Articles shall be considered as Articles of compact between the Original States and the people and States in the said territory, and forever remain unalterable, unless by common consent, to wit,

Article the First. No person demeaning himself in a peaceable and orderly manner shall ever be molested on account of his mode of worship or religious sentiments in the said territory.

Article the Second. The Inhabitants of the said territory shall always be entitled to the benefits of the writ of habeas corpus, and of the trial by Jury;

of a proportionate representation of the people in the legislature, and of judicial proceedings according to the course of the common law; all persons shall be bailable unless for capital offences, where the proof shall be evident, or the presumption great; all fines shall be moderate, and no cruel or unusual punishments shall be inflicted; no man shall be deprived of his liberty or property but by the judgment of his peers, or the law of the land; and should the public exigencies make it necessary for the common preservation to take any persons property, or to demand his particular services, full compensation shall be made for the same; and in the just preservation of rights and property it is understood and declared; that no law ought ever to be made, or have force in the said territory, that shall in any manner whatever interfere with, or affect private contracts or engagements, bona fide and without fraud previously formed.

Article the Third. Religion, Morality and knowledge being necessary to good government and the happiness of mankind, Schools and the means of education shall forever be encouraged. The utmost good faith shall always be observed towards the Indians, their lands and property shall never be taken from them without their consent; and in their property, rights and liberty, they never shall be invaded or disturbed, unless in just and lawful wars authorised by Congress; but laws founded in justice and humanity shall from time to time be made, for preventing wrongs being done to them, and for preserving peace and friendship with them.

Article the Fourth. The said territory, and the States which may be formed therein shall forever remain a part of this Confederacy of the United States of America, subject to the Articles of Confederation, and to such alterations therein as shall be constitutionally made; and to all the Acts and Ordinances of the United States in Congress Assembled, conformable thereto. The Inhabitants and Settlers in the said territory, shall be subject to pay a part of the federal debts contracted or to be contracted, and a proportional part of the expences of Government, to be apportioned on them by Congress, according to the same common rule and measure by which apportionments thereof shall be made on the other States; and the taxes for paying their proportion, shall be laid and levied by the authority and direction of the legislatures of the district or districts or new States, as in the original States, within the time agreed upon by the United States in Congress Assembled. The Legislatures of those districts, or new States, shall never interfere with the primary disposal of the Soil by the United States in Congress Assembled, nor with any regulations Congress may find necessary for securing the title in such soil to the bona fide purchasers. No tax shall be imposed on lands the property of the United States; and in no case shall non resident proprietors be taxed higher than residents. The navigable Waters leading into the Mississippi and St. Lawrence, and the carrying places between the same shall be common highways, and forever free, as well to the Inhabitants of the said territory, as to the Citizens of the United States, and those of any other States that may be admitted into the Confederacy, without any tax, impost or duty therefor.

Article the Fifth. There shall be formed in the said territory, not less than three nor more than five States, and the boundaries of the States, as soon as Virginia shall alter her act of cession and consent to the same, shall become fixed and established as follows, to wit: The Western State in the said territory, shall be bounded by the Mississippi, the Ohio and Wabash rivers; a direct line drawn from the Wabash and post Vincents due North to the territorial line between the United States and Canada, and by the said territorial line to the lake of the Woods and Mississippi. The middle State shall be bounded by the said direct line, the Wabash from post Vincents to the Ohio; by the Ohio, by direct line drawn due North from the mouth of the great Miami to the said territorial line, and by the said territorial line. The eastern State shall be bounded by the last mentioned direct line, the Ohio, Pennsylvania, and the said territorial line; provided however, and it is further understood and declared, that the boundaries of these three States, shall be subject so far to be altered, that if Congress shall hereafter find it expedient, they shall have authority to form one or two States in that part of the said territory which lies north of an east and west line drawn through the southerly bend or extreme of lake Michigan; and whenever any of the said States shall have sixty thousand free Inhabitants therein, such State shall be admitted by its Delegates into the Congress of the United States, on an equal footing with the original States, in all respects whatever; and shall be at liberty to form a permanent constitution and State government, provided the constitution and government so to be formed, shall be republican, and in conformity to the principles contained in these Articles; and so far as it can be consistent with the general interest of the Confederacy, such admission shall be allowed at an earlier period, and when there may be a less number of free Inhabitants in the State than sixty thousand.

Article the Sixth. There shall be neither Slavery nor involuntary Servitude in the said territory otherwise than in the punishment of crimes, whereof the party shall have been duly convicted; provided always that any person escaping into the same, from whom labor or service is lawfully claimed in any one of the original States, such fugitive may be lawfully reclaimed and conveyed to the person claiming his or her labor or service as aforesaid.

Be it Ordained by the Authority aforesaid, that the Resolutions of the 23d of April 1784 relative to the subject of this ordinance be, and the same are hereby repealed and declared null and void.

RESOLVE OF 1784[2]
BY THE UNITED STATES IN CONGRESS ASSEMBLED
[APRIL 23, 1784]

Resolved, That so much of the territory ceded, or to be ceded by individual states, to the United States, as is already purchased, or shall be purchased, of the Indian inhabitants, and offered for sale by Congress, shall be divided into distinct states in the following manner, as nearly as such cessions will admit; that is to say, by parallels of latitude, so that each state shall comprehend from north to south two degrees of latitude, beginning to count from the completion of forty-five degrees north of the equator; and by meridians of longitude, one of which shall pass through the lowest point of the rapids of Ohio, and the other through the western cape of the mouth the great Kanhaway: but the territory eastward of this last meridian, between the Ohio, lake Erie, and Pennsylvania, shall be one state, whatsoever may be its comprehension of latitude. That which may lie beyond the completion of the forty-fifth degree between the said meridians shall make part of the state adjoining it on the south; and that part of the Ohio, which is between the same meridians coinciding nearly with the parallel of thirty-nine degrees, shall be substituted so far in lieu of that parallel as a boundary line.

That the settlers on any territory so purchased and offered for sale, shall, either on their own petition, or on the order of Congress, receive authority from them, with appointments of time and place, for their free males of full age, within the limits of their state, to meet together, for the purpose of establishing a temporary government, to adopt the constitution and laws of any one of the original states; so that such laws nevertheless shall be subject to alteration by their ordinary legislature; and to erect, subject to a like alteration, counties, townships or other divisions, for the election of members for their legislature.

That when any such state shall have acquired twenty thousand free inhabitants, on giving due proof thereof to Congress, they shall receive from them authority, with appointment of time and place, to call a convention of representatives, to establish a permanent constitution and government for themselves. Provided that both the temporary and permanent governments be established on these principles as their basis.

FIRST. That they shall for ever remain a part of this confederacy of the United States of America.

SECOND. That they shall be subject to the article of confederation in all those cases, in which the original states shall be so subject; and to all the acts and ordinances of the United States in Congress assembled, conformable thereto.

THIRD. That they in no case shall interfere with the primary disposal of the soil by the United States in Congress assembled; nor with the ordinances and regulations which Congress may find necessary for securing the title in such soil to the bona fide purchasers.

FOURTH. That they shall be subject to pay a part of the federal debts, contracted or to be contracted; to be apportioned on them by Congress, according to the same common rule and measure by which apportionments thereof shall be make on the other states.

FIFTH. That no tax shall be imposed on lands the property of the United States.

SIXTH. That their respective governments shall be republican.

SEVENTH. That the lands of no-resident proprietors shall in no case be taxed higher than those of residents within any new state, before the admission thereof to a vote by its delegates in Congress.

That whensoever any of the said states shall have of free inhabitants, as many as shall then be in any one, the least numerous, of the thirteen original states, such state shall be admitted by its delegates into the Congress of the United States, on an equal footing with the said original states; provided the consent of so many states in Congress is first obtained as may at the time be competent to such admission. And in order to adapt the said articles of confederation to the state of Congress, when its number shall be thus encreased, it shall be proposed to the legislatures of the states, originally parties thereto, to require the assent of two thirds of the United States in Congress assembled, in all those cases, wherein by the said articles, the assent of nine states is now required; which being agreed to by them, shall be binding on the new states. Until such admission by their delegates into Congress, any of the said states after the establishment of their temporary government shall have authority to keep a member in Congress, with a right of debating, but not of voting.

That measures not inconsistent with the principles of the confederation, and necessary for the preservation of peace and good order among the settlers, in any of the said new states, until they shall assume a temporary government as aforesaid, may from time to time be taken by the United States in Congress assembled.

That the preceding articles shall be formed into a charter of compact; shall be duly executed by the president of the United States in Congress assembled, under his hand, and the seal of the United States; shall be promulgated; and shall stand as fundamental constitutions between the thirteen original states, and each of the several states now newly described, unalterable from and after the sale of any part of the territory of such state, pursuant to this resolve, but by the joint consent of the United States in Congress assembled, and of the particular state within which such alteration is proposed to be made.

Chapter Notes

Source Abbreviations: CVSP William P. Palmer, ed. *Calendar of Virginia State Papers.* 11 vols. Richmond, 1875–1893. **Cutler** William Parker Cutler, and Julia Perkins Cutler. *Life, Journals and Correspondence of Rev. Manasseh Cutler.* 2 vols. Cincinnati, 1888. **Draper** The Draper Manuscripts at the Wisconsin Historical Society. (For more information about this voluminous collection, see Josephine L. Harper. *Guide to the Draper Manuscripts.* Madison: State Historical Society of Wisconsin, 1983.) **Farrand** *The Records of the Federal Convention of 1787,* ed. Max Farrand. 3 vols. New Haven, CT: Yale University Press, 1911. *JCC Journals of the Continental Congress, 1774–1789,* ed. Worthington C. Ford et al. 34 vols. Washington, D.C.: U.S. Government Printing Office, 1904–1937. *LDC* Paul H. Smith et al., eds. *Letters of Delegates to Congress, 1774–1789.* 25 vols. Washington, D.C.: Library of Congress, 1976–2000. *MPHC Michigan Pioneer and Historical Collections.* 40 vols. Lansing, 1876–1929. *PCC* Papers of the Continental Congress, National Archives, Washington, D.C.

Foreword

1. James Oakes, *Freedom National: The Destruction of Slavery in the United States, 1861–1965* (New York: W. W. Norton, 2013), 13, 441.

2. According to Coles, President Madison told him: "Many individuals were members of both bodies [Constitutional Convention and Continental Congress], and thus were enabled to know what was passing in each—both sitting with closed doors and in secret sessions. The distracting question of slavery was agitating and retarding the labors of both, and led to conferences and inter-communications of the members, which resulted in a compromise by which the northern or anti-slavery portion of the country agreed to incorporate, into the Ordinance and Constitution, the provision to restore fugitive slaves; and this mutual and concurrent action was the cause of the similarity in the provision contained in both, and had its influence, in creating the great unanimity by which the Ordinance passed, and also in making the Constitution the more acceptable to the slave holders" [Edward Coles, *History of the Ordinance of 1787* (Philadelphia, 1856), 28–29, quoted in Staughton Lynd, "The Compromise of 1787," *Class Conflict, Slavery, and the United States Constitution,* new ed. (Cambridge: Cambridge University Press, 2009), 189.]

3. See Lynd, "Compromise of 1787," 191–194, citing the historian Richard Hildreth's recognition of this fact in 1849.

4. The dual delegates who traveled from Philadelphia to New York were Blount and Hawkins of North Carolina, and Pierce and Few of Georgia. Richard Henry Lee of Virginia took his seat in New York on July 9 after spending a week in Philadelphia en route. Lee was an active member of the new congressional committee that redrafted the Ordinance.

5. The facts undergirding this hypothesis are drawn from my previously cited paper and from Dr. Alexander's careful manuscript.

6. Henry Wiencek, *Master of the Mountain: Thomas Jefferson and His Slaves* (New York: Farrar, Straus & Giroux, 2012), 251.

Preface

1. Matthew J. Hegreness, "An Organic Law Theory of the Fourteenth Amendment: The Northwest Ordinance as the Source of Rights, Privileges, and Immunities," *Yale Law Journal* 120, no. 7 (May 2011): 1823.
2. Edward Coles, *History of the Ordinance of 1787, Read before the Historical Society of Pennsylvania, June 6, 1856* (Philadelphia, 1856), 28.
3. Draper 23 U 116–119; this speech was given at the Treaty of Fort Harmar, December 29, 1788; attribution is in Randolph C. Downes, *Council Fires on the Upper Ohio: A Narrative of Indian Affairs in the Upper Ohio Valley until 1795* (Pittsburgh: University of Pittsburgh Press, 1968), 307. In most quotes I have regularized and modernized spelling and punctuation, except where it seemed necessary for reasons of strict accuracy to leave the original language untouched.

Introduction

1. Cutler, 1:148.
2. The full text of the Northwest Ordinance can be found in Appendix D. For an account of the complete history of the Ordinance, the best single source is probably Jay A. Barrett, *Evolution of the Ordinance of 1787* (New York, 1891).
3. In the Proclamation of 1763, George III stated "that the several Nations or Tribes of Indians with whom We are connected, and who live under our Protection, should not be molested or disturbed in the Possession of such Parts of our Dominions and Territories as, not having been ceded to or purchased by Us, are reserved to them" ["Proclamation of October 7, 1763," *The Critical Period, 1763–1765*, vol. 10 of the *Collections of the Illinois State Historical Library* (1915), 43]. The region northwest of the Ohio River was never purchased by the Crown nor ceded to it.
4. After the Civil War, Jefferson Davis, former president of the Confederacy, wrote a two-volume history of secession, and as he explains, "It was not the passage of the 'personal liberty laws,' it was not the circulation of incendiary documents, it was not the raid of John Brown, it was not the operation of unjust and unequal tariff laws, nor all combined, that constituted the intolerable grievance, but it was the systematic and persistent struggle to deprive the Southern States of equality in the Union—generally to discriminate in legislation against the interests of their people, culminating in their exclusion from the Territories, the common

property of the States" [Jefferson Davis, *The Rise and Fall of the Confederate Government*, 2 vols. (1881; reprint, Richmond, VA, [1938]), 1:83].
5. As George Bancroft wrote, "Grayson, then the presiding officer of congress, had always opposed slavery. Two years before he had wished success to the attempt of King for its restriction; and everything points to him as the immediate cause of the tranquil spirit of disinterested statesmanship which took possession of every southern man in the assembly. Of the members of Virginia, Richard Henry Lee had stood against Jefferson on this very question; but now he acted with Grayson, and from the states of which no man had yielded before, every one chose the part which was to bring on their memory the benedictions of all coming ages. Obeying an intimation from the South, Nathan Dane copied from Jefferson the prohibition of involuntary servitude in the territory, and quieted alarm by adding from the report of King a clause for the delivering up of the fugitive slave. This at the second reading of the ordinance he moved as a sixth article of compact, and, on the thirteenth day of July 1787, the great statute forbidding slavery to cross the river Ohio was passed by the vote of Georgia, South Carolina, North Carolina, Virginia, Delaware, New Jersey, New York, and Massachusetts, all the states that were then present in congress. Pennsylvania and three states of New England were absent; Maryland only of the South. Of the eighteen members of congress who answered to their names, every one said 'aye' excepting Abraham Yates the younger of New York, who insisted on leaving to all future ages a record of his want of good judgment, right feeling, and common sense.

"Thomas Jefferson first summoned congress to prohibit slavery in all the territory of the United States; Rufus King lifted up the measure when it lay almost lifeless on the ground, and suggested the immediate instead of the prospective prohibition; a Congress composed of five southern states to one from New England, and two from the middle states, headed by William Grayson, supported by Richard Henry Lee, and using Nathan Dane as scribe, carried the measure to the goal in the amended form in which King had caused it to be referred to a committee; and, as Jefferson had proposed, placed it under the sanction of an irrevocable compact" [George Bancroft, *History of the Formation of the Constitution of the United States of America*, 2 vols. (New York, 1886), 2:115–116].

Paul Finkelman says of this (citing Bancroft in particular), "Nineteenth century historians sought to determine who deserved the credit for the Ordinance in general and Article VI in particular. Much of this writing was clearly filiopietistic" [Paul Finkelman, "Slavery and Bondage in the 'Empire of Liberty,'" *The Northwest Ordinance: Essays on Its Formulation, Provisions, and Legacy*, ed. Frederick L. Williams (East Lansing: Michigan State University Press, 1989), 89 *n*11].

6. Pierce Butler, July 13, 1787, Farrand, 1:605; John Rutledge, August 21, 1787, Farrand, 2:364.

7. In the post-Revolutionary South, the approximate overall percentage of slave population was forty percent; in some South Carolina counties, even before the invention of the cotton gin in 1793, the black population was over seventy percent; see, for example, Christopher Collier and James Lincoln Collier, *Decision in Philadelphia: The Constitutional Convention of 1787* (New York: Ballantine, 1986), 185. The extra Congressional (and Electoral College) representation afforded slave states by the three-fifths compromise was a hot-button issue throughout the antebellum era: "Disproportionate representation became the standard explanation for the Federalist loss of executive power in 1800. It was an easy argument to make. For there was little doubt that the three-fifths rule played a decisive role in John Adams's defeat. Adams's native Massachusetts had the largest free population in the nation but not the most electoral votes. Thanks to the three-fifths rule, Jefferson's Virginia had five more electoral votes than the Bay State. Virginia had six "slave" seats, the rest of the South, eight. In New England, Jefferson got trounced and lost the North as a whole by a margin of twenty electoral votes to fifty-six, but in the South he won fifty-three electoral votes to Adams's nine. In winning nationally by just eight electoral votes, he had the benefit of at least thirteen of the fourteen slave seats; some pundits thought he had all fourteen. In any event, without the so-called slave seats, he would have lost the election and John Adams would have served a second term" [Leonard L. Richards, *The Slave Power: The Free North and Southern Domination, 1780–1860* (Baton Rouge: Louisiana State University Press, 2000), 42].

8. Staughton Lynd, "The Compromise of 1787," *Class Conflict, Slavery, and the United States Constitution: Ten Essays* (Indianapolis: Bobbs-Merrill, 1967), 185–186, 207; Lynd is quoting Ulrich B. Phillips, *American Negro Slavery* (New York, 1918), 128. My analysis differs somewhat from Lynd's, particularly in my conclusion that the "agreement" originated in the Convention and traveled north to New York, and that Manasseh Cutler had little to do with it.

9. The various records of Congressional debates in the antebellum period—the *Annals of Congress*, *Register of Debates*, and *Congressional Globe* (all of which can be found online at

http://memory.loc.gov/ammem/amlaw/lawhome.html) contain increasing levels of detail in their recording of the debates, so that after 1851 one can read with stenographic accuracy a record of descent toward the breakdown of democracy. *The Journals of the Continental Congress*, however, are for the most part merely records of reports given to Congress by various committees, and of motions that passed. However, it should be remembered that "the United States in Congress Assembled" was for many years the only truly Federal body, having not only legislative but also judicial and executive authority, so Congress and its committees made decisions covering almost every aspect of governance; and its records, therefore, however rudimentary, contain enormous amounts of information. But the day-to-day debates are for the most part lost, and we have to rely on other sources to help reconstruct a record of Congressional events.

10. Nathan Dane to Rufus King, July 16, 1787, *LDC* 24:358. A more complete discussion of this letter occurs in a later chapter.

11. For example: "[It] is impossible that the vote in the Convention on the 12th could have been known by the Congress on the 13th, in time to affect the adoption of the Ordinance. And, of course, since the Ordinance was not adopted until the 13th, it seems unlikely that Article VI, which was not introduced until the 13th, could have affected a vote in Philadelphia the day before. It seems more likely that this is simply a coincidence of dates" [Paul Finkelman, "Slavery and Bondage," 71].

12. See Benjamin Franklin to Anthony Todd, Secretary of the General Post-Office, January 16, 1764: "I will now only just mention that we hope in the spring to expedite the communication between Boston and New York, as we have already that between New York and Philadelphia, by making the mails travel by night as well as by day, which has never heretofore been done in America. It passes now between Philadelphia and New York so quick that a letter can be sent from one place to another, and an answer received the following day, which before took a week, and when our plan is executed between Boston and New York, letters may be sent and answers received in four days, which before took a fortnight; and between Philadelphia and Boston in six days, which before required three weeks. We think this expeditious communication will greatly increase the number of letters from Philadelphia and Boston by the packets to Britain" [*The Complete Works of Benjamin Franklin*, ed. John Bigelow, vol. 10 (New York, 1888), 298].

13. It was crucial that the Pennsylvania legislature be informed overnight that Congress had voted to send the Constitution to the states

for their approval. The current session of the legislature was due to adjourn, and the incoming legislature would look much less favorably on any increase in Federal power—so it was necessary to the nationalists that the vote be taken before the deadline. "Sometime during the early morning, Bingham's messenger came spurring into town with the news that Congress had acted on the Constitution. By riding all night and changing horses at prearranged intervals along the way, he had managed to reach Philadelphia just twelve hours after the signing of the resolution in New York" [Robert C. Alberts, *The Golden Voyage: The Life and Times of William Bingham, 1752–1804* (Boston: Houghton Mifflin, 1969), 187]. As advertised a few years later, even a stagecoach could reach Philadelphia from northern New Jersey in one day: Advertisement, *Federal Gazette and Philadelphia Daily Advertiser*, Monday, June 14, 1790, 4, col. 1.

14. William Grayson to James Monroe, August 8, 1787, *LDC* 24:393.

15. Lynd, "Compromise," 191–193, 199.

16. For the details of Wilson's life, see Page Smith, *James Wilson, Founding Father, 1742–1796* (Westport, CT: Greenwood, 1973); for a more cerebral biography, see Geoffrey Seed, *James Wilson* (Millwood, NY: KTO Press, 1978). For Robert Morris, see Charles Rappleye, *Robert Morris: Financier of the American Revolution* (New York: Simon & Schuster, 2010).

17. H. W. Beckwith, *Historic Notes on the Northwest* (Chicago, 1879), 98.

18. *JCC* 32:340.

19. Article 6, Definitive Treaty of Peace between the United States of American and His Britannic Majesty, January 14, 1784, *JCC* 26:27.

20. *Johnson v. M'Intosh*, 21 U.S. 543 (1823), http://supreme.justia.com/us/21/543/case.html. M'Intosh is pronounced, and sometimes written, as McIntosh; excerpts are provided in Appendix B.

21. In St. John's, Newfoundland, in the world-famous Basilica of St. John the Baptist, to the left of the altar, there's a small shrine to Our Lady of Fatima, put there by the Portuguese community in 1955, memorializing a ceremony that celebrated the five hundredth anniversary of the Catholic Church in America. In 1455, as it happens, Pope Nicholas V issued a Papal Bull having to do with newly discovered lands just coming into the ken of Europeans. It followed upon the *Dum Diversas* of 1452, which gave permission to Christians to enslave the "heathens" of Africa, thus paving the way for the European slave trade. The *Romanus Pontifex*, issued on January 5, 1455, gave the Catholic nations of Europe dominion over the New World: "We weighing all and singular the premises with due meditation, and noting that

since we had formerly by other letters of ours granted among other things free and ample faculty to the aforesaid King Alfonso—to invade, search out, capture, vanquish, and subdue all Saracens and pagans whatsoever, and other enemies of Christ wheresoever placed, and the kingdoms, dukedoms, principalities, dominions, possessions, and all movable and immovable goods whatsoever held and possessed by them and to reduce their persons to perpetual slavery, and to apply and appropriate to himself and his successors the kingdoms, dukedoms, counties, principalities, dominions, possessions, and goods, and to convert them to his and their use and profit—by having secured the said faculty, the said King Alfonso, or, by his authority, the aforesaid infante, justly and lawfully has acquired and possessed, and doth possess, these islands, lands, harbors, and seas, and they do of right belong and pertain to the said King Alfonso and his successors" [Francis Gardiner Davenport, ed., *European Treaties Bearing on the United States and Its Dependencies to 1648* (Washington, D.C.: Carnegie Institution, 1917), 23]. For the ramifications of this document, see Steven T. Newcomb, *Pagans in the Promised Land: Decoding the Doctrine of Christian Discovery* (Golden, CO: Fulcrum Publishing, 2008).

22. "*Resolved*, That the Compact which exists between the North and the South is a 'covenant with death, and an agreement with hell,'—involving both parties in atrocious criminality,—and should be immediately annulled" ["Resolution adopted at the annual meeting of the Massachusetts Anti-Slavery Society, in Faneuil Hall, January 26, 1843," *The Liberator* (Boston), March 17, 1843, p. 3, col. 1]; this resolution was authored by William Lloyd Garrison, editor of *The Liberator*; the reference is to Isaiah 28:15: "We have made a covenant with death, and with hell are we at agreement."

23. For Gouverneur Morris's biography and character, see Richard Brookhiser, *Gentleman Revolutionary: Gouverneur Morris, the Rake Who Wrote the Constitution* (New York: Free Press, 2003).

24. As Charles Thomson wrote in 1786, "In the commencement of the present opposition these Committees had been revised, extended and reduced to system; so that when any intelligence of importance which it was necessary the people at large should be informed of reached the Capital, it was immediately dispatched to the county Committees and by them forwarded to the Committees of the districts, who disseminated it to the whole body of the people" [CT to Dr. David Ramsey, November 4, 1786, *Collections of the New-York Historical Society for the Year 1878* (New York, 1879), 218–219].

25. Rev. A. P. Peabody, "Manasseh Cutler," *New Englander and Yale Review* 46, no. 205 (April 1887): 319.

26. Peabody, "Manasseh Cutler," 325–327.

Chapter 1

1. George Washington to Thomas Jefferson, Philadelphia, May 30, 1787, Farrand, 3:31.

2. "Shays, with a party of about fifteen or sixteen hundred, approached General Shepherd's lines. The General sent a flag [of truce], wishing to know what he would have. Shays informed the messenger that he, with his men, determined to lodge in the barracks at Springfield. Upon which the General drew a line, and forbid his marching over; which, if he did, should certainly fire upon him. Shays, with his heretofore known folly, still kept on his march till he had exceeded the bounds prescribed. General Shepherd then ordered the artillery to fire two cannon [warning shots]—one on the right and the other on the left—which they paid no regard to. Then orders were given to fire among them; upon which three of Shays' men were killed and one wounded, and they retreated with haste and disorder, leaving their dead and wounded upon the spot" [Elisha Whitney to Manasseh Cutler, February 6, 1787, Cutler, 1:198]. The causes and progress of the rebellion are well laid-out in Leonard L. Richards, *Shays's Rebellion: The American Revolution's Final Battle* (Philadelphia: University of Pennsylvania Press, 2002).

3. Henry Knox to George Washington, October 23, 1786, Francis S. Drake, *Life and Correspondence of Henry Knox, Major-General in the American Revolutionary Army* (Boston, 1873), 91–93. (Knox's title, Secretary *at* War, was changed after the adoption of the Constitution to Secretary *of* War. The original phraseology presumably represented the notion that the position was only to be in effect while the nation was actually at war.) See also HK to the President of Congress, October 18, 1786: "I conceive my official duty obliges me to inform Congress, that it is my firm conviction, arising from the information I have received, that unless the present commotions are checked with a strong hand, that an armed tyranny may be established on the ruins of the present constitutions" [*JCC* 31:887]; also Edward Carrington to Edmund Randolph, December 8, 1786: "The Malcontents have assumed a deliberate and systematic conduct, and, every day, gain confidence and numbers. ... openly declare for an abolition of debts public and private, and a [re]distribution of property" [*LDC* 24:42–43].

For a good illustration of the "leveling" spirit which was sweeping the country after the Revolution, see the following by Thomas Anburey, a British army officer who toured America after his capture: "[April 10, 1779.] It appeared to me, that before the war, the spirit of equality or leveling principal was not so prevalent in Virginia, as in the other provinces; and that the different classes of people in the former supported a greater distinction than those of the latter; but since the war, that principle seems to have gained great ground in Virginia; an instance of it I saw at Colonel [Thomas Mann] Randolph's, at Tuckahoe, where three country peasants, who came upon business, entered the room where the Colonel and his company were sitting, took themselves chairs, drew near the fire, began spitting, pulling off their country boots all over with mud, and then opening their business, which was simply about some continental flour to be ground at the Colonel's mill. When they were gone, someone observed what great liberties they took; he replied, it was unavoidable, the spirit of independency was converted into equality, and every one who bore arms, esteemed himself upon a footing with his neighbour, and concluded with saying, 'No doubt, each of these men conceives himself, in every respect, my equal'" [(Thomas Anburey), *Travels through the Interior Parts of America*, 2 vols. (London, 1789), 2:370–371].

4. In contemporary American usage, *agrarian* would translate as *socialist*.

5. *JCC* 32:256.

6. Henry Knox describes Shays' defeat in some detail to Virginia Governor Edmund Randolph: "General Lincoln informs me that he marched at 8 o'clock on the evening of the 3d instant with his force, consisting of upwards of 3,000 troops of all descriptions, and after a fatiguing march of 30 miles, without halting but for a few moments, part of it through a violent storm of snow, after which succeeded a severe cold, so that most of his men were frozen in different places and degrees, he completely surprised the insurgents at Petersham at 9 o'clock Sunday morning, the 4th, and almost entirely dispersed them—took 150 prisoners—the rest fled in every direction. The leaders have escaped to New Hampshire and other States" [HK to ER, February 12, 1787, *CVSP* 4:236]. See also HK to the President of Congress, February 12, 1787, *JCC* 32:39.

7. As the Board of Treasury informed Congress, "There is no prospect of sufficient funds coming into the Treasury ... to enable this Board to make provision for payments on the foreign debt, which become due in the present year" [February 7, 1787, *JCC* 32:34].

8. James Madison to Edmund Randolph, February 25, 1787, *LDC* 24:121; Randolph was the governor of Virginia, and would soon be a delegate to the Constitutional Convention. See also Rufus King to Elbridge Gerry, January 7,

1787: "The anxiety and dissatisfaction still continues, which has for some time existed concerning the government of these states. God only knows what will prove the issue" [ibid., 63]; also William Grayson to William Short, April 16, 1787: "I am sorry to inform you that American affairs in general wear the worst aspect you can possibly conceive.... Congress annually vote requisitions for the foreign & domestic interest which are totally disregarded. It appears to me there is a considerable party in every State against the payment of the domestic debt: & though this matter has shewed itself openly only in Massachusetts yet I am satisfied a vigorous taxation would produce the same effect in many of the other states" [ibid., 226].

9. William Irvine to Josiah Harmar, February 27, 1787, *LDC* 24:123.

10. Wednesday, December 15, 1784, extract of a letter from Don J. Galvez, minister of his Catholick Majesty, to Congress: "Aranjues, June 26, 1784. Until the limits of Louisiana and the two Floridas shall be settled and determined with the United States of America, his Majesty commands that you should give the states and Congress to understand that they are not to expose to process and confiscation the vessels which they destine to carry on commerce on the River Mississippi, inasmuch as a treaty concluded between the United States and England, on which the former ground their pretensions to the navigation of that river, could not fix limits in a territory which that power did not possess, the two borders of the river being already conquered and possessed by our arms the day the treaty was made, namely, the 30th November, 1782" [*JCC* 27:690].

11. See, for example, François-Louis Hector, fourteenth Baron de Carondelet et Noyelles, Governor of Louisiana (1791–1797), Military Report: "A carbine and a little maize in a sack are enough for an American to wander about in the forests alone for a whole month.... With some tree trunks crossed one above another, in the shape of a square, he raises a house and even a fort that is impregnable to the savages by crossing a story above the ground floor" [quoted by Jon Kukla, *A Wilderness So Immense: The Louisiana Purchase and the Destiny of America* (New York: Knopf, 2003), 118].

12. As James Madison recorded in his notes for March 13, 1787, "Mr. Gardoqui would not listen to the idea of a right to the navigation of Mississippi by the U.S., contending that the possession of the two banks at the mouth shut the door against any such pretension. Spain never would give up this point. He lamented that he had been here so long without effecting any thing: and foresaw that the consequences would be very disagreeable.... He betrayed strongly the anxiety of Spain to retard the population of the Western Country; observing that whenever sufficient force should arise therein, it would be impossible for it [to] be controlled" [*LDC* 24:144–145]. Resolution of the Mississippi issue, by means of a treaty with Spain, did not occur until well after the new government under the Constitution had taken power—and any further dispute was obviated by the Louisiana Purchase in 1803. In this regard, it's interesting to note that free passage of the Mississippi would again become a key issue during the Civil War, and is in fact one of the major reasons that the political and military power of the Old Northwest was brought to bear on the Southern Confederacy: the farmers from the Midwest, as did their forebears in the 1780s, needed to ship their agricultural products to market by way of the Father of Waters. See, for example, Robert Alexander, *Five Forks: Waterloo of the Confederacy* (East Lansing: Michigan State University Press, 2003), 73.

13. Though a treaty required nine votes for approval, Congress, by a simple majority, had on 29 July 1786, at the behest of so-called Eastern delegates, issued orders to Jay to lay aside his original instructions for standing firm on the rights of passage (*JCC* 31:595–596). Were he to sign a treaty accepting closure of the Mississippi, Southern delegates feared that Jay would force the United States to abide by those agreements—despite the lack of nine votes as the Articles of Confederation stipulated—since any failure to do so could be treated, according to the Law of Nations, as a casus belli by the king of Spain. The notion that additional states west of the Appalachians—even if settled by Northerners—might share the desire for an open Mississippi could well have been among the "other political reasons" mentioned by William Grayson as reason for the Southern states' support of the Northwest Ordinance. See Staughton Lynd, "The Compromise of 1787," *Class Conflict, Slavery, and the United States Constitution: Ten Essays* (Indianapolis: Bobbs-Merrill, 1967), 194–198.

14. "A Copy of a Letter from a Gentleman at the falls of Ohio, to his friend in New England, dated December 4th, 1786," *The Diplomatic Correspondence of the United States, from the Signing of the Definitive Treaty of Peace ... to the Adoption of the Constitution,* 7 vols. (Washington, D.C., 1833–1834), 6:221 (henceforth cited as *Diplomatic Correspondence*); originally published in *Worcester Magazine* 3, no. 17 (July 1787).

15. George Washington to Benjamin Harrison, October 10, 1784, George Washington Papers, Library of Congress, Washington, D.C., http://memory.loc.gov/ammem/gwhtml/gwhome.html.

16. David Duncan to Josiah Harmar, Draper

1 W 269. See also George Muter, chief justice of the Kentucky District Court, to James Madison, February 20, 1787: "Our people here are greatly alarmed at the prospect of the navigation of the Mississippi being given up. And I have not met with one man, who would be willing to give the navigation up for ever so short a time, on any terms whatsoever" [Worthington Chauncey Ford, ed., *The Federal Constitution in Virginia, 1787–1788* (Cambridge, MA, 1903), 5]; also James Madison to George Washington, March 18, 1787: "I have a letter from Col. John Campbell dated at Pittsburg, from which I gather that the people of that quarter are thrown into great agitation by the reported intention of Congs. concerning the Mississippi, and that measures are on foot, for uniting the minds of all the different settlements which have a common interest at stake" [*LDC* 24:150].

17. "We have reason to believe [that] property has been plundered to a very considerable amount, and that it has been generally appropriated to private purposes.... [I]n the meantime, attempts are daily practised to augment the banditti at St. Vincennes, by delusive promises of lands, bounty and clothing from the officers appointed by General Clarke" ["A few private individuals to Governor Randolph, posted from Danville (District of Kentucky), 22 December 1786," *Diplomatic Correspondence*, 6: 211]; this letter was signed by T. Marshall, George Muter, Harry Innes. Edmund Lyne, Richard C. Anderson, Richard Taylor, James Wilkinson, J. Brown, Caleb Wallace, John Craig, Christ. Greenup, James Garrard, Charles Ewing, John Logan, and John Edwards.

18. "From a gentleman in Kentucky to his friend in Philadelphia, 12 December 1786," *LDC* 24:98. *Opost* was the term for Vincennes: "The post which the French established here in the first half of the seventeenth century was designated 'poste du Ouabache,' or, more commonly, simply 'au poste.' The early American settlers transformed this into 'the Post' or 'Opost'" [Milton Milo Quaife, ed., "A Narrative of Life on the Old Frontier: Henry Hay's Journal from Detroit to the Miami River," *Proceedings of the State Historical Society of Wisconsin at Its Sixty-Second Annual Meeting* (Madison, 1915), 231 *n*43]. See also Maj. John Wyllys to Col. Josiah Harmar, Rapids of Ohio, February 6, 1787: "I think it my duty to inform you that a party of men, not raised by any legal authority, as I can understand, have established themselves at Post St. Vincents: taking upon themselves to give and receive speeches and treat with the Indian nations inhabiting that country—how far such conduct may suit with the interests of the United States you can best judge" [PCC, item 150, 2:303; enclosed with Henry Knox's letter

to the President of Congress, April 16, 1787, ibid., 2:307].

19. James Madison to George Washington, April 16, 1787, *LDC* 24:231; see also John Jay, Secretary for Foreign Affairs, Report to Congress, April 12, 1787, *JCC* 32:189–204.

20. The Secretary at War to the President of Congress, April 16, 1787, *The Territory Northwest of the River Ohio, 1787–1803*, vol. 2 of Clarence Edwin Carter, ed., *The Territorial Papers of the United States* (Washington, D.C.: Government Printing Office, 1934), 26 (from PCC, item 150, 2:307). See also "Report of Secretary at War on intrusions in Western territory," April 19, 1787, *JCC* 32:222.

21. Proclamation of Gov. Edmund Randolph, January 25, 1787: "Authorizing surveys to be made on the lands allotted to the Virginia Line ... on the northwest side of the Ohio River ... in accordance with the act of Congress of the 9th of May, 1786" [*CVSP* 4:23].

22. Col. Levi Todd to Edmund Randolph, February 14, 1787, *CVSP* 4:237.

23. William Grayson to Beverley Randolph, June 25, 1787, *LDC* 24:341.

24. William Grayson to James Monroe, August 8, 1787, *LDC* 24:394.

25. Richard Butler to Henry Knox, Carlisle, March 28, 1787, PCC, item 150, 2:288; Maj. John Finley to Col. Josiah Harmar, April 16, 1787, Draper 1 W 291–292.

26. *JCC* 32:74.

27. Manasseh Cutler's journal entry for March 8, 1787, Cutler, 1:191–192. The use here of the word *adventurers* deserves mention: "Students of Ohio history, particularly of the original settlement, should note the significance of the word 'adventurer' which will be constantly found in the original records of the Ohio Company. The word was perhaps first used in the Fifteenth Century when Henry IV chartered the 'Merchant Adventurers'; in 1670 when Charles II granted to his cousin Prince Rupert a white empire in America the company formed to exploit it was called 'Adventurers of England Trading into Hudson Bay,' the present Hudson Bay Company. In colonial Maryland the Governor ordered that certain manors should bear the names given them by the 'adventurers' to whom they belonged. The word should convey an emigrant-gamester significance, though it was used of both actual emigrants and absentee speculators. It was used with all the old, time-honored significance when the Ohio pioneers on the Youghiogheny named their principal craft 'The Adventure Galley'; as an after-thought the boat was later rechristened the 'Mayflower.' The old name was richer, more signicant and typical, and should always be preferred" [Archer Butler Hulbert, ed., *The Records of the Original Proceedings of*

the Ohio Company, vol. 1 (Marietta, OH, 1917), xxvii *n*14].

28. Manasseh Cutler to Major Winthrop Sargent, Ipswich, March 16, 1787, Cutler, 1:192.

29. A geographic township is a square six miles on a side, and a range of townships is a vertical column—thus seven ranges would extend forty-two miles west of the Pennsylvania border. See Manasseh Cutler to Nathan Dane, March 16, 1787: "You are doubtless acquainted with the institution of a Company in the New England States by the name of the Ohio Company, for the purpose of making a large settlement on the federal lands on the river Ohio.... The directors entertain hopes that Congress, notwithstanding their land ordinance, will not refuse to make a private sale to this company, as it will greatly accelerate the settlement, save the company a large expense, and enable them to purchase the whole in one body" [Cutler, 1:194–195]. Cutler was also hoping to convince Congress to lower their price, which had been set at one dollar per acre—so he also mentioned in his letter that there was land available for sale in the existing states for much less: "The high price at which Congress have set the federal lands has operated much against the company; for the lands belonging to this, and several of the other states, are sold at half a dollar per acre, which is the highest price the company will give for the lands on the Ohio. Though the federal lands may be of a better quality, yet their distance from the northward states, and the hazards to which the first settlers must be exposed in the neighborhood of numerous tribes of Indians, are no small discouragements to adventurers, and will be admitted, I conceive, as a reason for lowering the price" [ibid., 194].

30. *Articles of an Association by the Name of the Ohio Company* (Worcester, 1786); on the opening page is a copy of the Resolution made March 4, at the Bunch of Grapes Tavern in Boston, by the "Convention" that established the company; following the text of the pamphlet is a series of blank pages on which are handwritten names of subscribers. When the author bought a photocopy of the pamphlet, it turned out to be a reproduction of Sargent's personal copy!

31. Josiah Harmar—for whom the fort was named—described it to a friend as a most pleasant spot: "The Muskingum river is about one hundred and eighty miles distant from [Pittsburgh], at the mouth of which the fort stands. I have often wished during the hunting season (viz., the months of November and December), for the honor of your company at my post. Venison, bear, turkey, geese, ducks, etc., etc. You should have regaled upon the greatest abundance" [JH to Thomas Mifflin, Speaker of the Pennsylvania Assembly (and later delegate to the Constitutional Convention), Fort Pitt, March 17, 1787, Appendix 1, *Military Journal of Major Ebenezer Denny* (Philadelphia, 1859), 217].

32. James Madison to Edmund Pendleton, April 22, 1787: "Congress are at present deliberating on the most proper plan for disposing of the Western lands, and providing a criminal and civil administration for the Western settlements beyond the Ohio. The latter subject involves great difficulties" [*LDC* 24:245]. As John Jay wrote Jefferson, "I fear that western country will one day give us trouble. To govern them will not be easy, and whether after two or three generations they will be fit to govern themselves is a question that merits consideration" [JJ to TJ, April 24, 1787, *The Correspondence and Public Papers of John Jay, 1782–1793*, ed. Henry P. Johnston, 4 vols. (New York: 1890–1893), 3:245]. The situation at Vincennes—where George Rogers Clark had been "playing hell"—was a case in point, and it demanded immediate attention: "*Resolved*, That the Secretary at War direct the commanding officer of the troops of the United States on the Ohio to take immediate and efficient measures for dispossessing a body of men who have in a lawless and unauthorised manner taken possession of post St. Vincents in defiance of the proclamations and authority of the United States and that he employ the whole or such part of the force under his command as he shall judge necessary to effect the Object" [April 24, 1787, *JCC* 32:231].

33. *JCC* 32:242.

34. *JCC* 32:274–275.

35. "Description of the Tract": this piece of land was to be "bounded on the east by the western boundary of the seventh range of townships, on the south by the Ohio river, on the west by the river Scioto, and on the north by a due east and west line run from the northwest corner of the south township of the seventh range (reckoning from the Ohio) until it shall intersect the Scioto.... The price to be three shillings and sixpence, lawful money, or one-twelfth of a dollar, per acre, payable in any of the securities of the United States" [Charles S. Hall, *Life and Letters of Samuel Holden Parsons: Major-General in the Continental Army and Chief Judge of the Northwestern Territory, 1737–1789* (Binghamton, NY, 1905), 500; also PCC, item 41, 8:234].

36. The summary of the day's proceedings can be found at *JCC* 32:283. The original minutes can be found in PCC, item 1, 38:245. Also on May 10, a debate took place about the negotiations with Spain concerning American use of the lower Mississippi. A parliamentary maneuver the previous September initiated by

Rufus King, delegate from Massachusetts, had succeeded in stifling Congressional discussion of the issue—but finally on May 10 the coalition of seven Northern states collapsed (*JCC* 32: 278–279). Delegates from Pennsylvania and New Jersey switched their votes, perhaps concerned at the level of agitation out west. This represented a victory for the Southern faction, who favored an open river for trade. In studying the events of 1787, it's important to keep in mind this conflict and the sectional conflict it represented—which was a driving force behind some of the decisions made in Philadelphia. As James Madison wrote in his notes on April 26, "It was considered on the whole that the project of shutting the Mississippi was at an end; a point deemed of great importance in reference to the approaching Convention for introducing a change in the federal Government, and to the objection to an increase of its powers foreseen from the jealousy which had been excited by that project" [Notes of Debates, Thursday, April 26, 1787, *LDC* 24:260 n2].

Patrick Henry was a case in point. He decided not to attend the Constitutional Convention because, he was quoted as saying, he "smelt a rat," and he felt his energy would be better spent in Virginia (for the quote from Henry, see Hugh Blair Grigsby, *History of the Virginia Convention of 1788*, 2 vols. [Richmond, VA, 1890], 1:32; quoted by Jon Kukla, "A Mysteriously Transcendent Quality? The Secessionist Crisis of 1785–1786 and Some of Its Implications," *Secessions: From the American Revolution to Civil War*, Filson Institute Academic Conference, October 22, 2010, 27). As James Madison wrote to Jefferson in France, "Mr. Henry's disgust exceeded all measure and I am not singular in ascribing his refusal to attend the Convention to the policy of keeping himself free to combat or espouse the result of it according to the result of the Missisipi business among other circumstances" [JM to TJ, New York, March 19, 1787, *LDC* 24:153].

At the Virginia Ratifying Convention the following spring, one of the major objections to the new Constitution was precisely that it would make it easier for the northern states to achieve their goal of trading away rights to free passage of the Mississippi; for example, on Friday, June 13, 1788, "Mr. Monroe added several other observations, the purport of which was, that the interest of the western country would not be as secure, under the proposed Constitution, as under the Confederation; because, under the latter system, the Mississippi could not be relinquished without the consent of nine states—whereas, by the former, he said, a majority, or Seven states, could yield it. His own opinion was, that it would be given up by a majority of the senators present in the Senate, with

the President, which would put it in the power of less than seven states to surrender it; that the Northern States were inclined to yield it; that it was their interest to prevent an augmentation of the southern influence and power; and that, as mankind in general, and states in particular, were governed by interest, the Northern States would not fail of availing themselves of the opportunity, given them by the Constitution, of relinquishing that river, in order to depress the western country, and prevent the southern interest from preponderating" [Jonathan Elliot, ed., *The Debates in the Several State Conventions on the Adoption of the Federal Constitution*, 2nd ed., 5 vols., 1836–1859 (Washington, D.C., 1836), 3:340].

37. Nathan Dane to Rufus King, May 31, 1787, *LDC* 24:297. See also Charles Thomson to William Bingham, June 25, 1787: "You cannot imagine what an alarm the secession of the Members from Congress at this crisis has spread through the eastern states. Were I to hazard an Opinion it would be that the peace of the Union & the happy termination of the measures of the Convention depend on the meeting & continuance of Congress & keeping up the form of government until the New plan is ready for Adoption" [ibid., 343].

38. Josiah Harmar to Henry Knox, May 14, 1787, *The St. Clair Papers: The Life and Public Services of Arthur St. Clair*, ed. William Henry Smith, 2 vols. (Cincinnati, 1882), 2:20, quoting PCC, item 150, 2:360. See also William Blount to Thomas Blount, July 30, 1787, *LDC* 24:380.

39. David Duncan to Josiah Harmar, Pittsburgh, June 17, 1787, Draper 1 W 301–302.

Chapter 2

1. Charles A. Beard, *An Economic Interpretation of the Constitution of the United States* (New York: Macmillan, 1921), 23.

2. Farrand, 1:15. These quotes are for the most part excerpts from James Madison's notes, and unless otherwise indicated are taken from Max Farrand's *Records of the Federal Convention of 1787*. Subsequent references to Farrand are included in brackets in the text. The fact that one person's speech follows right after another does not necessarily mean that one followed another directly in "real time." But I have attempted to be accurate in following the train of thought of the debate.

3. These comments are from Robert Yates's notes of the Convention.

4. John Adams, "Thoughts on Government," *The Works of John Adams*, ed. Charles Francis Adams (Boston, 1851), 4:195. For a complete discussion of these issues and how they played out in the early Republic, see Gordon S. Wood, *The Creation of the American Republic,*

1776–1787 (1969; Chapel Hill: University of North Carolina Press, 1998).

5. For example, in the Massachusetts Constitution, "The House of Representatives is intended as the Representatives of the Persons, and the Senate of the property of the Common Wealth"—or as Benjamin Lincoln phrased it, "Men possessed of property are entitled to a greater share in political authority than those who are destitute of it" [Wood, *Creation of the American Republic*, 218, 220].

6. Alan Taylor, *American Colonies* (New York: Viking, 2002), 238.

7. *JCC* 19:217.

8. *JCC* 24:260.

9. At this stage of the Republic's evolution, Federal taxes were assessed upon states and not upon individuals. In fact, at one point in the proceedings Gouverneur Morris stated that "It is idle to suppose that the General Government can stretch its hand directly into the pockets of the people scattered over so vast a Country" [Farrand, 2:223].

10. The best biography of John Rutledge, and his brother Edward, is James Haw, *John and Edward Rutledge of South Carolina* (Athens: University of Georgia Press, 1977). Also of interest is Richard Barry, *Mr. Rutledge of South Carolina* (New York: Duell, Sloan & Pearce, 1942).

11. In this regard, see the satiric pamphlet by Thomas Paine, *Public Good, Being an Examination into the Claim of Virginia to the Vacant Western Territory...* (Philadelphia, 1780).

12. "An act for declaring and asserting the rights of this Commonwealth, concerning purchasing lands from Indian natives. To remove and prevent all doubt concerning purchases of lands from the Indian natives," quoted in *Johnson v. M'Intosh*, 21 U.S. 543 (1823), fn e, http://supreme.justia.com/us/21/543/case.html.

13. Barry, *Mr. Rutledge*, 315.

14. This of course was previous to the invention of the cotton gin in 1793, which revolutionized commercial production of short-staple cotton; though cotton also existed in its long-staple sea-island form, it was not a major export item before that date; in fact, the word *cotton* never appears in the Constitutional debates as recorded by James Madison.

15. Barry, *Mr. Rutledge*, passim; also David O. Stewart, *The Summer of 1787: The Men Who Invented the Constitution* (New York: Simon & Schuster, 2007).

Chapter 3

1. John Penn, "To the Chiefs and Warriors of the Shawanese Indians," 1774, *The St. Clair Papers: The Life and Public Services of Arthur St. Clair*, ed. William Henry Smith, 2 vols. (Cincinnati, 1882), 1:336.

2. Josiah Harmar to Henry Knox, March 18, 1787, Josiah Harmar Papers, Letter Book B, Letter XL, p. 59, William L. Clements Library, University of Michigan, Ann Arbor.

3. "A Treaty Held at the Town of Lancaster ... with the Indians of the Six Nations in June, 1744," C. Van Doren, and J. P. Boyd, eds., *Indian Treaties Printed by Benjamin Franklin, 1736–1762* (Philadelphia: Historical Society of Pennsylvania, 1938), 56, 60–61.

4. Jared Sparks, ed., *The Writings of George Washington*, 12 vols. (New York, 1847), 2:479.

5. Sparks, *Writings of George Washington*, 2:480. A note following the excerpt states that Sparks is quoting from the "MS Journal of the Commissioners." For the account that Sparks is quoting, see "The Treaty of Logg's Town, 1752" (1906), *Virginia Magazine of History and Biography* 13 (1906): 154–174; the speech about the "sun-setting," made by Tanacharison, the Half-King—a Seneca chief—can be found on p. 168.

6. Richard Hofstadter, *America at 1750: A Social Portrait* (New York: Random House, 1971), 159–160.

7. For an exhaustive treatment of this subject, see Shaw Livermore, *Early American Land Companies: Their Influence on Corporate Development* (New York: Commonwealth Fund, 1939). See also a letter from George Mason to Edmund Randolph, written in 1782, which elucidates these land grants, quoted by Kate Mason Rowland, *The Life of George Mason, 1725–1792*, 2 vols. (New York, 1892), 2:23–24.

The King's minister in charge of western affairs, Lord Hillsborough, cast a jaundiced eye on Franklin's proposal for a new colony: "If a vast territory be granted to any set of gentlemen who really mean to people it, and actually do so, it must draw and carry out a great number of people from Great Britain, and I apprehend they will soon become a kind of separate and independent people and who will set up for themselves; and they will soon have manufactures of their own; that they will neither take supplies from the mother country nor from the provinces at the back of which they are settled; that being at a distance from the seat of government, courts, and magistrates, they will be out of the reach and control of law and government; that it will become a receptacle and kind of asylum for offenders who will flee from justice to such new country or colony" [*Report of the Lords Commissioners for Trade and Plantations, on the Petition of the Honorable Thomas Walpole, Benjamin Franklin ... and their Associates, for a Grant of Lands on the River Ohio, in North America* (1772; reprint, [Gloucester, UK]: Dodo, 2008), 13].

8. Camilla Townsend, *Pocahontas and the Powhatan Dilemma* (New York: Hill and Wang, 2004), 129–130.

9. James Hall, *Sketches of History, Life, and Manners in the West,* 2 vols. (Cincinnati, 1834–1835), 1:68.

10. John Locke, *Two Treatises of Government, a New Corrected Edition* (1689; London, 1821), 213.

11. Alice Beck Kehoe, "Deconstructing John Locke," *Postcolonial Perspectives in Archaeology: Proceedings of the 39th (2006) Annual Chacmool Archaeological Conference,* ed. Peter Bikoulis, Dominic Lacroix, and Meaghan Peuramaki-Brown (Calgary, Alberta: University of Calgary Archaeological Association, 2009), 125–132.

12. William Byrd to Charles Boyle, the Earl of Orrery, July 5, 1726; quoted by Eugene D. Genovese, *Roll, Jordan, Roll: The World the Slaves Made* (New York: Vintage, 1976), 75.

13. Peter [Pehr] Kalm, *Travels in North America* [1770], trans. and ed., Adolph R. Benson, 2 vols. (1937; reprint, New York: Dover, 1966), 1:367–374. Kalm was a great naturalist, student and later colleague of Linnaeus, and his journal makes for fascinating reading.

14. See, for example, Neville Craig, ed., *The Olden Time,* 2 vols. (1876; reprint, Lewisburg, PA: Wennawoods Publishing, 2002), 1:30–33. For a comprehensive treatment of the entirety of the Seven Years' War in America, see Fred Anderson, *Crucible of War: The Seven Years' War and the Fate of Empire in British North America, 1754–1766* (New York: Knopf, 2000).

15. Philippe de Rigaud Vaudreuil, Governor-General of New France, to the French Minister [Étienne François, duc de Choiseul], June 24, 1760, *Collections of the State Historical Society of Wisconsin* (Madison, 1908), 18:218.

16. Archer Butler Hulbert, *Waterways of Westward Expansion: The Ohio River and Its Tributaries* (Cleveland, 1903), 48.

17. Le Comte de Vergennes, as quoted by George Bancroft, *History of the United States of America: From the Discovery of the Continent,* The Author's Last Revision, vol. 2 (New York, 1891), 564–565.

18. See, for example, David Curtis Skaggs and Larry Lee Nelson, eds., *The Sixty Years' War for the Great Lakes* (East Lansing: Michigan State University Press, 2010). For a good look at the consequences of the Seven Years' War in America, see Colin G. Calloway, *The Scratch of a Pen: 1763 and the Transformation of North America* (New York: Oxford University Press, 2006).

19. For a history and discussion of these and other issues regarding the financial affairs of the Early Republic, see Bray Hammond, *Banks and Politics in America: From the Revolution to the Civil War* (Princeton: Princeton University Press, 1957). For a concise treatment of the various French-British wars before 1763, see

Howard H. Peckham, *The Colonial Wars, 1689–1762* (Chicago: University of Chicago Press, 1964).

20. "Proclamation against Settling" [*Archives,* series A, 26:10], *Report on Canadian Archives, 1889,* Douglas Brymner, archivist (Ottawa, 1890), 73.

21. Amherst's attempt to use germ warfare against the First Nations came during Pontiac's Rebellion. As he wrote his second-in-command, Colonel Henry Bouquet, "Could it not be contrived to send the small pox among the disaffected tribes of Indians? We must on this occasion use every stratagem in our power to reduce them." And then nine days later: "You will do well to try to inoculate the Indians by means of blankets, as well as to try every other method that can serve to extirpate this execrable race" [JA to HB, July 7, 1763, and July 16, 1763, quoted by Kevin Kenny, *Peaceable Kingdom Lost: The Paxton Boys and the Destruction of William Penn's Holy Experiment* (New York: Oxford University Press, 2009), 121]. For photocopies of the original letters, see "Jeffrey Amherst and Smallpox Blankets," http://www.nativeweb.org/pages/legal/amherst/lord_jeff.html.

22. See, for example, Gregory Evans Dowd, *War under Heaven: Pontiac, the Indian Nations, and the British Empire* (Baltimore: Johns Hopkins University Press, 2002).

23. "Proclamation of October 7, 1763," *The Critical Period, 1763–1765,* ed. Clarence Walworth Alvord and Clarence Edwin Carter, vol. 10 of the *Collections of the Illinois State Historical Library* (Springfield, 1915), 43–44.

24. For an excellent discussion of these issues, see Thomas Perkins Abernethy, *Western Lands and the American Revolution* (New York: Russell & Russell, 1959).

25. Daniel Boone, "The Adventures of Col. Daniel Boon," in John Filson, *The Discovery and Settlement of Kentucke* (1784; reprint, Ann Arbor: University Microfilms, 1966), 51. Colonel Richard Henderson, *Journal of an Expedition to Cantuckey in 1775,* quoted (without citation) in Edna Kenton, *Simon Kenton: His Life and Period, 1755–1836* (1930; reprint, Salem, NH: Ayer, 1993), 7. Felix Walker, "The First Settlement of Kentucky: Narrative of an Adventure in Kentucky in the Year 1775," *De Bow's Review* 16, no. 2 (Feb. 1854): 152–153.

26. George Washington to William Crawford, September 21, 1767, *The Washington-Crawford Letters,* ed. C. W. Butterfield (Cincinnati, 1877), 3.

27. "Treaty of Fort Stanwix" [1768], E. B. O'Callaghan, ed., *Documents Relative to the Colonial History of the State of New-York,* , vol. 8 (Albany, 1857), 120; can also be found at http://earlytreaties.unl.edu/treaty.00007.html.

28. William Johnson to the Lords of Trade and Plantation, November 1763, quoted in Berthold Fernow, *The Ohio Valley in Colonial Days* (Albany, 1890), 36–37.

29. Hulbert, *Waterways*, 49.

30. "Deed Determining the Boundary Line between the Whites and the Indians," "Treaty of Fort Stanwix," O'Callaghan, *Documents*, 135–137.

31. "[Kentucky] was a common hunting ground for many tribes, who visited it from a great distance, roaming over its rich pastures during the season for taking game, and making it their temporary residence during a part of every year, for that purpose. It was also the great battle ground of the Indians, who met here in desperate conflict, either accidentally, when engaged in hunting, or by concert, in the mutual pursuance of a policy which induced them to carry their wars as far as possible from home. The name applied to it by the savages— *the dark and bloody ground*—is terribly significant of the sanguinary character of those conflicts" [Hall, *Sketches*, 1:80–81].

32. "Treaty of Hard Labor" [1768], William Laurence Saunders, ed., *The Colonial Records of North Carolina,* , vol. 7 (Raleigh, 1890), 851–855; can also be found at http://jeffersonswest. unl.edu/archive/view_doc.php?id=jef.00089.

33. As William Walker later noted, in a personal interview with Lyman Coleman Draper, "There never did exist much of the *entente cordiale* between the Wyandotts and Delawares on the one side, and the Mohawks on the other, since the old Iroquois wars of the [seventeenth] century" [Draper 11 F 59; note on p. 51: "William Walker was Territorial Governor of Kansas, was born near Brownstown, mouth of the Detroit River, Nov. [?] 5, 1799—his mother a half-blood Wyandott, his father a white prisoner.—LCD"].

34. Boone, "Adventures," 50.

35. Hulbert, *Waterways*, 49.

36. See W. J. Eccles, "The Fur Trade and Eighteenth-Century Imperialism," *William and Mary Quarterly* 40, no. 3 (July 1983): 341–362. For a broader picture, see Eric Jay Dolin, *Fur, Fortune, and Empire: The Epic History of the Fur Trade in America* (New York: Norton, 2010). For another good look at the whole history, and the ecological consequences, of the trade in beaver fur, see Frances Backhouse, *Once They Were Hats: In Search of the Mighty Beaver* (Toronto: ECW Press, 2015). In return for beaver pelts and other animal skins, the Native Americans were supplied with various items of "civilization"—objects which soon seemed almost necessities of life—cooking gear (brass kettles), which were more transportable than clay pots, weapons for hunting and warfare (guns and gunpowder, which were

more effective for killing at a distance than bows and arrows), and above all, addictive beverages (French brandy and British rum), as well as blankets, pipes, and articles of personal clothing and adornment. One list of goods supplied includes "blankets, buckles, armbands, earrings, belts, fishhooks, awls, spears, mirrors, knives, razors, scissors, combs, thimbles, jew's harps, rifles, pistols, powder, shot, flints, lead, beads, needles, tomahawks, pipes, tobacco, laced hats, flags, plumes, medals, coats, bridles, kettles, lace, ribbon, rum" [Colin G. Calloway, *Crown and Calumet: British-Indian Relations, 1783-1815* (Norman: University of Oklahoma Press, 1967), 61].

For an even more detailed list, see "Estimate of Merchandise Wanted for Indian Presents at Detroit from August 1782 to 20th August 1783," *MPHC* 11:382–383; this is an itemized list from the last year of the Revolution, which represents the needs of only one post held at that time by the British forces, albeit perhaps the most important post in the west, at a time when they were most desperate to keep the alliance of the western Indians.

37. See, for example, Henry Harvey, *History of the Shawnee Indians: From the Year 1681 to 1854, Inclusive* (Cincinnati, 1855); and for a more modern treatment, Jerry E. Clark, *The Shawnee* (Lexington: University Press of Kentucky, 1993).

38. *Lenape* simply means *people*, or *the people*, and they were also known as the Lenni Lenape, or True People. According to their oral history, they originated west of the Mississippi and later displaced another people who inhabited the eastern part of the continent and were the builders of the earthworks to be found in Ohio and elsewhere; see John Heckewelder, *History, Manners, and Customs of the Indian Nations Who Once Inhabited Pennsylvania and the Neighbouring States*, a New and Revised Edition (1819; Philadelphia, 1876), 47–50. The best guide to historical Native communities is Helen Hornbeck Tanner's *Atlas of Great Lakes Indian History* (Norman: University of Oklahoma Press, 1987). See also Michael N. McConnell, *A Country Between: The Upper Ohio Valley and Its Peoples* (Lincoln: University of Nebraska Press, 1992); also Richard White, *The Middle Ground: Indians, Empires, and Republics in the Great Lakes Region, 1650-1815* (Cambridge: Cambridge University Press, 1991). One of the best contemporary descriptions of a Native American village during this period was written not about the Ohio country but rather a town of the Sauk Nation along the Wisconsin River: "It contains about ninety houses, each large enough for several families. These are built of hewn plank, neatly jointed and covered with bark so compactly as to keep out the most

penetrating rains. Before the doors are placed comfortable sheds, in which the inhabitants sit, when the weather will permit, and smoke their pipes. The streets are regular and spacious; so that it appears more like a civilized town than the abode of savages" [Jonathan Carver, *Three Years Travels throughout the Interior Parts of North America* (Boston, 1802), 29].

39. Rufus King, *Ohio: First Fruit of the Ordinance of 1787* (Boston, 1903), 25. The author was the grandson of Rufus King of Massachusetts, delegate to the Constitutional Convention.

Chapter 4

1. William Pierce, "Character Sketches of Delegates to the Federal Convention," Farrand, 3:94–95.

2. See, for example, David C. Hendrickson, *Peace Pact: The Lost World of the American Founding* (Lawrence: University Press of Kansas, 2003), particularly Part One.

3. For a biography of Baldwin, see E. Merton Coulter, *Abraham Baldwin: Patriot, Educator, and Founding Father* (Arlington, VA: Vandamere Press, 1897).

4. Hamilton's estimate of forty thousand for the population of Delaware differs slightly from that of Rufus King—thirty-five thousand—which he gives about a week later, on July 6 (Farrand, 1:541). According to the census of 1790, Delaware's population was about fifty-nine thousand [U.S. Bureau of the Census, *A Century of Population Growth: From the First Census of the United States to the Twelfth, 1790–1900* (Washington, D.C.: Government Printing Office, 1909), 47].

5. See, for example, Robert W. Barnwell, Jr., "Rutledge, 'The Dictator,'" *Journal of Southern History* 7, no. 2 (May 1941): 215–224.

6. George Mason to Beverly Randolph, June 30, 1787, Farrand, 3:50. In the absence of Edmund Randolph, who was in Philadelphia, his cousin Beverly was acting governor of Virginia.

7. "The Genuine Information, Delivered to the Legislature of the State of Maryland, Relative to the Proceedings of the General Convention, Held at Philadelphia, in 1787," Farrand, 3:188. There may be another reason that Baldwin switched his vote. According to Richard Barry, in his well-researched but poorly documented biography of John Rutledge, on the evening of June 30 Rutledge entertained Sherman at the Indian Queen. There, according to Barry, Rutledge and Sherman agreed to the compromise that would later be embodied in the Constitution, by which the Northerners would agree to a twenty-year moratorium on putting an end to the slave trade in return for the Southerners backing off on their demand that

a two-thirds vote in the Senate be necessary to pass any navigation acts. This would have protected the Southern states from Northern control of the so-called carrying trade—that is, the ability of the Northern shipping interests to restrict competition and require the Southerners to pay top dollar to get their agricultural products to market. If we accept this supposition, there is no reason to doubt that Rutledge and Sherman could also have come to an understanding regarding proportional representation in the House of Representatives (including, perhaps, some percentage of the slave population) in return for each state having an equal vote in the Senate. Given Baldwin's close connection to the Connecticut delegates, he may have been included in those privy to this understanding, and that may have influenced his vote [Richard Barry, *Mr. Rutledge of South Carolina* (New York: Duell, Sloan & Pearce, 1942), 329–332]. If this is reasoning is accurate, it might explain why Baldwin's brother-in-law, Joel Barlow, later became the front man in Paris for the Scioto Group of speculators who—as we'll see—helped pave the way for Congressional approval of the Ohio Company's plans. That is to say, perhaps the Connecticut investors in the venture realized they owed Baldwin a favor for switching his vote on July 2. For a good treatment of Joel Barlow's part in the fraudulent sale of Ohio land to unsuspecting Frenchmen and their resulting disastrous experience in Gallipolis, see John McGovern, "The Gallipolis Colony in Ohio, 1788–1795," *Records of the American Catholic Historical Society* 37 (March 1926): 29–72.

8. Coulter, *Abraham Baldwin*, 97.

9. Alexander Hamilton to George Washington, 3 July 1787, Farrand, 3:54.

Chapter 5

1. James Wilson, *On the Improvement and Settlement of Lands in the United States* (1795?; Philadelphia: Free Library of Philadelphia, 1946), 11.

2. See Thomas Perkins Abernethy, *Western Lands and the American Revolution* (New York: Russell & Russell, 1959), 116–122.

3. For a brief history of the enterprise, see "Memorial Communicated to the House of Representatives, 21 December 1819, by the United Illinois and Wabash Land Companies," *American State Papers: Public Lands*, 8 vols. (1834–1861), 2:88–89, 96. For Wilson's ownership, see Charles Page Smith, *James Wilson, Founding Father, 1742–1796* (Westport, CT: Greenwood, 1973), 160. For a fuller history of the topic, see Clarence Walworth Alvord, *The Illinois Country, 1673–1818* (Chicago, 1922), 300–307, 340–341, and 380–387.

4. Thomas Paine, *Common Sense* (1775; New York, 1918), 44.

5. *JCC* 18:915–916.

6. The best discussion of this process, and its political ramifications, can be found in Merrill Jensen, *The Articles of Confederation: An Interpretation of the Social-Constitutional History of the American Revolution, 1774–1781* (1940; reprint, Madison: University of Wisconsin Press, 1948).

7. See John Heckewelder, *A Narrative of the Mission of the United Brethren among the Mohegan and Delaware Indians ... to the Close of the Year 1808* (Philadelphia, 1820), 317–320.

8. Quoted by Robert Morgan, *Boone: A Biography* (Chapel Hill, NC: Algonquin Books, 2007), 309.

9. Edwin Danson, *Drawing the Line: How Mason and Dixon Surveyed the Most Famous Border in America* (New York: Wiley, 2001), 178–179.

10. "28 November 1782. In Pursuance of an Order of the Executives of the States of Virginia and Pennsylvania ... we have extended Dixon's and Mason's Line, twenty-three miles to a small poplar in the extended forks of Fish Creek, & from thence extended a meridian of sixty-one miles and two hundred and thirty-six perches to the Ohio River ... about two and one-half miles above the mouth of Yellow Creek" ["Report of Jos. Nevill, State of Virginia, and Alexander McHan, State of Pennsylvania, to the Governor of Virginia," *CVSP* 3:380].

11. May 1, 1782, *JCC* 22:230.

12. September 13, 1783, *JCC* 25:558.

13. In its acceptance of the Virginia cession, Congress added the following clause: "*Provided always*, that the acceptance of the said cession, in manner and form aforesaid, shall not be considered as implying any opinion or decision of Congress respecting the extent or validity of the claim of the Commonwealth of Virginia, to western territory, by charter or otherwise" [March 1, 1784, *JCC* 26:116]. By so ruling (as a result of pressure from different land companies on the various state delegations), Congress neither supported nor denied Virginia's position that the Illinois and Wabash Companies' purchase from the First Nations was null and void because only the government of Virginia—which claimed to own the land—could sell it.

14. For the continuing saga in Congress of pleas and rejections, see *American State Papers: Public Lands* 1:63–65, 1:66, 1:173, 2:220.

15. See Appendix B for excerpts from John Marshall's decision.

16. George Washington to General [Rufus] Putnam, June 2, 1783, Cutler, 1:141.

17. Brig. Gen. Allan Maclean to Gen. Frederick Haldimand, May 18, 1783, *MPHC* 20:118–119.

18. Indian Council at Detroit, Major De Peyster Commandant, June 28, 1783, *MPHC* 11:370.

19. Sir John Johnson, July 23, 1783, quoted by Walter Mohr, *Federal Indian Relations, 1774–1788* (Philadelphia: University of Pennsylvania Press, 1933), 128.

20. Joseph Hadfield, *An Englishman in America, 1785: Being the diary of Joseph Hadfield*, ed. Douglas S. Robertson (Toronto: Hunter-Rose, 1933), 185.

21. May 1, 1783, *JCC* 24:319–320.

22. William Irvine to Benjamin Lincoln, Fort Pitt, August 17, 1783, *Washington-Irvine Correspondence*, ed. C. W. Butterfield (Madison, WI, 1882), 193. See also Philip Schuyler to the President of Congress, July 29, 1783: "It will be little or no obstacle to our future improving the very country [the Indians] may retain, whenever we shall want it, for as our settlements approach their country, they must, from the scarcity of game, which that approach will induce to, retire farther back, and dispose of their lands ... and thus leave us the country without the expence of a purchase, trifling as that will probably be" [PCC, item 153, 3:603]. Schuyler was correct about the effect on game of the expanding western settlements—but he was dead wrong about the Native Americans' willingness to part with their land. For example, according to one report in September 1783, "the Shawanese & Cherokees [gave] several speeches tending to assure the Six Nations of their willingness to join in defence of their country ... as the Americans were encroaching upon different parts of it" [Alexander McKee, Deputy Agent for Indian Affairs, "Minutes of Transactions with Indians at Lower Sandusky," *MPHC* 20:175].

23. George Washington to James Duane, Rocky Hill, September 7, 1783, George Washington Papers, Library of Congress, Washington, D.C.; http://memory.loc.gov/ammem/gw html/gwhome.html].

24. *JCC* 25:602.

25. David Howell to James Manning, September 27, 1783, *LDC* 20:728. See also DH to Paul Allen, 18 [December] 1783: "three hundred & twenty millions of acres ... at one eighth of a dollar per acre would extinguish a debt of forty millions of dollars. It is a general opinion they will & ought to fetch a dollar per acre" [*LDC* 21:209].

26. Virginia Delegates to [Governor] Benjamin Harrison, November 1, 1783, *LDC* 21:139.

Chapter 6

1. Mercy Warren to Mrs. Macauley, September 28, 1787, quoted by Jackson Turner Main, *The Antifederalists: Critics of the Consti-*

tution, 1781–1788 (1961; reprint, New York: Norton, 1974), 186.

2. John Adams, Diary, September 5, 1774, *The Works of John Adams*, ed. Charles Francis Adams, vol. 2 (Boston, 1850), 366.

3. September 6, 1774, *JCC* 1:25.

4. Adams, Diary, 367.

5. Connecticut Delegates to Governor Jonathan Trumbull, Sr., October 10, 1774, *LDC* 1:168.

6. *JCC* 2:221.

7. After declaring Independence on July 4, 1776, Congress turned on July 12 to a draft of the Articles of Confederation, the original constitution of the United States. The first draft of Article 11, as introduced on July 12, reads in part as follows: "All Charges of Wars and all other Expences that shall be incurred for the common Defence, or general Welfare ... shall be defrayed out of a common Treasury, which shall be supplied by the several Colonies in Proportion to the Number of Inhabitants of every Age, Sex and Quality, except Indians not paying Taxes, in each Colony, a true Account of which, distinguishing the Inhabitants who are not slaves, shall be triennially taken" [*JCC* 5:548]. During the debate, the words "who are not slaves" were struck out and "white" was inserted before the word "inhabitants." This was the first, though by no means the last occasion on which various circumlocutions were used to avoid mentioning the word *slave*.

Here are some excerpts from the debates that summer, as recorded by both Jefferson and Adams; Jefferson's notes are rendered in italics, Adams' in roman typeface:

"Samuel Chase [of Maryland]: The negroes are wealth. Numbers are not a certain rule of wealth.... Negroes [are] a species of property, personal estate. If negroes are taken into the computation of numbers to ascertain wealth, they ought to be in settling the representation. The Massachusetts fisheries, and navigation, ought to be taken into consideration" [*JCC* 6:1079].

"John Adams: The numbers of people were taken by this article as an index of the wealth of the state and not as subjects of taxation.... it was of no consequence by what name you called your people, whether by that of freemen or of slaves.... in some countries the labouring poor were called freemen, in others they were called slaves.... Certainly 500 freemen produce no more profits, no greater surplus for the payment of taxes than 500 slaves.... Suppose by any extraordinary operation of nature or of law, one half the labourers of a state could in the course of one night be transformed into slaves: would the state be made the poorer or the less able to pay taxes? ... the condition of the labouring poor in most countries, that of the fishermen particularly of the

Northern states, is as abject as that of slaves. It is the number of labourers which produce the surplus for taxation, and numbers therefore indiscriminately are the fair index of wealth" [1099–1100].

"[Benjamin] Harrison [of Virginia] proposed a compromise, that two slaves should be counted as one freeman. He affirmed that slaves did not do so much work as freemen, and doubted if two effected more than one ... this was proved by the price of labor, the hire of a labourer in the Southern colonies being from 8 to 12 £, while in the Northern it was generally 24 £" [1100].

8. *JCC* 6:1080.

9. For an excellent discussion of antebellum slave patrols, see Sally E. Hadden, *Slave Patrols: Law and Violence in Virginia and the Carolinas* (Cambridge, MA: Harvard University Press, 2001).

10. *JCC* 19:215.

11. John Adams to Abigail Adams, July 29, 1776, *JCC* 5:616 n1.

12. *JCC* 6:1102.

13. *JCC* 6:1081. At this time, James Wilson made a comment similar to one he would make in Philadelphia in 1787: "It has been said that Congress is a representation of states, not of individuals. I say that the objects of its care are all the individuals of the states. It is strange that annexing the name of 'State' to ten thousand men, should give them an equal right with forty thousand. This must be the effect of magic, not of reason. as to those matters which are referred to Congress, we are not so many states; we are one large state. We lay aside our individuality whenever we come here" [ibid., 1105].

14. *JCC* 19:215–221.

15. *JCC* 5:762–763. According to Archer Butler Hulbert, "The first provision for granting lands to soldiers who should serve to the close of the war was passed in September, 1776; though this act does not specify that it was western or trans-Allegheny land ... it seems to have been the general opinion at the time that such was to be the case. From the very beginning of hostilities the 'Old Northwest' seems to have been looked upon as the tangible prize of the war" [Introduction, *The Records of the Original Proceedings of the Ohio Company* (Marietta, OH, 1917), xv]. This is precisely the same sort of guarantee that was made to Virginia troops at the start of the previous war in 1754 by Governor Dinwiddie: "I do hereby notify and promise, by and with the advice and consent of his Majesty's council of this Colony, that over and above their pay, two hundred thousand acres of his Majesty the King of Great Britain's lands, on the east side of the river Ohio, within his dominion ... shall be laid off and granted to such persons, who by their voluntary engagement, and good behaviour, in the

said service, shall deserve the same. By the Honourable Robert Dinwiddie, Esqr." [Kenneth P. Bailey, ed., *The Ohio Company Papers, 1752–1817: Being Primarily Papers of the "Suffering Traders" of Pennsylvania* (Arcata, CA: [n.p.], 1947), 25].

16. The best discussion of the economics of the Revolution and the post-Revolutionary era is Elmer James Ferguson, *The Power of the Purse: A History of American Public Finance, 1776–1790* (Chapel Hill: University of North Carolina Press, 1961).

17. Shays' Rebellion was not an isolated incident in Massachusetts—see Robert Joseph Taylor, *Western Massachusetts in the Revolution* (Providence, RI: Brown University Press, 1954).

18. See Main, *The Antifederalists*, 72–102.

19. January 28, 1783, *JCC* 25:878.

20. Quoted by Kate M. Rowland, *The Life of George Mason, 1725–1792*, 2 vols. (New York, 1892), 2:51.

21. *JCC* 25:948.

22. *JCC* 25:948–949. Madison also reports the specific reasoning used on both sides of the debate: "The arguments used by those who were for rating slaves high were, that the expence of feeding & clothing them was as far below that incident to freemen as their industry & ingenuity were below those of freemen; and that the warm climate within which the States having slaves lay, compared with the rigorous climate & inferior fertility of the others, ought to have great weight in the case & that the exports of the former States were greater than of the latter. On the other side it was said that Slaves were not put to labor as young as the children of laboring families—that, having no interest in their labor, they did as little as possible, & omitted every exertion of thought requisite to facilitate & expedite it; that if the exports of the States having slaves exceeded those of the others, their imports were in proportion, slaves being employed wholly in agriculture, not in manufactures; & that in fact the balance of trade formerly was much more against the Southern States than the others" [ibid., 949]. The notes of the committee itself can be found in PCC, item 26, 433–434.

23. Jonathan Elliot, ed., *The Debates in the Several State Conventions on the Adoption of the Federal Constitution*, 5 vols. (Philadelphia, PA, and Washington, D.C., 1836–1859), 1:93.

Chapter 7

1. William Pierce, "Character Sketches of Delegates to the Federal Convention," Farrand, 3:91–92.

2. The seventh resolution can be found in Farrand, 1:236: "Resd. that the rights of suffrage in the 1st branch of the National Legislature,

ought not to be according to the rule established in the articles of confederation but according to some equitable ratio of representation, namely, in proportion to the whole number of white & other free citizens & inhabitants, of every age sex and condition, including those bound to servitude for a term of years, & three fifths of all other persons, not comprehended in the foregoing description, except Indians not paying taxes in each State."

3. James H. Hutson, ed., *Supplement to Max Farrand's The Records of the Federal Convention of 1787* (New Haven: Yale University Press, 1987), 150.

4. In Mason's will, among other assets, he left his heirs "sixty thousand acres of among the finest lands in Kentucky" and "some three hundred slaves" [Kate Mason Rowland, *The Life of George Mason, 1725–1792*, 2 vols. (New York, 1892), 2:368].

5. Hugh Williamson to Thomas Ruston, February 12, 1787, *LDC* 21:354.

6. For land sales in the Ohio Country, see Albion Morris Dyer, "First Ownership of Ohio Lands," *New England Historical and Genealogical Register* 64 (1910): 167–180, 263–282, 356–369, and also vol. 65 (1911): 51–62, 139–150, 220–228; reissued as a single volume, *First Ownership of Ohio Lands* (1911; reprint, Baltimore: Genealogical Publishing, 1969).

Chapter 8

1. Farrand, 1:135.

2. Harriet Martineau, *Society in America*, 3rd ed., 2 vols. (New York, 1837), 1:382.

3. For the arrival of the ship carrying news of the peace treaty, see Mary Barney, ed., *Biographical Memoir of the Late Commodore Joshua Barney: From Autographical Notes and Journals in Possession of His Family, and Other Authentic Sources* (Boston, 1832), 138–139. The ship that Commodore Barney captained, the *Washington*, was owned by Robert Morris, and it was rumored that Barney told Morris of the treaty before anyone else was informed, enabling Morris to make transactions in the money market that ensured him a tidy profit when the news became general that peace had broken out after nearly eight years of war.

4. Timothy Pickering to [Samuel] Hodgdon, April 7, 1783, Cutler, 1:149, 156, 158.

5. PCC, item 42, 6:62–71; also Cutler, 1:160–167 (which lists the names of all 288 petitioners).

6. George Washington to the President of Congress, June 17, 1783, Cutler, 1:172–174.

7. "In case the quantity of good lands on the southeast side of the Ohio … prove insufficient for their legal bounties, the deficiency should be made up to the said troops, in good lands,

to be laid off between the rivers Scioto, and Little Miami, on the northwest side of the river Ohio, in such proportions as have been engaged to them by the laws of Virginia" [*JCC* 26:114–115]. See William E. Peters, *Ohio Lands and their Subdivision*, 2nd ed. (Athens, OH, 1918), 102–117.

8. Archer Butler Hulbert, ed., Introduction to *The Records of the Original Proceedings of the Ohio Company*, 2 vols. (Marietta, OH, 1917), 1:xviii.

9. See map of the Ohio Country below, preceding Chapter 12.

10. Hugh Williamson to Thomas Ruston, February 12, 1784, *LDC* 21:352–353.

11. Charles Thomson to Hannah Thomson, October 15, 1783, *LDC* 21:60–61. For this entire fascinating correspondence, which took place during the time that Congress was away from Philadelphia and Charles Thomson was separated from his wife, see Eugene R. Sheridan and John M. Murrin, eds., *Congress at Princeton: Being the Letters of Charles Thomson to Hannah Thomson, June–October 1783* (Princeton: Princeton University Library, 1985).

12. David Howell to Jonathan Arnold, February 21, 1784, *LDC* 21:380–381. Howell was a professor of mathematics, natural history, Latin, French, and Hebrew at Rhode Island College (now Brown University). Earlier in this letter Howell presents an interesting picture of the life of a Congressman: "You cannot easily conceive the *tedium* of our present situation. Had my education in youth—or did my present taste admit of my participating in the amusements of this place such as plays, balls, concerts, routs, hops, fandangoes & fox hunting—or I may add did my finances admit of mixing with the *bon ton*—time might pass off agreeably; but four dollars a day, altho' as much as I wish, or expect from the state at present, burdened as the people are with accumulated debts, will not admit of seeing much company, as you well know. You will ask then how I spend my time? I have perused the letters from Europe on our files & some of the extracts are sent to the state. I sometimes read. Gov. Jefferson, who is here a Delegate from Virginia, and one of the best members I have ever seen in Congress, has a good Library of French books, & has been so good as to lend me [some]" [380].

13. *LDC* 21:382.

14. *JCC* 26:117.

15. "The deed of cession of Virginia, March 1, 1784, finally gave the United States title to a large strip north of the Ohio River. New York had yielded a more shadowy claim to the same region three years earlier. Deeds of cession by Massachusetts, April 19, 1785, and by Connecticut, May 28, 1786, extended the national jurisdiction until it covered the whole of the North-west, except Connecticut's western reserve along the south shore of Lake Erie" [Elbert Jay Benton, "Establishing the American Colonial System in the Old Northwest," *Transactions of the Illinois State Historical Society for the Year 1918* (Springfield, 1919), 47].

16. *JCC* 26:119. The entire document can be found in Appendix D. One can argue that this was Thomas Jefferson's finest hour regarding the peculiar institution. As a younger man, it is true, he argued in court for the freedom of a black slave, based upon the notion that all men are born free—but he lost that case, and in any event it only concerned the fate of one man. If, on the other hand, the proposal submitted that March day in Annapolis had become the law of the land, it would—as Jefferson said later—have affected the lives of millions of men and women yet to be born. His attitude toward the abolition of slavery would change over the years, particularly with regard to the Federal government's power to mandate such a momentous change. Two decades later, President Jefferson engineered the purchase of the immense Louisiana Territory from Napoleon—but he made no attempt to restrict the growth of slavery across the Mississippi (where, to be sure, it already existed under French law). And nearly twenty years after that, at the time of the Missouri Crisis, he opposed Congressional attempts to extend the free-soil line of the Ohio River further westward. The best treatment of Jefferson's tangled relationship with slavery is John Chester Miller, *The Wolf by the Ears: Thomas Jefferson and Slavery* (1977; reprint, Charlottesville: University Press of Virginia, 1991).

17. *JCC* 26:246–247.

18. TJ to Jean-Nicolas Démeunier, June 22, 1786, *The Works of Thomas Jefferson*, ed. Paul Leicester Ford, vol. 5 (New York, 1904), 65. See also TJ to James Madison, April 25, 1784: "The [slavery clause] was lost by an individual vote only. Ten states were present. The 4 Eastern states, [and] N. York, Pennsva. were for the clause. Jersey would have been for it, but there were but two members, one of whom was sick in his chambers. South Carolina, Maryland & !Virginia! voted against it. N. Carolina was divided as would have been Virginia had not one of its delegates been sick in bed" [*LDC* 21:545]. The Virginia delegate who was absent was James Monroe.

19. *JCC* 26:275–279. The full text of the Resolve of 1784, along with the Northwest Ordinance, can be found in Appendix D.

20. *American Lands and Funds* Broadside, Printed Ephemera Collection, Library of Congress, Portfolio 42, Folder 18; http://hdl.loc.gov/loc.rbc/rbpe.04201800.

21. *JCC* 26:324.

22. William Grayson to Timothy Pickering, April 27, 1785, *LDC* 22:359; see also Rufus King to Elbridge Gerry, April 26, 1785, ibid., 357.

23. Geographically, this is a tale of two great river systems, the Mississippi and the St. Lawrence, which together drain the entire mid-continent of North America. Across the Midwest are several places where the two river systems are divided by a short portage. The one at the Miami Villages (now Fort Wayne, Indiana) would be of crucial importance in the years following the passage of the Northwest Ordinance, becoming a military objective for the national troops attempting to subdue the Native inhabitants of the Ohio Country. In 1792, units under the command of Arthur St. Clair sustained—at the Battle of the Wabash—one of the worst defeats ever inflicted upon an American army, at the hands of Native American warriors under the command of Little Turtle. Not until two years later, at Fallen Timbers, would Anthony Wayne—in command of a larger army made possible by Federal taxing power under the Constitution—defeat the forces of the First Nations. The Treaty of Greenville followed in 1795, which ceded all of southern Ohio to the American settlers. For a magisterial discussion of the various portages and their importance in American history, see Archer Butler Hulbert, *Portage Paths: The Keys of the Continent* (Cleveland, 1903).

24. For a complete discussion of the retention of the frontier posts in British foreign policy, see A. L. Burt, *The United States, Great Britain, and British North America: From the Revolution to the Establishment of Peace after the War of 1812* (New York: Russell & Russell, 1961), 82–105.

25. GW to Jacob Read, November 3, 1784, George Washington Papers, Library of Congress, Washington, D.C.; http://memory.loc.gov/ammem/gwhtml/gwhome.html. Another writer speaks of an "infatuation" with western land: Dorsey Pentecost to James Wilson, June 26, 1783, quoted in full in E. Douglas Branch and Dorsey Pentecost, "Plan for the Western Lands, 1783," *Pennsylvania Magazine of History and Biography* 60, no. 3 (July 1936): 288–292; stable URL: http://www.jstor.org/stable/20086990.

26. "Treaty of Fort Stanwix, in 1784," Neville Craig, ed., *The Olden Time*, 2 vols. (1876; reprint, Lewisburg, PA: Wennawoods Publishing, 2002), 2:414.

27. "Joseph Brant's account of the treaty of Fort Stanwix" [1784], Draper 23 U 2–3.

28. "[B]eginning at the mouth of a creek about four miles east of Niagara ... upon the lake named by the Indians Oswego, and by us Ontario; from thence southerly ... [to] Lake Erie; thence south to the north boundary of the state of Pennsylvania; thence west to the end of the said north boundary; thence south along the west boundary of the said state, to the river Ohio" ["Treaty with the Six Nations, 1784," Charles J. Kappler, ed., *Indian Affairs: Laws and Treaties*, 2 vols. (Washington, D.C.: Government Printing Office, 1904), 2:6].

29. Arthur Lee to Jacob Read, October 29, 1784, Draper F 11 4.

30. "Arthur Lee's Journal," December 17, 1784, Craig, *Olden Time*, 2:339.

31. Josiah Harmar to Thomas Mifflin, January 31, 1785, Draper 1 W 35; see also JH to John Dickinson, January 15, 1785, Consul Wilshire Butterfield, ed., "Dickinson-Harmar Correspondence of 1784–5," Appendix to *Journal of Capt. Jonathan Heart* (Albany, 1885), 53. (This second letter also appears in Draper 1 W 32–33.) The speech of the commissioners at Fort McIntosh is as follows: "The King of Great Britain in his treaty with the United States, has not stipulated any thing in favour of you & of the other Indian Nations who joined him in the war against us. You are therefore left to obtain peace from the U. States, & to be received under their government and protection, upon such conditions as seem proper to Congress, the Great Council of the United States" [Draper 1 W 26–27].

32. "The boundary line between the United States and the Wiandot and Delaware nations shall begin at the mouth of the river Cayahoga, and run thence up the said river to the portage between that and the Tuscarawas branch of Meskingum ... then westerly to the portage of the Big Miami, which runs into the Ohio ... then along the said portage to the Great Miami or Ome river, and down the south-east side of the same to its mouth; thence along the south shore of lake Erie, to the mouth of Cayahoga where it began" ["Treaty with the Wyandot, etc., 1785," Kappler, *Indian Affairs*, 2:6–7].

33. "Proclamation of the Commissioners for Indian Affairs, January 24, 1785: Surveying or settling the lands not within the limits of any particular State being forbidden by the United States in Congress assembled, the commander will employ such force as he may judge necessary in driving off persons attempting to settle on the lands of the United States" [*The St. Clair Papers: The Life and Public Services of Arthur St. Clair*, ed. William Henry Smith, 2 vols. (Cincinnati, 1882), 2:3 *n*1; also Draper 1 W 40].

34. David Howell to William Greene, February 9, 1785, *LDC* 22:177. See also Hugh Williamson to Thomas Ruston, March 2, 1785: "Our Commissioners have just finished a second Indian treaty at which the several Tribes concerned have ceded to the United States about 12 or 14 millions of Acres. I presume that we shall soon open an office for the sale of those

lands. I think the price will hardly be lower than a dollar per acre, hardly so little, but public securities will be taken in payment and they may be purchased much below par" [ibid., 240].

35. Richard Henry Lee to George Washington, February 14, 1785, *LDC* 22:198. For the changing distribution of Indian villages throughout the historical period, see Helen Hornbeck Tanner, *Atlas of Great Lakes Indian History* (Norman: University of Oklahoma Press, 1987). For a Native account of how the Shawnees had inhabited the Ohio Country for many years, see various remarks at the Treaty of Greenville, particularly by Blue Jacket and Little Turtle, in Jacob Burnet, *Notes on the Early Settlement of the North-Western Territory* (New York, 1847), 222, 226.

36. See, for example, David Howell to Jabez Bowen, March 7, 1785: "It is proposed to hold another Treaty about the first of June … at St. Vincents on the Wabash river. This, it is hoped, will finish this business for the present" [*LDC* 22:251–252].

37. "Advertisement," March 12, 1785, Draper 1 W 39–40. This "advertisement" also appears in a couple of other places, with various slight modifications: Smith, *St. Clair Papers*, 2:5 fn; and Butterfield, "Dickinson-Harmar Correspondence," 65–66 fn; see also Charles Thomson to Peter Miller, May 9, 1785, *LDC* 22:389. The name Menzons is also spelled Mancer and Manser, and Emerson also appears as Amberson.

38. "At the time of the Treaty of Fort Stanwix in 1768, tribes in the Great Lakes Region probably numbered about 60,000 persons.… Most eighteenth-century population data in original sources are given in terms of warriors, with the ratio of warrior count to total population figured as 1:5, although ratios of 1:5 and 1:6 are also mentioned. In modern studies, the recommended ration varies from 1:3.5 to 1:6" [Tanner, *Atlas*, 65]. This would indicate a total number of Indian warriors in the greater Midwest above 10,000. If even one-fourth of these men were available at any given time, that would mean somewhere around two thousand superb wilderness fighters, certainly enough to defeat a similar number of militiamen with a small complement of regular troops.

Consider these remarks of James Smith: "Nothing can be more unjustly represented than the different accounts we have had of [the Indians'] number from time to time both by their own computations, and that of the British. While I was among them, I saw the account of the number, that they in those parts gave to the French, and kept it by me. When they in their own council-house, were taking an account of their number, with a piece of bark newly stripped, and a small stick, which answered the end of a slate and pencil, I took an account of

the different nations and tribes, which I added together, and found there were not half the number which they had given the French: and though they were then their allies, and lived among them, it was not easy finding out the deception, as they were a wandering set, and some of them almost always in the woods hunting. I asked one of the chiefs what was their reason for making such different returns. He said it was for political reasons, in order to obtain greater presents from the French, by telling them they could not divide such and such quantities of goods among so many.

"In [the] year of General Bouquet's last campaign, 1764, I saw the official return made by the British officers, of the number of Indians that were in arms against us that year, which amounted to thirty thousand. As I was then a lieutenant in the British service, I told them I was of opinion that there was not above one thousand in arms against us.… The British officers hooted at me, and said they could not make England sensible of the difficulties they labored under in fighting them, as England expect that their troops could fight the undisciplined savages in America, five to one, as they did the East-Indians, and therefore my report would not answer their purpose, as they could not give an honorable account of the war, but by augmenting their number. I am of opinion that from Braddock's war until the present time there never were more than three thousand Indians at any time, in arms against us, west of Fort Pitt, and frequently not half that number" [*An Account of the Remarkable Occurrences in the Life and Travels of Col. James Smith* (1799; Cincinnati, 1907), 154–156].

39. "There were, by 1785, a hundred thousand people in what we know as West Virginia and Kentucky" [Archer Butler Hulbert, *Waterways of Westward Expansion: The Ohio River and Its Tributaries* (Cleveland, OH, 1903), 55.]; "By 1800 there are forty-five thousand inhabitants in the entire Northwest Territory, of which probably twenty-five thousand are in the Ohio Valley" [ibid., 70]. As an estimate, therefore, fifty thousand settlers in Kentucky and north of the Ohio, around 1785, seems a reasonable assumption.

40. Josiah Harmar to John Armstrong, March 29, 1785, Draper 1 W 40–41.

41. George Washington to Hugh Williamson, Mount Vernon, March 15, 1785, George Washington Papers, Library of Congress, Washington, D.C.; http://memory.loc.gov/ammem/gwhtml/gwhome.html.

42. David Howell to Jonathan Arnold, February 21, 1784, *LDC* 21:383.

43. [Pliny Durant, et al.], *History of Clinton County Ohio*, ed. Albert J. Brown (Indianapolis, 1915), 79.

44. Durant, *History*, 78.
45. David Howell to Jonathan Arnold, February 21, 1784, *LDC* 21:383.
46. *JCC* 28:114.
47. Timothy Pickering to Rufus King, March 8, 1785, *The Life and Correspondence of Rufus King*, ed. Charles R. King, vol. 1 (New York, 1894), 45–46.
48. *JCC* 28:164.
49. *JCC* 28:165.
50. *JCC* 28:239. According to a footnote, "this report … was read on this day [April 6] and Thursday April 14 assigned for consideration."
51. In a letter to James Madison, William Grayson suggested that King withdrew his motion so it wouldn't interfere with the passage of the Land Ordinance, which was already tangled up in Congressional debate: "Mr. King of Massachusets has a resolution ready drawn, which he reserves till the [Land] Ordinance is passed, for preventing slavery in the new State. I expect Seven States may be found liberal enough to adopt it" [WG to JM, 1 May 1785, *LDC* 22:366]. But apparently there exists no explanation of why King failed to reintroduce his motion after the Land Ordinance had passed.
52. [Harry Innes?], Danville, Kentucky, March 1, 1785, quoted in full by G. Hubert Smith, "A Letter from Kentucky," *Mississippi Valley Historical Review* 19, no. 1 (June 1932): 90–95; note on p. 91: "The following letter … first appeared in the *Boston Magazine* for September, 1785. The writer's name is not given, but it seems likely that he was Judge Harry Innes, who removed to Kentucky about that time"; originally appeared in *Boston Magazine* 2 (1785): 342–345. See also David Howell to William Greene, New York, April 29, 1785, *LDC* 22:361–362.
53. "Message from the Shawanese Towns to Alexander McKee," March 20, 1785, *MPHC* 25:691. This letter can also be found in Draper 23 U 16.
54. Josiah Harmar to Henry Knox, April 13, 1785, Draper 1 W 55.
55. John Armstrong, Ensign, to Col. Josiah Harmar, April 13, 1785, Smith, *St. Clair Papers*, 2:3 *n*2; also Draper 1 w 47. See also Col. Josiah Harmar to Richard Henry Lee, President of Congress, Fort McIntosh, May 1, 1785: "The number of settlers lower down the river is very considerable, and, from all accounts, daily increasing" [Smith, *St. Clair Papers*, 2:3].
56. "An Ordinance for Ascertaining the Mode of Disposing of Lands in the Western Territory," *JCC* 28:371–385. Here is one example of the reaction in Congress: "I inclose you a copy of the Ordinance: & if it is not the best in the world, it is I am confident the best that could be procured for the present. There was

such a variety of interests most of them imaginary, that I am only surprised it is not more defective. The Eastern people who before the revolution never had an idea of any quantity of earth above a hundred acres, were for selling in large tracts of 30,000 acres while the Southern people who formerly could scarce bring their imaginations down so low as to comprehended the meaning of a hundred acres of ground were for selling the whole territory in lots of a mile square. In this situation we remained for eight days, with great obstinacy on both sides, until a kind of compromise took effect" [William Grayson to James Madison, May 28, 1785, *LDC* 22:406]. For this May 4–5 compromise, see *JCC* 28:335–339.
57. John Jay to William Bingham, 31 May 1785, *The Correspondence and Public Papers of John Jay, 1782–1793*, ed. Henry P. Johnston, 4 vols. (New York, 1890–1893), 3:154.
58. Josiah Harmar to Francis Johnston, June 1, 1785, Draper 1 W 71–72.
59. "Captain Johnny, a Shawnee, speaking on behalf of the Shawnee, the Mingo, and the Delaware, at a Council held at Wakitumikee," May 18, 1785 [*MPHC* 25:691]. See also Captain [Alexander] McKee to Sir John Johnson, Detroit, June 2, 1785: "I have received from Simon Girty (Interpreter) who is returned from the Indian Country where I had sent him upon service: the enclosed copy of a meeting held by the several nations Inhabiting the country contiguous to the Ohio, which fully declares their sentiments respecting the impolitic terms imposed by the American Commissioners: and I find the same opinion is general amongst all the nations to the Westward, and that they appear unanimously determined to support their right to the country as long as they are able. They say they did not call out for peace, they always thought the Americans desired it, and they listened to it thro' the advice of their father; but never entertained an Idea that the Americans looked upon them [as] a conquered people until the declaration of their Commissioners informed them thereof" [*MPHC* 11:457].
60. See, for example, Lord Sydney, UK Secretary of State, to Colonel Henry Hope, Lieutenant Governor of Quebec, May 7, 1786: "To afford them open and avowed assistance, should hostilities commence, must at all events in the present state of this country be avoided; but His Majesty's Ministers at the same time do not think it either consistent with justice or good policy entirely to abandon them, and leave them to the mercy of the Americans, as from motives of resentment it is not unlikely that they might hereafter be led to interrupt the peace and prosperity of the Province of Quebec. It is utterly impracticable for His Majesty's

Ministers to prescribe any direct line for your conduct should matters be driven to the extremity, and much will depend upon your judgment and discretion in the management of a business so delicate and interesting, in which you must be governed by a variety of circumstances which cannot at this moment be foreseen" [quoted by Isabel Thompson Kelsay, *Joseph Brant, 1743-1807: Man of Two Worlds* (Syracuse, NY: Syracuse University Press, 1984), 398]. See also David Howell to William Greene, August 23, 1785: "While these posts are held by the British too the Indians will hardly be prevailed on, by seeing only paper & parchments, to believe that the U. States are in fact the Sovereigns of that Country" [*LDC* 22:588].

For an overall picture of Native resistance and its tangled relationship with the British government, see Gregory Evans Dowd, *A Spirited Resistance: The North American Indian Struggle for Unity, 1745-1815* (Baltimore: Johns Hopkins University Press, 1992). For a discussion of these issues from the British point of view, see A. L. Burt, *The United States, Great Britain, and British North America: From the Revolution to the Establishment of Peace after the War of 1812* (New York: Russell & Russell, 1961).

61. Arthur Lee to Josiah Harmar, 12 Sept 1785, Draper 1 W 91.

Chapter 9

1. "A Treaty Held at the Town of Lancaster ... with the Indians of the Six Nations in June, 1744," C. Van Doren and J. P. Boyd, eds., *Indian Treaties Printed by Benjamin Franklin, 1736–1762* (Philadelphia: Historical Society of Pennsylvania, 1938), 63–64.

2. See letters of William Blount and Benjamin Hawkins to Governor Richard Caswell of North Carolina, New York, July 10, 1787, *LDC* 24:350-351.

3. Edward Coles, *History of the Ordinance of 1787, Read before the Historical Society of Pennsylvania, June 6, 1856* (Philadelphia, 1856), 28–29.

4. Alexander Hamilton to George Washington, July 3, 1787, Farrand, 3:54.

5. *JCC* 32:297.

6. James E. Dupriest, *William Grayson: A Political Biography of Virginia's First United States Senator* (Manassas, VA: Prince William County Historical Commission, 1977), 42.

7. Mannasseh Cutler's journal entry for July 6, 1787, Cutler, 1:230.

8. For the information about Arthur Lee being a member of the Ohio Company, see Albion Morris Dyer, "First Ownership of Ohio Lands," *New England Historical and Genealogical Register* 65 (1911): 54–55, 149; reprinted as

First Ownership of Ohio Lands (Baltimore: Genealogical Publishing, 1969).

9. "Yesterday there was a Congress of seven states. Your communications respecting Indian affairs were laid before them, & were referred to the Secretary at war for report. This may be expected in a day or two.... Indeed it is very difficult to get anything done with so thin a representation" [William Grayson to Beverley Randolph, July 7, 178, *LDC* 24:348]; this letter can also be found in *CVSP* 4:312.

10. Richard Henry Lee to Francis Lightfoot Lee, July 14, 1787, *LDC* 24:353. For RHL's admission to Congress, see *JCC* 32:310. For Lee having been in Philadelphia, see RHL to Thomas Lee Shippen, July 22, 1787, LDC 24:367.

11. *JCC* 32:310.

12. For a list of Ohio Company purchasers, see Dyer, "First Ownership of Ohio Lands," 61–62, 139-150, 220-228.

13. Nathan Dane to Rufus King, July 16, 1787, *LDC* 24:358. For a complete record of the lengthy progress of the ordinance through Congress, see *JCC* for March 27, May 10, July 13 and 19, and September 21, 1786; also April 26, May 9 and 10, and July 9, 11, 12, and 13, 1787.

14. Peter Force, "The Ordinance of 1787, and Its History," Appendix 1, *The St. Clair Papers: The Life and Public Services of Arthur St. Clair*, ed. William Henry Smith, 2 vols. (Cincinnati, 1882), 2:610–611; first published in the *National Intelligencer* in 1847.

15. PCC, item 30, 95–96; a transcription of this broadside (with printed emendations) can be found in *JCC* 32:281-283.

16. *JCC* 32:281 fn 1; the Rough Journals for May 10 can be found in PCC, item 1, 38:245.

17. PCC, item 1, 38:245.

18. *JCC* 32:313-320.

19. "In printed form this report is in Papers of the Continental Congress Broadsides, with Mss. changes by Charles Thomson and Mr. William Grayson and with a Mss. copy of the sixth Article in the writing of Mr. Dane attached to it. From the indorsement it appears that the corrected printed form represents the second reading on July 12" [*JCC* 32:314, *n*1]. The printed broadside can be found at http://hdl. loc.gov/loc.rbc/bdsdcc.224a1. In the printed broadside of the Ordinance as passed on July 13, Article 6 (together with some other changes) are underlined, and the note in the *Journals* indicates that the underlined portions "were added to the original report by amendment during the debate" [ibid., 334 *n*3]—but the editor remains silent as to the precise date on which this debate took place. The July 13 broadside can be found at http://hdl.loc.gov/loc.rbc/ bdsdcc.22501.

20. *JCC* 32:343; for the full text of the Northwest Ordinance, see pp. 334-343. It can also be

found, along with the Resolve of 1784, in Appendix D.

21. Nathan Dane to Rufus King, July 16, 1787, *LDC* 24:358.

22. Manasseh Cutler's journal for July 9, 1787, Cutler, 1:236–238.

23. Cutler, 1:240–241. Another dinner that Cutler shared with Duer would be a key event in bringing the Ohio Company land deal to fruition—but that occurred a week *after* the Northwest Ordinance had become the law of the land (see Cutler, 1:295–296). Duer was instrumental in bringing in other investors, the so-called Scioto Associates, who would help close the deal, expanded to include five million acres. This group of speculators has been studied in great detail by Archer Butler Hulbert: "The office of Colonel Duer in New York was the business center of the group. Closely associated with him were Andrew Craigie of New York and Cambridge, Massachusetts—of Craigie House fame—Royal Flint of New York and Boston, William Constable, Melancthon Smith, Seth Johnson, and Richard Platt of New York, and Christopher Gore and Samuel Osgood of Boston. The connections abroad were with Daniel Parker and Company, and Smith, Wright, and Gray in London; N. and Th. Van Staphorst and Company in Amsterdam; and the Delasserts in Paris.... The principals and chief agents resided at Philadelphia; New York; Boston; Alexandria; Marietta, Ohio; and London, Amsterdam, and Paris" ["The Methods and Operations of the Scioto Group of Speculators," *Mississippi Valley Historical Review* 1, no. 4 (March 1915): 507]. See also Joseph Stancliffe Davis, "The Board of Treasury and the Scioto Flotation," *Essays in the Earlier History of American Corporations* (Cambridge, MA, 1917), 124–150. For the best picture of Duer and his business dealings, see Robert F. Jones, *The King of the Alley: William Duer, Politician, Entrepreneur, and Speculator, 1768–1799* (Philadelphia: American Philosophical Society, 1992).

24. *JCC* 32:311.

25. Cutler, 1:242.

26. Archer Butler Hulbert, ed., Introduction to *The Records of the Original Proceedings of the Ohio Company*, 2 vols. (Marietta, OH, 1917), 1:lix–lx.

27. Cutler, 1:254. For a complete account of the various men Cutler meets with, many of whom are involved in one way or another with western land speculation, see ibid., 253–271.

28. Hulbert, Introduction, 1:lix.

29. Rev. A. P. Peabody, "Manasseh Cutler," *New Englander and Yale Review* 46, no. 205 (April 1887): 326–327.

30. Cutler, 1:293. The one amendment not adhered to involves taxation. As Cutler explains, "The amendments I proposed have all been made except one, and that is better qualified. It was, that we should not be subject to Continental taxation until we were entitled to a full representation in Congress.... They have granted representation, with right of debating, but not of voting, upon our being first subject to taxation."

31. *JCC* 32:327–331.

Chapter 10

1. Samuel Montgomery, "Journal of Samuel Montgomery [1785]," *Mississippi Valley Historical Review* 2, no. 2 (Sept. 1915): 273.

2. Charles S. Hall, *Life and Letters of Samuel Holden Parsons: Major-General in the Continental Army and Chief Judge of the Northwestern Territory, 1737–1789* (Binghamton, NY, 1905), 482.

3. The trip of the commissioners and the soldiers down the Ohio River, and the construction of the fort and its several outbuildings took months, and we are fortunate that Richard Butler kept a journal throughout the whole process, including two side trips—one to Big Bone Lick and one to the fledgling community of Louisville at the Falls of the Ohio: "Journal of Richard Butler," Neville Craig, ed., *The Olden Time*, 2 vols. (1876; reprint, Lewisburg, PA: Wennawoods Publishing, 2002), 2:433–464, 481–531. For another point of view of the actual treaty talks, see Robert Walsh, "From the notes of an old officer," Draper 11 J 60.

4. Ebenezer Denny, *Military Journal of Major Ebenezer Denny* (Philadelphia, 1859), 72–73; for a full account of his journey, the treaty, and its aftermath, see pp. 56–76. Black strings and belts of wampum indicated war; white indicated peace. A good description of wampum comes from Thomas Forsyth: "The wampum belts are woven together by thread made of the deer's sinews, the thread is passed through each grain of wampum and the grains lay [*sic*] in the belt parallel to each other, the Belts are of various sizes, some more than two yards in length; if for peace or friendship the Belts are composed solely of white grained wampum, if for war, they are made of the blue grained wampum painted red with vermillion; the greater the size of the Belt, the more force of expression is meant by it to convey. In forming alliances other Belts are made of white wampum, representing the various nations with whom they are in alliance or friendship" [Thomas Forsyth, "An Account of the Manners and Customs of the Sauk and Fox Nations of Indians Tradition," *The Indian Tribes of the Upper Mississippi Valley and Region of the Great Lakes*, ed. Emma Helen Blair, 2 vols. (Cleveland, 1911), 2:185]. According to Blair, "The early white explorers found everywhere among the natives shells or beads made

from them, in use as currency, and for personal adornment; and the English colonists adopted the name for this article that was current among the New England Indians, 'wampum.' This term was afterward extended to the glass or porcelain beads brought from Europe by traders. The beads were strung upon cords or sinews, and when woven into plaits about as broad as the hand formed 'wampum belts'; these constituted practically the official form of presents sent by one tribe or one village to another, and were used in negotiating and in recording treaties" [ibid., 185 fn].

5. Don Greene, *Shawnee Heritage II: Selected Lineages of Notable Shawnee, with Contributions by Noel Schutz* (n.p.: Lulu, 2008), 316–317, 343–344, 442, 446, 458.

6. Butler, "Journal," *Olden Time*, 2:521–531.

7. Hector de Crevecoeur discusses this phenomenon in great detail: "By what power does it come to pass, that children who have been adopted when young among these people, can never be prevailed on to re-adopt European manners? Many an anxious parent I have seen [after the] last war, who at the return of the peace, went to the Indian villages where they knew their children had been carried in captivity; when to their inexpressible sorrow, they found them so perfectly Indianized, that many knew them no longer, and those whose more advanced ages permitted them to recollect their fathers and mothers, absolutely refused to follow them, and ran to their adopted parents for protection against the effusions of love their unhappy real parents lavished on them! Incredible as this may appear, I have heard it asserted in a thousand instances, among persons of credit.... [Life among the Indians] cannot be, therefore, so bad as we generally conceive it to be; there must be in their social bond something singularly captivating, and far superior to any thing to be boasted of among us; for thousands of Europeans are Indians, and we have no examples of even one of those Aborigines having from choice become Europeans! There must be something more congenial to our native dispositions, than the fictitious society in which we live; or else why should children, and even grown persons, become in a short time so invincibly attached to it? ... For, take a young Indian lad, give him the best education you possibly can, load him with your bounty, with presents, nay with riches; yet he will secretly long for his native woods, which you would imagine he must have long since forgot; and on the first opportunity he can possibly find, you will see him voluntarily leave behind him all you have given him, and return with inexpressible joy to lie on the mats of his fathers.... Without temples, without priests, without kings, and without laws, they are in many instances superior to us; and the proofs of what I advance, are, that they live without care, sleep without inquietude, take life as it comes, bearing all its asperities with unparalleled patience, and die without any kind of apprehension for what they have done, or for what they expect to meet with hereafter. What system of philosophy can give us so many necessary qualifications for happiness?" [*Letters from an American Farmer* (1782; New York, 1904), 305–308].

8. The reader will have noticed the discrepancy in the two accounts, as to which American it was who insulted the Shawnees by smashing the string of wampum. The following note by Neville Craig, the original editor of Butler's journal, may shed some light: "We have no doubt that [Butler's] account of the speech in reply to Kekewepellethe, the Shawanese, will greatly surprise many of our readers. Gen. Clarke is so commonly regarded as the principal actor in that striking incident, that our publication will by some persons, be viewed as an attempt to do him injustice. We certainly have no bias in the case; we have long admired the daring and enterprising spirit of the conqueror of the Illinois country; and would be loth, indeed, to deprive him of a single laurel. But let us do justice, though the heavens should fall. Clarke had *earned* glory enough without *filching* one particle from his equally gallant fellow Commissioner, Richard Butler. It would, in fact, be casting a stigma upon the memory of Clarke, to suppose that he had ever given any countenance to the story which assigned to him the decisive reply to the Shawanese chief" [Butler, "Journal," 525].

9. "Treaty with the Shawnee, 1786," *Indian Affairs: Laws and Treaties*, ed. Charles J. Kappler, 2 vols. (Washington, 1904), 2:16–17.

10. "Message from the Shawanese to the British Indian Agents, April 29, 1786," *MPHC* 24:25; the same letter can be found in Draper 23 U 33–34.

11. Archer Butler Hulbert, ed., *The Records of the Original Proceedings of the Ohio Company*, 2 vols. (Marietta, OH, 1917), 1:1–3.

12. Manasseh Cutler to Winthrop Sargent, March 24, 1786, Cutler, 1:188.

13. "A Speech of the Six United Nations by the Speaker a Cayuga Chief called the Fish Carrier, to the Western Indians, Fort Schlosser, March 27, 1786," Draper 23 U 32.

14. David Duncan to Josiah Harmar, March 28, 1786, Draper 1 W 115.

15. March 27, 1786, *JCC* 30:139 *n*1.

16. *Pennsylvania Packet and Advertiser*, May 30, 1786, Draper 11 F 2.

17. Board of Treasury to the Secretary at War, April 1, 1786, PCC, item 150, 1:463.

18. April 6, 1786, *JCC* 30:155.

19. "*Resolved*, That the Geographer of the United States, and the surveyors appointed pursuant to the ordinance of Congress, passed May 20, 1785, for ascertaining the mode of disposing of lands in the western territory, and who have accepted their appointments, proceed in the execution of the said ordinance" [May 9, 1786, *JCC* 30:248].

20. *JCC* 30:252–255.

21. *JCC* 30:346. For the condition of the western posts, see Rufus King to Theodore Sedgwick, May 21, 1786: "[John] Adams demanded the Evacuation of the Posts, and has been officially refused. Repeal your laws against the recovery of British debts before you demand a compliance with the treaty on our part, is the language of the reply to Mr. Adams's demand" [*LDC* 23:305].

22. Congress to Henry Knox, *JCC* 30:353. Knox's full orders to Josiah Harmar, June 27, 1786, are as follows: "An Indian war in the present moment would exceedingly embarrass the United States. It ought to be avoided, if possible consistently with the dignity of the nation. You will therefore act in the double capacity of negotiator and commanding officer. Endeavor to prevent or remove every just cause of complaint on the part of the Indians, but if they will wantonly be the agressors, and attack the troops, make them if possible repent it with bitterness. But you will remark that this conduct is only to be dictated by the principle of unprovoked agression on their part" [Draper 1 W 133]. As Major Walter Finney wrote Harmar on July 3, "I am convinced that military force only can make a permanent peace with Indians & circumscribe their bounds. The treasure expended in treaties might be much more advantageously applied in equipping troops for that purpose" [Draper 1 W 137].

23. Charles Nisbet to David Erskine, the Earl of Buchan, June 24, 1786, quoted by Samuel Miller, *Memoir of the Rev. Charles Nisbet, D.D., Late President of Dickinson College, Carlisle* (New York, 1840), 165.

24. *JCC* 30:390–394. For an interesting discussion of the genesis of this clause, see Jorge M. Robert, "James Monroe and the Three-To-Five Clause of the Northwest Ordinance," http://www.earlyamerica.com/early-america-review/volume-5/northwest-ordinance.

25. *JCC 30*:402–406. On July 19, Nathan Dane was added to the committee [ibid., 418 *n*1].

26. Levi Todd to Patrick Henry, July 12, 1786, *CVSP* 4:155.

27. Col. Josiah Harmar to Capt. John Hamtramck, Fort Harmar, September 6, 1786: "I wrote you on the 18th inst. acquainting you that I had received information that a body of Indians were at the Shawanese Towns, prepared for war. Since which, the information has been further interpreted, that a large body of them were assembled there to council, but their designs are not yet perfectly known" [Draper 1 W 201]. In fact, this is the council that was later interrupted by Logan's Raid; see Chapter 12.

28. "An extract of a letter from an officer commanding at Fort McIntosh," *Maryland Journal*, Tuesday, October 3, 1786, Draper 3 JJ 305.

29. *JCC* 31:670–673.

30. The population of Delaware was estimated by Alexander Hamilton in 1787 at forty thousand (Farrand, 1:466) and by Rufus King at less than thirty-five thousand (ibid., 541). According to the census of 1790, Delaware's population was about fifty-nine thousand, and one-thirteenth of the U.S. population would total about three hundred thousand people: 3,893,635 ÷ 13 = 299,510 [Bureau of the Census, *A Century of Population Growth: From the First Census of the United States to the Twelfth, 1790–1900* (Washington, D.C.: Government Printing Office, 1909), 47]. In Article 5 of the Northwest Ordinance, a minimum of sixty thousand inhabitants is necessary for new states to qualify for admission to the Union, though "such admission shall be allowed … when there may be a less number of free Inhabitants" if "consistent with the general interest of the Confederacy" [*JCC* 32:342–343].

31. Nathan Dane to Rufus King, August 11, 1786, *LDC* 23:489 *n*1.

32. See Henry Knox to Congress, September 28, 1786, *JCC* 31:699.

33. See, for example, Samuel Parsons to William Johnson, October 2, 1786, in Hall, *Life and Letters*, 469. See also Henry Knox to the President of Congress, October 3, 1786, *JCC* 31:752–753.

34. Henry Knox to the President of Congress, October 18, 1786, *JCC* 31:887. See also George Washington to James Madison, November 5, 1786: "Without some alteration in our political creed, the superstructure we have been seven years raising at the expence of much blood and treasure, must fall. We are fast verging to anarchy & confusion! … How melancholy is the reflection that in so short a space, we should have made such large strides towards fulfill[ing] the prediction of our transatlantic foes!—'leave them to themselves, and their government will soon dissolve'" [George Washington Papers, Library of Congress, Washington, D.C.; http://memory.loc.gov/ammem/gwhtml/gwhome.html].

35. James Monroe to Thomas Jefferson, October 12, 1786, *LDC* 23:59.

Chapter 11

1. William Pierce, "Character Sketches of Delegates to the Federal Convention," Farrand, 3:92.

2. *JCC* 24:260.

3. *JCC* 32:74.

4. Though approved by eleven states, this change to Article 8 had never become law because the Articles of Confederation required all thirteen states to approve any amendment.

5. George Washington to Alexander Hamilton, July 10, 1787, Farrand, 3:56–57.

6. "Rufus King in the Senate of the United States" [March 1819], Farrand, 3:428–430. For threats of war, see, for example, the comment by Thomas Cobb of Georgia, on March 2, 1820, in the House of Representatives: "He believed that they were kindling a fire which all the waters of the ocean could not extinguish. It could be extinguished only in blood!" [*Annals of Congress*, 15th Cong., 2nd session, 1437].

7. Here, for the sake of clarity, is the precise language the delegates were voting on (note that the first part of the resolution had already been approved on July 9, and the vote on July 12 encompassed both the original clause and the amendment):

"But as the present situation of the States may probably alter as well in point of wealth as in the number of their inhabitants that the Legislature be authorised from time to time to augment the number of representatives: and in case any of the States shall hereafter be divided, or any two or more States united, or any new State created within the limits of the United States the Legislature shall possess authority to regulate the number of representatives in any of the foregoing cases upon the principles of their wealth and number of inhabitants" [Farrand, 1:557–558].

"Provided always that representation ought to be proportioned according to direct Taxation and in order to ascertain the alteration in the direct Taxation which may be required from time to time by the changes in the relative circumstances of the States—Resolved that a Census be taken within six years from the first meeting of the Legislature of the United States and once within the term of every Ten years afterwards of all the inhabitants of the United States in the manner and according to the ratio recommended by Congress in their resolution of April 18, 1783—and that the Legislature of the U. S. shall proportion the direct Taxation accordingly" [ibid., 590–591].

8. Hamilton was one of the men whom Manasseh Cutler mentions meeting on the evening of July 12 at the Indian Queen Tavern in Philadelphia (Cutler, 1:254). James Hutson disputes the veracity of Cutler's diary, citing "the definitive edition of Hamilton's papers" [that is, *The Papers of Alexander Hamilton*, vol. 4, *January 1787–May 1788*, ed. Harold C. Syrett and Jacob E. Cooke (New York: Columbia University Press, 1962), 223]; according to Hutson,

Hamilton was not actually in Philadelphia at that time—but Staughton Lynd, in a personal communication to the author (November 23, 2014), states that Syrett (who was Lynd's graduate adviser) "readily conceded that he had made a mistake" about this fact. See James H. Hutson, "Riddles of the Federal Constitutional Convention," *William and Mary Quarterly* 44, no. 3 (July 1987): 417.

9. Where was Morris between Friday and Tuesday? My notion is that he took the weekend off to travel to New York (though he is a delegate from Pennsylvania, his home is in New York), perhaps using that opportunity to adjust his investments. He was a business associate of William Duer, whose meeting with Manasseh Cutler the following week was, as we'll see, the key to Cutler's mission coming to fruition—and perhaps Morris took part in the bargaining. Once Duer got involved in the Ohio purchase, the group of potential investors expanded widely. As a twentieth-century writer explains, "[Duer's] son, writing some years later, names among those who were frequently at the house [John] Jay, [Henry] Knox, [Friedrich von] Steuben, Gouverneur Morris, Egbert Benson, James Duane, John Lawrence, Chancellor and Brockholst Livingston, as well as a number of less prominent persons. Among the occasional guests were the presidents of Congress, James Madison, Arthur Lee, Robert Morris, Rufus King, Philip Schuyler, Ralph Izard, and John Kean, later cashier of the first Bank of the United States" [Joseph Stancliffe Davis, "The Board of Treasury and the Scioto Flotation," *Essays in the Earlier History of American Corporations* (Cambridge, MA, 1917), 126, citing William A. Duer, *New York as It Was, During the Latter Part of the Last Century* (New York, 1849), 28–29].

10. At the beginning of August, the draft Constitution comes back to the floor after having been rewritten by the Committee of Detail. This provides one more opportunity for the three-fifths compromise to be debated and, perhaps, overturned. at the beginning of August, when the draft Constitution comes back to the floor after having been rewritten by the Committee of Detail. This provides one more opportunity for the three-fifths compromise to be debated and, perhaps, overturned. Article IV, Sect. 4., then reads, "As the proportions of numbers in different States will alter from time to time; as some of the States may hereafter be divided; as others may be enlarged by addition of territory; as two or more States may be united; as new States will be erected within the limits of the United States. the Legislature shall, in each of these cases, regulate the number of representatives by the number of inhabitants, according to the provisions herein after made,

at the rate of one for every forty thousand" [Farrand, 2:219]. On August 8, Gouverneur Morris makes a motion "to insert 'free' before the word 'inhabitants.'" He follows this motion with an impassioned speech, which shows the depth of his anti-slavery feeling, making his apparent change of sentiment between Wednesday afternoon, July 11, and Thursday morning, July 12, even more remarkable:

"Much he said would depend on this point. He never would concur in upholding domestic slavery. It was a nefarious institution—it was the curse of heaven on the States where it prevailed. Compare the free regions of the Middle States, where a rich & noble cultivation marks the prosperity & happiness of the people, with the misery & poverty which overspread the barren wastes of Va. Maryd. & the other States having slaves. Travel thro' the whole Continent & you behold the prospect continually varying with the appearance & disappearance of slavery. The moment you leave the E. Sts. & enter N. York, the effects of the institution become visible; passing thro' the Jerseys and entering every criterion of superior improvement witnesses the change. Proceed Southwdly, & every step you take thro' the great regions of slaves, presents a desert increasing with the increasing proportion of these wretched beings" [Farrand, 2:221–223].

Morris's motion goes down in defeat, with only one state—New Jersey—voting aye. And despite his strong language, Morris will end up voting to approve the Constitution, complete with three-fifths compromise.

11. W. R. Davie to James Iredell, July 17, 1787, Farrand, 3:60. James Iredell was a close friend of James Wilson, and both served together as justices of the Supreme Court—in fact, it is while visiting Iredell that Wilson, on the run from his creditors, died in a room above a tavern in Edenton, North Carolina; see Page Smith, *James Wilson, Founding Father, 1742–1796* (Westport, CT: Greenwood, 1973), 384–388.

12. In his masterful treatment of slavery in the politics of the early American republic, George William Van Cleve agrees that an "extraconstitutional side bargain" concerning the Northwest Ordinance took place during July 1787, which resulted in "the western expansion of slavery" [George William Van Cleve, *A Slaveholders' Union: Slavery, Politics, and the Constitution in the Early American Republic* (Chicago: University of Chicago Press, 2010), 180]. Van Cleve, however, argues for an "alternative view of the quid pro quo" that has to do with the sectional conflict over the Mississippi River [163]. He suggests that "the Southern states ... proffered their support of the Northwest Ordinance of 1787 in return for the abandonment of the [terms of the Jay-Gardoqui] treaty by the Northern states ... in effect compensating the Northern states for their loss" [162]. To be sure, on July 10, 1787, one day after the committee considering the draft Northwest Ordinance limited its scope to the territory northwest of the Ohio, Benjamin Hawkins of North Carolina wrote that "our right to the free and common navigation of the Mississippi" had been "put in a better situation than heretofore" by "a variety of circumstances unnecessary as well perhaps as improper to relate" [BH to Richard Caswell, *LDC* 24:351]—but Van Cleve fails to take into account the crucial vote on May 10, 1787, in which the Northern coalition opposing free passage of the Mississippi collapsed (*JCC* 32:278–279). Subsequently, the bargaining chip which Van Cleve asserts the Northerners could use in return for a slave-free Northwest Territory was in fact of much less significance, and it is my opinion they would need to offer the Southerners something in addition for them to agree to limit the expansion of slavery—that is, the three-fifths ratio in the formula for apportionment.

13. Advertisement, *Federal Gazette and Philadelphia Daily Advertiser*, Monday, June 14, 1790, 4, col. 1.

Chapter 12

1. James W. Taylor, *History of the State of Ohio: First Period, 1650–1787* (Cincinnati, 1854), 327.

2. Keren Jane Gaumer, "Mac-O-Chee Valley," *Ohio History* 26, no. 4 (Oct. 1917): 459–460.

3. There are many biographies of Boone, and many descriptions of the Battle of Blue Licks. See, for example, Daniel Boone, "Colonel Boone's Narrative," *A Collection of Some of the Most Interesting Narratives of Indian Warfare in the West*, comp. Samuel L. Metcalf (Lexington, KY, 1821), 29–30; for a more recent treatment, see Robert Morgan, *Boone: A Biography* (Chapel Hill, NC: Algonquin Books, 2008), 316–331.

4. Colin G. Calloway, *The Shawnees and the War for America* (New York: Penguin, 2007), 63.

5. There are many accounts of this event; one of the most moving, by the minister of the Moraviantowns congregation, is by John Heckewelder, *A Narrative of the Mission of the United Brethren among the Mohegan and Delaware Indians ... to the Close of the Year 1808* (Philadelphia, 1820), 311–324.

6. "Colonel Crawford's Death at the Stake: William Croghan's Report on the Tragic Aftermath of the Battle of the Olentangy, 1782," *The Ohio Frontier: An Anthology of Early Writings*, ed. Emily Foster (Lexington: University Press of Kentucky, 1996), 65–67.

7. Benjamin Logan to Edmund Randolph, December 17, 1786, *CVSP* 4:204. As one Kentucky old-timer reported, many years later, "Near Old Town, perhaps a mile south, a fellow made off with an officer's horse, & gave the Indians intelligence—then Logan made forced marches day & night—reached Meckacheck on Saturday about 2 o'clock" [General Henry Lee to Lyman C. Draper, Draper 9 BB 60 (1); Draper's note: "From General Henry Lee of Marion [?] County, Ky., July 1843 (who settled at Lex., Ky., in 1779")].

8. Henry Clay Alder, *A History of Jonathan Alder: His Captivity and Life with the Indians*, ed. Larry L. Nelson (Akron, OH: University of Akron Press, 2002), 77. According to a footnote on p. 195, "The combined village settlement ... was comprised of Mequashake (Mack-a-chack), Wapakoneta, Piqua, Blue Jacket's Town, Wakatomica, Kispoko or McKee's Town, and Zane's Town. Logan's men destroyed the entire settlement on October 6 and 7." See Helen Hornbeck Tanner, *Atlas of Great Lakes Indian History* (Norman: University of Oklahoma Press, 1987), 84–86.

9. There are traditionally five different "divisions" of the Shawnee Nation, each devoted to one particular trade or life-practice, and the Mackachack, or Mekoche, of which Moluntha was chief, are the healers and peacemakers. Tecumseh, who was a teenager at this time, was from the Chalakatha division—the warriors. See James Henri Howard, *Shawnee! The Ceremonialism of a Native Indian Tribe and Its Cultural Background* (Athens: Ohio University Press, 1981).

10. Obidiah Robins to Richard Butler, New Coshocton, September 29, 1786, Draper 1 W 249.

11. William Lytle, quoted by Henry Howe, *Historical Collections of Ohio* (Cincinnati, 1848), 299–301.

12. John Mason Peck, quoted by Morgan, *Boone*, 328.

13. The Delaware Chief White-Eyes was another such cultural mediator who was murdered: see Gregory Schaaf, *Wampum Belts and Peace Trees: George Morgan, Native Americans, and Revolutionary Diplomacy* (Golden, CO: Fulcrum Publishing, 1990).

14. Simon Girty to Capt. Alexander McKee, October 11, 1786, *MPHC* 24:34. See also Capt. Walter Finney to Col. Harmar, October 31, 1786, Draper 1 W 242–243; also the account of Gen. Henry Lee, Draper 9 BB 60 (7–8); also "Information from Mr. Lewis Wetsell [*sic*], Muskingum, November 14, 1786," Draper 1 W 263–264 (probably Lewis Wetzel [1763–1808], a noted "Indian fighter"); also an undated letter, Alexander McKee to John Johnson, Draper 23 U 38.

15. Wyandot Chiefs to Gen. Richard Butler, Superintendent of Indian Affairs, October 28, 1786, Draper 1 W 252–253; note on p. 253 states that "This letter appeared in the *Columbian Magazine*, Dec. 1786"; this letter also appeared in the *New-York Packet*, no. 653 (December 12, 1786): 3; it is reprinted in Archer Butler Hulbert, ed., *Ohio in the Time of the Confederation* (Marietta, OH, 1918), 94, citing PCC, item 60, 289. The Indian conference at the Shawnee Towns was attended by Joseph Brant, according to a letter received by Thomas Hutchins, the Geographer of the United States, who was in charge of surveying the Seven Ranges: "A letter dated October 27, 1786, informed Hutchins that 'Joseph Brant with 56 of the Six Nations had gone to the Shawnees Towns. In a council he had with some of the Indians at Casheckton [*sic*] he expressed a wonder that the surveyors should proceed to survey the land that did not belong to them.' Hutchins Papers, vol. 3, p. 32, Hist. Soc. of Penn" [Albion Morris Dyer, "First Ownership of Ohio Lands," *New England Historical and Genealogical Register* 64 (1910): 366 *n*65; this note can be found on p. 46 in the reprint edition of Dyer's article (1911; Baltimore: Genealogical Publishing, 1969). Apparently Brant and many of the other chiefs at the council were out hunting and therefore were absent from the fighting at the Shawnee Towns—see letter from W. Ancrum of the British Indian Agency, October 20, 1786, *MPHC* 24:37. Because the council was interrupted by Logan's Raid, the Indians met later in the year at the Huron Town south of Detroit.

16. "Proceedings of a General Court Martial, Wednesday, March 21, 1787," *CVSP* 4:258–260.

17. "When the sun rose in the morning it looked upon a strange and sorrowful scene.... The Capitol Square, seeming to be safest from the conflagration, was covered over with piles of furniture dragged from the burning houses, among which were huddled together women and children, whose only homes were now beneath the open sky; even here the air was dim with smoke, and blinding with a snow of fiery cinders. The sun was an hour high when from the rear of the motley crowd pressing up Main Street arose the ominous cry of 'The Yankees! The Yankees!'" [Alfred H. Guernsey and Henry M. Alden, eds., *Harper's Pictorial History of the Civil War* (1866; New York: Gramercy Books, 1996), 765].

18. "Court Martial of Hugh McGary, Bardstown, March 21, 1787," Draper 12 S 133–134, 136–137, 139.

19. William Littell, *The Statute Law of Kentucky*, vol. 3 (Frankfort, KY, 1811), 344; various of the promissory notes issued in 1786 can be found in the Kentucky Historical Society

archives, Kentucky Militia Collection, 1786–1864, 90 M 5.

20. Lord Dorchester to Sir John Johnson, Quebec, November 27, 1786, *MPHC* 24:39.

21. "Speech of the [Six] Nations to the Western Indians, Nov. 1786," Draper 23 U 45–46.

22. Joseph Brant to Henry Knox, Secretary at War, December 18, 1786: "I have the honor to enclose to you a Speech from our united Confederacy to be laid before the Honorable Congress of the United States of America" [PCC, item 150, 2:401]. The reason for the long delay in delivery is no mystery. First, just as the conference ended, there was a major storm, followed by an unusually severe winter, and the Indian messengers had been confined by heavy snow to their villages: "On Saturday morning began, and continued for 24 hours, a snow-storm equally severe and violent with that which we experienced on the Monday and Tuesday preceeding. The quantity of snow is supposed to be greater now than has been seen in this country at any time since that which fell about 70 years ago, commonly called the *great snow.* The traveling is exceedingly difficult and in many places impracticable" [*American Mercury* (Hartford), vol. 3, no. 128 (Monday, December 18, 1786): 3, col. 1]. To make matters worse, the following spring, when travel again became possible, Richard Butler was in a riding accident and broken his leg so badly that "the ends of both bones appeared through his stocking" [Capt. Walter Finney to Josiah Harmar, Philadelphia, April 19, 1787, Draper 1 W 289]; see also Henry Knox to JH, June 19, 1787: "Genl. Butler, having unfortunately broken his leg near Lancaster on his way to Congress about 6 or 7 weeks ago, all information through him respecting Indian Affairs has been suspended" [Draper 1 W 303].

23. "Speech of the United Indian Nations, at their Confederate Council, held near the mouth of the Detroit river, the 28th November and 18th December, 1786," *American State Papers: Indian Affairs,* 2 vols. (1832–1834), 1:8–9; also PCC, item 150, 2:381–387. The full text of this speech can be found in Appendix C. For a transcription in the Mohawk language, see PCC, item 150, 1:215–228.

Chapter 13

1. *Independent Gazetteer* (Philadelphia), February 29, 1788, quoted by Jackson Turner Main, *The Antifederalists: Critics of the Constitution, 1781–1788* (1961; New York: Norton, 1974), 174.

2. *JCC* 32:333.

3. *JCC* 32:343. The Ordinance itself, with a table of the vote, can be found on pp. 334–343. It is also reprinted, along with the Resolve of 1784, in Appendix D.

4. These essays are reprinted in full in Appendix A, where I also give my reasons for believing that Abraham Yates was their author.

5. "Neither slavery nor involuntary servitude, except as a punishment for crime whereof the party shall have been duly convicted, shall exist within the United States, or any place subject to their jurisdiction" [13th Amendment, Section 1—passed by Congress January 31, 1865; ratified December 6, 1865].

6. Richard Henry Lee to George Washington, July 15, 1787, *LDC* 24:356; see also RHL to Francis Lightfoot Lee, July 14, 1787: "We owe much money, the pressure of taxes is very great & much complained of—we have now something to sell that will pay the debt & discharge the greatest part of the taxes" [ibid., 353–354].

7. Nathan Dane to Rufus King, *LDC* 24:358.

8. *JCC* 32:369.

9. William Blount to Richard Caswell, *LDC* 24:362–363; see also William Irvine to Richard Butler, New York, July 19, 1787, ibid., 364.

10. According to the Law of Nations, conditions of a treaty entered into by a sovereign power (in this case, the British Crown) are for the most part binding upon any future government that occupies the same territory (that is, the United States): see Emmerich de Vattel, *The Law of Nations* (1758; Philadelphia, 1883), book 2:207–208, 215, and book 3:387.

11. *JCC* 32:376.

12. William E. Peters, *Ohio Lands and Their Subdivision,* 2nd ed. (Athens, OH, 1918), 178; for a full history of the Ohio Company purchase, see ibid., 237–258.

13. This group of men has been studied in great detail by Archer Butler Hulbert: "The office of Colonel Duer in New York was the business center of the group. Closely associated with him were Andrew Craigie of New York and Cambridge, Massachusetts—of Craigie House fame—Royal Flint of New York and Boston, William Constable, Melancton Smith, Seth Johnson, and Richard Platt of New York, and Christopher Gore and Samuel Osgood of Boston. The connections abroad were with Daniel Parker and Company, and Smith, Wright, and Gray in London; N. and Th. Van Staphorst and Company in Amsterdam; and the Delasserts in Paris…. The principals and chief agents resided at Philadelphia; New York; Boston; Alexandria; Marietta, Ohio; and London, Amsterdam, and Paris" ["The Methods and Operations of the Scioto Group of Speculators," *Mississippi Valley Historical Review* 1, no. 4 (March 1915): 507]. See also Joseph Stancliffe Davis, "The Board of Treasury and the Scioto Flotation," *Essays in the Earlier History of American Corporations* (Cambridge, MA, 1917), 124–150.

14. *JCC* 33:385.
15. *JCC* 33:399–400.
16. *JCC* 33:401.
17. Edward Carrington to James Madison, New York, July 25, 1787, *LDC* 24:373. As Cutler wrote in his journal, "My friends had made every exertion in private conversation to bring over my opposers in Congress. In order to get at some of them, so as to work powerfully on their minds, [we] were obliged to engage three or four persons before we could get at them. In some instances we engaged one person, who engaged a second, and he a third, and so on to a fourth, before we could effect our purpose" [Cutler, 1:297].
18. To advertise the land which will soon be available for purchase, Cutler published a brochure—perhaps the first real-estate hype north of the Ohio River: "The toils of agriculture will here be rewarded with a greater variety of valuable productions than in any part of America. The advantages of almost every climate are here blended together; every considerable commodity, that is cultivated in any part of the United States, is here produced in the greatest plenty and perfection. The high dry lands are of a deep, rich soil, producing in abundance, wheat, rye, Indian corn, buckwheat, oats, barley, flax, hemp, tobacco, indigo, silk, wine, and cotton. The tobacco is of a quality superior to that of Virginia; and the crops of wheat are larger than in any other part of America" [Cutler, 2:400; this paragraph is an excerpt from Appendix C, "An Explanation of the Map which Delineates that Part of the Federal Lands ... Now Ready for Settlement" (Salem, MA, 1787)].
19. William Blount to Thomas Blount, *LDC* 24:379–380.
20. Edward Carrington to James Monroe, *LDC* 24:391.
21. William Grayson to James Monroe, *LDC* 24:394.
22. Charles A. Beard, *An Economic Interpretation of the Constitution of the United States* (New York: Macmillan, 1921), 23.
23. Nathan Dane to Rufus King, *LDC* 24: 401.
24. Josiah Harmar to Henry Knox, Appendix 1, *Military Journal of Major Ebenezer Denny* (Philadelphia, 1859), 221.

Appendix A

1. Linda Grant De Pauw, *The Eleventh Pillar: New York State and the Federal Constitution* (Ithaca, NY: Cornell University Press, 1966), 283–292. More recent scholarship also supports the notion that Abraham Yates used "Cato" as a pseudonym; see, for example, Tony Gronowicz, "Yates, Abraham, Jr. (1724–96)," *Blooms-*

bury Encyclopedia of the American Enlightenment, ed. Mark G. Spencer, 2 vols. (New York: Bloomsbury, 2015), 1:1149.
2. Staughton Lynd, "Abraham Yates's History of the Movement for the United States Constitution," *William and Mary Quarterly* 20, no. 2 (April 1963): 241 *n*41.
3. Major General [Anthony] Wayne to the Secretary of War, August 14, 1794, *American State Papers: Indian Affairs*, 2 vols. (1832–1834) 1:490.
4. *JCC* 33:386.

Appendix B

1. Alexis de Tocqueville, *Democracy in America* (1848; New York: Random House, 1945), 352–63.
2. *American State Papers: Public Lands*, 8 vols. (1834–1861), 2:220. The course of this process previous to this date is exemplified by the following: ibid., 1:63–65, 66, 173.
3. For an excellent discussion of *Johnson v. M'Intosh*, its causes and consequences, see Lindsay G. Robertson, *Conquest by Law: How the Discovery of America Dispossessed Indigenous Peoples of Their Lands* (New York: Oxford University Press, 2005).
4. *Washington Post*, Thursday, December 16, 2010, http://www.washingtonpost.com/wp-dyn/content/article/2010/12/16/AR2010121603136.html. For the complete text of the Declaration on the Rights of Indigenous Peoples, see http://www.un.org/esa/socdev/unpfii/documents/DRIPS_en.pdf (the quote is from Article 26). For the State Department "Announcement of U.S. Support for the United Nations Declaration on the Rights of Indigenous Peoples," see http://www.state.gov/documents/organization/184099.pdf.
5. For the complete opinion, see https://supreme.justia.com/cases/federal/us/21/543/case.html.

Appendix C

1. *American State Papers: Indian Affairs*, 2 vols. (1832–1834), 1:8–9; also PCC, item 150, 2:381–387; for a transcription of this speech in the Mohawk language, see PCC, item 150, 1:215–228.

Appendix D

1. July 13, 1787, *JCC* 32:334–343. Various drafts of the Northwest Ordinance can be found as follows in the *Papers of the Continental Congress*: the May 9 printing—heavily edited (presumably during the committee meeting of July 9)—is in PCC, item no. 30, 95–96. The July 11 version is in PCC, item no. 56, 497–502; the

Library of Congress Broadside Collection has an annotated copy of this version with Article 6 in the handwriting of Nathan Dane: http://www.loc.gov/resource/bdsdcc.224a1?sp=3. The July 13 printing is in PCC, item no. 59, 229–30. Finally, the version as rewritten to conform to the Constitution—"An Act to Provide for the Government of the Territory North-west of the River Ohio," which was one of the first acts of the "new" Congress, passed on August 7, 1789, can be found in *The Public Statutes at Large of the United States of America*, ed. Richard Peters (Boston, 1845), 1:50–53.

2. April 23, 1784, *JCC* 26:275–279.

Bibliography

Abernethy, Thomas Perkins. *From Frontier to Plantation in Tennessee: A Study in Frontier Democracy.* Chapel Hill: University of North Carolina Press, 1932.

_____. *Western Lands and the American Revolution.* New York: Russell & Russell, 1959. First published 1937 by Appleton-Century.

Ablavsky, Gregory. "The Savage Constitution." *Duke Law Journal* 63, no. 5 (February 2014): 999–1089.

Adams, John. Diary. *The Works of John Adams.* Edited by Charles Francis Adams. Vol. 2. Boston, 1850, 1–422.

_____. "Thoughts on Government." 1776. *The Works of John Adams.* Edited by Charles Francis Adams. Vol. 4. Boston, 1851, 188–200.

Alberts, Robert C. *The Golden Voyage: The Life and Times of William Bingham, 1752–1804.* Boston: Houghton Mifflin, 1969.

Alder, Henry Clay. *A History of Jonathan Alder: His Captivity and Life with the Indians.* Edited by Larry L. Nelson. Akron, OH: University of Akron Press, 2002.

Alvord, Clarence Walworth. *The Illinois Country, 1673–1818.* Chicago, 1922.

Alvord, Clarence Walworth, and Clarence Edwin Carter, eds. *The Critical Period, 1763–1765.* Vol. 10 of the *Collections of the Illinois State Historical Library.* Springfield, IL, 1915.

American Lands and Funds. Broadside. Printed Ephemera Collection, Library of Congress. Portfolio 42, Folder 18. http://hdl.loc.gov/loc.rbc/rbpe.04201800.

American State Papers. 38 vols. Washington, D.C., 1832–1861.

[Anburey, Thomas]. *Travels through the Interior Parts of America.* 2 vols. London, 1789.

Anderson, Fred. *Crucible of War: The Seven Years' War and the Fate of Empire in British North America, 1754–1766.* New York: Knopf, 2000.

Anderson, James Donald. "Vandalia: The First West Virginia?" *West Virginia History* 40, no. 4 (Summer 1979): 375–92.

Articles of an Association by the Name of the Ohio Company. Worcester, 1786.

Axtell, James. *Natives and Newcomers: The Cultural Origins of North America.* New York: Oxford University Press, 2001.

_____. "The White Indians of Colonial America." *William and Mary Quarterly* 32, no. 1 (January 1975): 55–88.

Backhouse, Frances. *Once They Were Hats: In Search of the Mighty Beaver.* Toronto: ECW Press, 2015.

Bailey, Kenneth P., ed. *The Ohio Company Papers, 1752–1817: Being Primarily Papers of the "Suffering Traders" of Pennsylvania.* Arcata, CA: [n.p.], 1947.

_____. *The Ohio Company of Virginia and the Westward Movement, 1748–1792: A Chapter in the History of the Colonial Frontier.* Glendale, CA: Arthur H. Clark, 1939.

Bancroft, George. *History of the Formation of the Constitution of the United States of America.* 2 vols. New York, 1886.

_____. *History of the United States of America: From the Discovery of the Continent.* The Author's Last Revision. Vol. 2. New York, 1891.

Barnwell, Robert W., Jr. "Rutledge, 'The Dictator.'" *Journal of Southern History* 7, no. 2 (May 1941): 215–224.

Barr, Daniel P., ed. *The Boundaries Between Us: Natives and Newcomers Along the Frontiers of the Old Northwest Territory, 1750–1850.* Kent, OH: Kent State University Press, 2006.

Barrett, Jay A. *Evolution of the Ordinance of 1787.* New York, 1891.

Barry, Richard H. *Mr. Rutledge of South Carolina.* New York: Duell, Sloan & Pearce, 1942.

Beard, Charles A. *An Economic Interpretation of the Constitution of the United States.* New York: Macmillan, 1921.

Beckwith, H. W. *Historic Notes on the Northwest.* Chicago, 1879.

Benezet, Anthony. *Some Observations on the Situation, Disposition, and Character of the Indian Natives of This Continent.* Philadelphia, 1784.

Benton, Elbert Jay. "Establishing the American Colonial System in the Old Northwest." *Transactions of the Illinois State Historical Society for the Year 1918.* Springfield, IL, 1919, 47–63.

Berkhofer, Robert F., Jr. "Jefferson, the Ordinance of 1784, and the Origins of the American Territorial System." *William and Mary Quarterly* 29, no. 2 (April 1972): 231–262.

Bielinski, Stefan. *Abraham Yates, Jr., and the New Political Order in Revolutionary New York.* Albany: New York State American Revolution Bicentennial Commission, 1975.

Blumrosen, Alfred W., and Ruth G. *Slave Nation: How Slavery United the Colonies and Sparked the American Revolution.* Naperville, IL: Sourcebooks, 2005.

Bond, Beverly W., Jr. "American Civilization Comes to the Old Northwest." *Mississippi Valley Historical Review* 19, no. 1 (June 1932): 3–29.

Boone, Daniel. "The Adventures of Col. Daniel Boon." In *The Discovery and Settlement of Kentucke,* by John Filson. 1784. Ann Arbor: University Microfilms, 1966.

Bowen, Catherine Drinker. *Miracle at Philadelphia: The Story of the Constitutional Convention, May to September 1787.* Boston: Little, Brown, 1966.

Boyd, Julian P., ed. *Indian Treaties Printed by Benjamin Franklin, 1736–1762.* Introduction by Carl Van Doren. Philadelphia: Historical Society of Pennsylvania. 1938.

Branch, E. Douglas, and Dorsey Pentecost. "Plan for the Western Lands, 1783." *Pennsylvania Magazine of History and Biography* 60, no. 3 (July 1936): 287–292.

Breen, T. H. *Tobacco Culture: The Mentality of the Great Tidewater Planters on the Eve of Revolution.* Princeton: Princeton University Press, 1985.

Brookhiser, Richard. *Gentleman Revolutionary: Gouverneur Morris, the Rake Who Wrote the Constitution.* New York: Free Press, 2003.

Brymner, Douglas. *Report on Canadian Archives, 1889.* Ottawa, ON, 1890.

Buell, Rowena, ed. *The Memoirs of Rufus Putnam and Certain Official Papers and Correspondence.* Boston, 1903.

Burnet, Jacob. *Notes on the Early Settlement of the North-Western Territory.* New York, 1847.

Burt, A. L. *The United States, Great Britain, and British North America: From the Revolution to the Establishment of Peace after the War of 1812.* New York: Russell and Russell, 1961.

Butler, Mann. *A History of the Commonwealth of Kentucky.* Louisville, 1834.

Butler, Richard. "Journal of Richard Butler." In *The Olden Time,* edited by Neville Craig.

2 vols. Cincinnati, 1876, 2:433–464, 481–531. Reprint, Lewisburg, PA: Wennawoods Publishing, 2002.

Butterfield, Consul Wilshire, ed. "Dickinson-Harmar Correspondence of 1784–5." Appendix to *Journal of Capt. Jonathan Heart*. Albany, 1885.

_____. *History of the Girtys*. Cincinnati, 1890.

_____, ed. *The Washington-Crawford Letters ... Concerning Western Lands*. Cincinnati, 1877.

_____, ed. *Washington-Irvine Correspondence ... 1781 to 1783*. Madison, WI, 1882.

Calloway, Colin G. *Crown and Calumet: British-Indian Relations, 1783–1815*. Norman: University of Oklahoma Press, 1967.

_____. *New Worlds for All: Indians, Europeans, and the Remaking of Early America*. Baltimore, MD: Johns Hopkins University Press, 1987.

_____. *The Scratch of a Pen: 1763 and the Transformation of North America*. New York: Oxford University Press, 2006.

_____. *The Shawnees and the War for America*. New York: Penguin, 2007.

Carey, Matthew, ed. *The American Museum; or, Annual Register of Fugitive Pieces, Ancient and Modern, for the year 1798*. Philadelphia, 1799.

Carter, Clarence Edwin, ed. *The Territory Northwest of the River Ohio, 1787–1803*. Vol. 2 of *The Territorial Papers of the United States*. Washington, D.C.: Government Printing Office, 1934.

Carver, Jonathan. *Three Years Travels throughout the Interior Parts of North America*. Boston, 1802.

Cayton, Andrew R. L. *The Frontier Republic: Ideology and Politics in the Ohio Country, 1780–1825*. Kent, OH: Kent State University Press, 1986.

_____. "Land, Power, and Reputation: The Cultural Dimension of Politics in the Ohio Country." *William and Mary Quarterly* 47, no. 2 (April 1990): 266–286.

Cayton, Andrew R. L., and Stuart D. Hobbs, eds. *The Center of a Great Empire: The Ohio Country in the Early American Republic*. Athens: Ohio University Press, 2005.

Clark, Jerry E. *The Shawnee*. Lexington: University Press of Kentucky, 1993.

Coles, Edward. *History of the Ordinance of 1787, Read Before the Historical Society of Pennsylvania, June 6, 1856*. Philadelphia, 1856.

Collections of the New-York Historical Society for the Year 1878. New York, 1879.

Collections of the State Historical Society of Wisconsin. 20 vols. Madison: Wisconsin State Historical Society, 1888–1931.

Collier, Christopher, and James Lincoln Collier. *Decision in Philadelphia: The Constitutional Convention of 1787*. New York: Ballantine, 1986.

Cooper, Thomas, ed. *Some Information Respecting America*. 2nd ed. London, 1795.

Craig, Neville, ed. *The Olden Time: A Monthly Publication Devoted to the Preservation of Documents and Other Authentic Information in Relation to ... the Country Around the Head of the Ohio*. 1846–1848. 2 vols. Lewisburg, PA: Wennawoods Publishing, 2002. First published as a collected edition in Cincinnati, 1876.

Coulter, E. Merton. *Abraham Baldwin: Patriot, Educator, and Founding Father*. Arlington, VA: Vandamere Press, 1897.

Cresswell, Nicholas. *The Journal of Nicholas Cresswell, 1774–1777*. New York: Dial Press, 1924.

Cutler, William Parker, and Julia Perkins Cutler. *Life, Journals and Correspondence of Rev. Manasseh Cutler*. 2 vols. Cincinnati, 1888.

Danson, Edwin. *Drawing the Line: How Mason and Dixon Surveyed the Most Famous Border in America*. New York: Wiley, 2001.

Davenport, Francis Gardiner, ed. *European Treaties Bearing on the United States and Its Dependencies to 1648*. Washington, D.C.: Carnegie Institution, 1917.

Davis, David Brion. "Constructing Race: A Reflection." *William and Mary Quarterly* 54, no. 1 (January 1997): 7–18.

Davis, Joseph Stancliffe. "The Board of Treasury and the Scioto Flotation." *Essays in the Earlier History of American Corporations.* Cambridge, MA, 1917, 124–150.

Dawes, E. C. "The Beginning of the Ohio Company and the Scioto Purchase." *Ohio Archaeological and Historical Publications* 4 (1895): 1–29.

de Crevecoeur, J. Hector St. John. *Letters from an American Farmer.* 1782. New York, 1904.

De Pauw, Linda Grant. *The Eleventh Pillar: New York State and the Federal Constitution* Ithaca, NY: Cornell University Press, 1966.

de Tocqueville, Alexis. *Democracy in America.* 1848. 2 vols. New York: Random House, 1945.

de Vattel, Emmerich. *The Law of Nations.* 1758. Philadelphia, 1883.

de Warville, J. P. Brissot. *New Travels in the United States of America: Performed in 1788 by J. P. Brissot de Warville.* Translated from the French. Dublin, 1792.

Denny, Ebenezer. *Military Journal of Major Ebenezer Denny.* Philadelphia, 1859.

Diener, Mary Alice Ferry. *The Honorable Dorsey Pentecost, Esquire.* Fresno, CA: Pioneer Publishing, 1978.

Doddridge, Joseph. *Notes on the Settlement and Indian Wars of the Western Parts of Virginia and Pennsylvania from 1763 to 1783, Inclusive.* Pittsburgh, PA, 1912.

Dolin, Eric Jay. *Fur, Fortune, and Empire: The Epic History of the Fur Trade in America.* New York: Norton, 2010.

Dowd, Gregory Evans. *A Spirited Resistance: The North American Indian Struggle for Unity, 1745–1815.* Baltimore: Johns Hopkins University Press, 1992.

_____. *War under Heaven: Pontiac, the Indian Nations, and the British Empire.* Baltimore: Johns Hopkins University Press, 2002.

Downes, Randolph C. *Council Fires on the Upper Ohio: A Narrative of Indian Affairs in the Upper Ohio Valley until 1795.* Pittsburgh: University of Pittsburgh Press, 1968.

_____. "George Morgan, Indian Agent Extraordinary, 1776–1779," *Pennsylvania History* 1, no. 4 (October 1934): 202–216.

Drake, Francis S. *Life and Correspondence of Henry Knox, Major-General in the American Revolutionary Army.* Boston, 1873.

Draper Manuscripts. Wisconsin State Historical Society, Madison.

Duer, William A. *New York as It Was, During the Latter Part of the Last Century* New York, 1849.

Dupriest, James E. *William Grayson: A Political Biography of Virginia's First United States Senator.* Manassas, VA: Prince William County Historical Commission, 1977.

Durant, Pliny, et al. *History of Clinton County Ohio.* Edited by Albert J. Brown. Indianapolis, 1915.

Dyer, Albion Morris. *First Ownership of Ohio Lands.* 1911. Reprint, Baltimore: Genealogical Publishing, 1969. First published in *New England Historical and Genealogical Register* 64 (1910): 167–180, 263–282, 356–369, and vol. 65 (1911): 51–62, 139–150, 220–228.

Eccles, W. J. "The Fur Trade and Eighteenth-Century Imperialism." *William and Mary Quarterly* 40, no. 3 (July 1983): 341–362.

Elliot, Jonathan, ed. *The Debates in the Several State Conventions on the Adoption of the Federal Constitution.* 5 vols. Philadelphia, PA, and Washington, D.C., 1836–1859.

Ellis, Joseph J. *American Creation: Triumphs and Tragedies at the Founding of the Republic.* New York: Knopf, 2007.

Farrand, Max. *The Framing of the Constitution of the United States.* New Haven: Yale University Press, 1913.

_____, ed. *The Records of the Federal Convention of 1787.* 3 vols. New Haven: Yale University Press, 1911.

Fehrenbacher, Don E. *The Dred Scott Case: Its Significance in American Law and Politics.* New York: Oxford University Press, 1978.

Ferguson, Elmer James. *The Power of the Purse: A History of American Public Finance, 1776–1790.* Chapel Hill: University of North Carolina Press, 1961.

Ferling, John. *A Leap in the Dark: The Struggle to Create the American Republic.* New York: Oxford University Press, 2003.

Fernow, Berthold. *The Ohio Valley in Colonial Days.* Albany, 1890.

Finkelman, Paul. *Slavery and the Founders.* 3rd ed. Armonk, NY: Sharpe, 2014.

Fleming, Thomas. *The Perils of Peace: America's Struggle for Survival After Yorktown.* New York: Smithsonian Books, 2007.

Force, Peter. "The Ordinance of 1787, and Its History." 1847. Appendix 1 of *The St. Clair Papers.* Edited by William Henry Smith. Cincinnati, 1882, 2:603–617.

Ford, Paul Leicester, ed. *Essays on the Constitution of the United States, Published During Its Discussion by the People, 1787–1788.* Brooklyn, NY, 1902.

Ford, Worthington Chauncey, ed. *The Federal Constitution in Virginia, 1787–1788.* Cambridge, MA, 1903.

Forsyth, Thomas. "An Account of the Manners and Customs of the Sauk and Fox Nations of Indians Tradition." In *The Indian Tribes of the Upper Mississippi Valley and Region of the Great Lakes*, edited by Emma Helen Blair. 2 vols. Cleveland, 1911, 2:183–245.

Foster, Emily, ed. *The Ohio Frontier: An Anthology of Early Writings.* Lexington: University Press of Kentucky, 1992.

Franklin, Benjamin. *The Complete Works of Benjamin Franklin.* Edited by John Bigelow. 10 vols. New York, 1887–1888.

Friedenberg, Daniel M. *Life, Liberty, and the Pursuit of Land: The Plunder of Early America.* Buffalo, NY: Prometheus Books, 1992.

Gaumer, Keren Jane. "Mac-O-Chee Valley." *Ohio Archaeological and Historical Quarterly* 26, no. 4 (Oct. 1917): 455–469.

Genovese, Eugene D. *Roll, Jordan, Roll: The World the Slaves Made.* New York: Vintage, 1976.

Gibson, Alan. *Understanding the Founding: The Crucial Questions.* Lawrence: University Press of Kansas, 2007.

Goldstone, Lawrence. *Dark Bargain: Slavery, Profits, and the Struggle for the Constitution.* New York: Walker, 2005.

[Green, John]. *State of the British and French Colonies in North America.* London, 1755.

Greene, Don, *Shawnee Heritage II: Selected Lineages of Notable Shawnee.* With contributions by Noel Schutz. N.p.: Lulu, 2008.

Gronowicz, Tony. "Yates, Abraham, Jr. (1724–96)." In *Bloomsbury Encyclopedia of the American Enlightenment*, edited by Mark G. Spencer. 2 vols. New York: Bloomsbury, 2015, 1:1149.

Guernsey, Alfred H., and Henry M. Alden, eds. *Harper's Pictorial History of the Civil War.* 1866. New York: Gramercy Books, [1996].

Hadden, Sally E. *Slave Patrols: Law and Violence in Virginia and the Carolinas.* Cambridge, MA: Harvard University Press, 2001.

Hadfield, Joseph. *An Englishman in America, 1785: Being the Diary of Joseph Hadfield.* Edited by Douglas S. Robertson. Toronto: Hunter-Rose, 1933.

Hall, Charles S. *Life and Letters of Samuel Holden Parsons: Major-General in the Continental Army and Chief Judge of the Northwestern Territory, 1737–1789.* Binghamton, NY, 1905.

Hall, James. *Sketches of History, Life, and Manners in the West.* 2 vols. Cincinnati, 1834–1835.

Hammond, Bray. *Banks and Politics in America: From the Revolution to the Civil War.* Princeton: Princeton University Press, 1957.

Harley, Lewis R. *The Life of Charles Thomson: Secretary of the Continental Congress and Translator of the Bible from the Greek.* Philadelphia, 1900.

Harmar, Josiah. Josiah Harmar Papers, 1681–1937. William L. Clements Library, University of Michigan, Ann Arbor, MI.

Harper, John Robinson. "Revolution and Conquest: Politics, Violence, and Social Change in the Ohio Valley, 1765–1795." PhD diss., University of Wisconsin–Madison, 2008.

Harpster, John W., ed. *Pen Pictures of Early Western Pennsylvania.* Maps and illustrations by Harvey Cushman. Pittsburgh: University of Pittsburgh Press, 1938.

Hartley, David, and Thomas Jefferson. 1784. [A map of the United States east of the Mississippi River in which the land ceded by the Treaty of Paris is divided by parallels of latitude and longitude into fourteen new states]. William L. Clements Library, University of Michigan, Ann Arbor.

Harvey, Henry. *History of the Shawnee Indians: From the Year 1681 to 1854, Inclusive.* Cincinnati, 1855.

Haw, James. *John and Edward Rutledge of South Carolina.* Athens: University of Georgia Press, 1977.

Heckewelder, John. *History, Manners, and Customs of the Indian Nations Who Once Inhabited Pennsylvania and the Neighbouring States.* 1819. New and Revised Edition. Philadelphia, 1876.

_____. *A Narrative of the Mission of the United Brethren Among the Mohegan and Delaware Indians … to the Close of the Year 1808.* Philadelphia, 1820.

Hegreness, Matthew J. "An Organic Law Theory of the Fourteenth Amendment: The Northwest Ordinance as the Source of Rights, Privileges, and Immunities." *Yale Law Journal* 120, no. 7 (May 2011): 1820–1884.

Henderson, H. James. *Party Politics in the Continental Congress.* New York: McGraw-Hill, 1976.

Hendrickson, David C. *Peace Pact: The Lost World of the American Founding.* Lawrence: University Press of Kansas, 2003.

Hildreth, Samuel P., ed. *Biographical and Historical Memoirs of the Pioneer Settlers of Ohio.* Cincinnati, 1852.

_____. *Pioneer History: Being an Account of … the Early Settlement of the Northwest Territory.* Cincinnati, 1848.

[Lord Hillsborough], *Report of the Lords Commissioners for Trade and Plantations, on the Petition of the Honorable Thomas Walpole, Benjamin Franklin. .. and Their Associates, for a Grant of Lands on the River Ohio, in North America.* 1772. Reprint, [Gloucester, UK]: Dodo, 2008.

Hinderaker, Eric. *Elusive Empires: Constructing Colonialism in the Ohio Valley, 1673–1800.* Cambridge: Cambridge University Press, 1997.

Hinsdale, B. A. *The Old Northwest: The Beginnings of Our Colonial System.* Rev. ed. Boston, 1899.

Hofstadter, Richard. *America at 1750: A Social Portrait.* New York: Random House, 1971.

Holton, Woody. *Unruly Americans and the Origins of the Constitution.* New York: Hill and Wang, 2007.

Horsman, Reginald. "American Indian Policy in the Old Northwest, 1783–1812," *William and Mary Quarterly* 18, no. 1 (Jan. 1961): 35–53.

_____. *Expansion and American Indian Policy, 1783–1812.* With a new preface by the author. East Lansing: Michigan State University Press, 1967.

_____. *Matthew Elliott, British Indian Agent.* Detroit: Wayne State University Press, 1964.

_____. "Thomas Jefferson and the Ordinance of 1784." *Illinois Historical Journal* 79, no. 2 (Summer 1986): 99–112.

Howard, James Henri. *Shawnee! The Ceremonialism of a Native Indian Tribe and Its Cultural Background.* Athens: Ohio University Press, 1981.

Howe, Henry. *Historical Collections of Ohio.* Cincinnati, 1848.

Hulbert, Archer Butler. "The Methods and Operations of the Scioto Group of Speculators." *Mississippi Valley Historical Review* 1, no. 4 (March 1915): 502–515, and vol.
2, no. 1 (June 1915): 56–73.

_____, ed. *Ohio in the Time of the Confederation.* Marietta, OH, 1918.

_____. *Portage Paths: The Keys of the Continent.* Cleveland, OH, 1903.

_____, ed. *The Records of the Original Proceedings of the Ohio Company.* 2 vols. Marietta,
OH, 1917.

_____. *Waterways of Westward Expansion: The Ohio River and Its Tributaries.* Cleveland,
OH, 1903.

Hunter, Robert. *From Quebec to Carolina in 1785–1786: Being the Travel Diary and Observations of Robert Hunter, a Young Merchant of London.* Edited by Louis B. Wright
and Marion Tinling. San Marino, CA: Huntington Library, 1943.

Hurt, R. Douglas. *The Ohio Frontier: Crucible of the Old Northwest, 1720–1830.* Bloomington: Indiana University Press, 1996.

Hutson, James H. *The Northwest Ordinance of 1787.* Lynchburg, VA: H. E. Howard, 1987.

_____. "Riddles of the Federal Constitutional Convention." *William and Mary Quarterly*
44, no. 3 (July 1987): 411–423.

_____, ed. *Supplement to Max Farrand's* The Records of the Federal Convention of 1787.
New Haven: Yale University Press, 1987.

Imlay, Gilbert. *A Topographical Description of the Western Territory of North America.*
London, 1792.

Jacobs, Wilbur R. *Dispossessing the American Indian: Indians and Whites on the Colonial
Frontier.* New York: Scribner's, 1972.

James, Alfred P. *The Ohio Company: Its Inner History.* [Pittsburgh, PA]: University of
Pittsburgh Press, [1959].

James, James Alton, ed. *George Rogers Clark Papers, 1781–1784.* Vol. 19 of the *Collections
of the Illinois State Historical Library.* Springfield, 1926.

_____. "Some Phases of the History of the Northwest, 1783–1786." In *Proceedings of the
Mississippi Valley Historical Association for 1913–1914,* vol. 7, edited by Benjamin
F. Shambaugh. Cedar Rapids, IA, 1914, 168–195.

Jay, John. *The Correspondence and Public Papers of John Jay, 1782–1793.* Edited by Henry
P. Johnston. 4 vols. New York, 1890–1893.

Jefferson, Thomas. *The Works of Thomas Jefferson.* Edited by Paul Leicester Ford. 12
vols. New York, 1904–1905.

Jennings, Francis. *The Invasion of America: Indians, Colonialism, and the Cant of Conquest.* Chapel Hill: University of North Carolina Press, 1975.

Jensen, Merrill. *The Articles of Confederation: An Interpretation of the Social-Constitutional History of the American Revolution, 1774–1781.* 1940. Reprint, Madison:
University of Wisconsin Press, 1948.

_____. *The New Nation: A History of the United States during the Confederation, 1781–
1789.* New York: Knopf, 1962.

Johnson v. M'Intosh. 21 U.S. 543 (1823). http://supreme.justia.com/us/21/543/case.html.

Jones, Robert F. *The King of the Alley: William Duer, Politician, Entrepreneur, and Speculator, 1768–1799.* Philadelphia: American Philosophical Society, 1992.

_____. "William Duer and the Business of Government in the Era of the American Rev-
olution." *William and Mary Quarterly* 32, no. 3 (Jul. 1975): 393–416.

Journals of the Continental Congress, 1774–1789. Edited by Worthington C. Ford et al.
34 vols. Washington, D.C., 1904–1937.

Kades, Eric. "History and Interpretation of the Great Case of *Johnson v. M'Intosh.*" *Law
and History Review* 19, no. 1 (2001). http://www.historycooperative.org/journals/
lhr/19.1/kades.html.

Kalm, Peter [Pehr]. *Travels in North America*. 1770. Translated and edited by Adolph R. Benson. 2 vols. 1937. Reprint, New York: Dover, 1966.

Kaminski, John P. *A Necessary Evil: Slavery and the Debate Over the Constitution*. Madison, WI: Madison House, 1995.

Kappler, Charles J., ed. *Indian Affairs: Laws and Treaties*. 2 vols. Washington, D.C.: Government Printing Office, 1904.

Kehoe, Alice Beck. "Deconstructing John Locke." In *Postcolonial Perspectives in Archaeology: Proceedings of the 39th (2006) Annual Chacmool Archaeological Conference*, edited by Peter Bikoulis, Dominic Lacroix, and Meaghan Peuramaki-Brown. Calgary, Alberta: University of Calgary Archaeological Association, 2009, 125–132.

Kellogg, Louise Phelps, ed. *Early Narratives of the Northwest, 1634–1699*. New York, 1917.

Kelsay, Isabel Thompson. *Joseph Brant, 1743–1807: Man of Two Worlds*. Syracuse, NY: Syracuse University Press, 1984.

Kemper, Charles E., ed. "The Early Westward Movement of Virginia, 1722–1734: As Shown by the Proceedings of the Colonial Council." *Virginia Magazine of History and Biography* 13, no. 1 (July 1905): 1–16.

Kenny, Kevin. *Peaceable Kingdom Lost: The Paxton Boys and the Destruction of William Penn's Holy Experiment*. New York: Oxford University Press, 2009.

Kenton, Edna. *Simon Kenton: His Life and Period, 1755–1836*. 1930. Reprint, Salem, NH: Ayer, 1993.

King, Charles R., ed. *The Life and Correspondence of Rufus King*. 6 vols. New York, 1894–1900.

King, Rufus. *Ohio: First Fruit of the Ordinance of 1787*. Boston, 1903.

Konkle, Burton Alva. *James Wilson and the Constitution*. Philadelphia, 1907.

Kukla, Jon. "A Mysteriously Transcendent Quality? The Secessionist Crisis of 1785–1786 and Some of Its Implications." *Secessions: From the American Revolution to Civil War*. Filson Institute Academic Conference, 22 October 2010.

_____. *A Wilderness So Immense: The Louisiana Purchase and the Destiny of America*. New York: Knopf, 2003.

Littell, William. *The Statute Law of Kentucky*. 3 vols. Frankfort, KY, 1809–1811.

Livermore, Shaw. *Early American Land Companies: Their Influence on Corporate Development*. New York: Commonwealth Fund, 1939.

Locke, John. *Two Treatises of Government*. 1689. New Corrected Edition. London, 1821.

Lynd, Staughton. "Abraham Yates's History of the Movement for the United States Constitution." *William and Mary Quarterly* 20, no. 2 (April 1963): 223–245.

_____. "The Compromise of 1787." *Class Conflict, Slavery, and the United States Constitution: Ten Essays*. Indianapolis: Bobbs-Merrill, 1967, 185–213. First published in *Political Science Quarterly* 81, no. 2 (June 1966): 225–250.

Madison, James. *The Writings of James Madison*. Edited by Gaillard Hunt. New York, 1900–1910.

McClung, John A. *Sketches of Western Adventure*. Cincinnati, 1839.

McColley, Robert. *Slavery and Jeffersonian Virginia*, 2nd ed. Urbana: University of Illinois Press, 1973.

McConnell, Michael N. *A Country Between: The Upper Ohio Valley and Its Peoples*. Lincoln: University of Nebraska Press, 1992.

McCormick, Richard P. "The 'Ordinance' of 1784?" *William and Mary Quarterly* 50, no. 1 (Jan. 1993): 112–122.

McGaughy, J. Kent. *Richard Henry Lee of Virginia: A Portrait of an American Revolutionary*. Lanham, MD: Rowman & Littlefield, 2003.

McGovern, John. "The Gallipolis Colony in Ohio, 1788–1795." *Records of the American Catholic Historical Society* 37 (March 1926): 29–72.

McLaughlin, Andrew C. *James Wilson in the Philadelphia Convention*. Boston, 1897.
Main, Jackson Turner. *The Antifederalists: Critics of the Constitution, 1781–1788*. 1961. Reprint, New York: Norton, 1974.
Martineau, Harriet. *Society in America*. 3rd ed. 2 vols. New York, 1837.
Mason, George. *The Papers of George Mason*. Edited by Robert A. Rutland. 3 vols. Chapel Hill: University of North Carolina Press, 1970.
Metcalf, Samuel L., comp. *A Collection of Some of the Most Interesting Narratives of Indian Warfare in the West*. Lexington, KY, 1821.
Michigan Pioneer and Historical Collections. 40 vols. Lansing, 1876–1929.
Miller, John Chester. *The Wolf by the Ears: Thomas Jefferson and Slavery*. 1977. Reprint, Charlottesville: University Press of Virginia, 1991.
Miller, Samuel. *Memoir of the Rev. Charles Nisbet, D.D., Late President of Dickinson College, Carlisle*. New York, 1840.
Mohr, Walter H. *Federal Indian Relations, 1774–1788*. Philadelphia: University of Pennsylvania Press, 1933.
Mombert, J. I. *An Authentic History of Lancaster County in the State of Pennsylvania*. Lancaster, PA, 1869.
Montgomery, Samuel. "Journal of Samuel Montgomery [1785]." *Mississippi Valley Historical Review* 2, no. 2 (Sept. 1915): 262–273.
Moore, Charles. *The Northwest Under Three Flags, 1635–1796*. New York, 1900.
Morgan, Robert. *Boone: A Biography*. Chapel Hill, NC: Algonquin Books, 2008.
Nash, Gary B. *The Unknown American Revolution: The Unruly Birth of Democracy and the Struggle to Create America*. New York: Viking, 2005.
Nelson, Larry L. *A Man of Distinction Among Them: Alexander McKee and the Ohio Country Frontier, 1754–1799*. Kent, OH: Kent State University Press, 1999.
Newcomb, Steven T. *Pagans in the Promised Land: Decoding the Doctrine of Christian Discovery*. Golden, CO: Fulcrum Publishing, 2008.
Nobles, Gregory H. "Breaking into the Backcountry: New Approaches to the Early American Frontier, 1750–1800," *William and Mary Quarterly* 46, no. 4 (Oct. 1989): 641–670.
O'Callaghan, E. B., ed. *Documents Relative to the Colonial History of the State of New-York*. Vol. 8. Albany, 1857, 111–137.
O'Donnell, James H., III. *Ohio's First Peoples*. Athens: Ohio University Press, 2004.
Ohio Archaeological and Historical Quarterly. 43 vols. Columbus, OH, 1887–1934.
Ohio Company. *Articles of an Association by the Name of the Ohio Company*. Worcester, 1786.
Ohline, Howard A. "Republicanism and Slavery: Origins of the Three-Fifths Clause in the United States Constitution," *William and Mary Quarterly* 28, no. 4 (Oct. 1971): 563–584.
Onuf, Peter S. "Liberty, Development, and Union: Visions of the West in the 1780s," *William and Mary Quarterly* 43, no. 2 (April 1986): 179–213.
_____. *Statehood and Union: A History of the Northwest Ordinance*. Bloomington: Indiana University Press, 1987.
O'Toole, Fintan. *White Savage: William Johnson and the Invention of America*. New York: Farrar, Straus and Giroux, 2005.
Paine, Thomas. *Common Sense*. 1775. New York, 1918.
_____. *Public Good, Being an Examination into the Claim of Virginia to the Vacant Western Territory, and of the Right of the United States to the Same*. Philadelphia, 1780.
Palmer, William P., ed. *Calendar of Virginia State Papers*. Vols. 3 and 4. Richmond, 1883–1884.
Papers of the Continental Congress, 1774–1789. National Archives, Washington, D.C.
Pathways to the Old Northwest: An Observance of the Bicentennial of the Northwest Ordi-

nance. Proceedings of a Conference Held at Franklin College of Indiana, July 10–11, 1987. Indianapolis: Indiana Historical Society, 1988.

Pattison, William D. "The Survey of the Seven Ranges." *Ohio History Quarterly* 68, no. 2 (April 1959): 115–140.

Peabody, A. P. "Manasseh Cutler." *New Englander and Yale Review* 46, no. 205 (April 1887): 319–335.

Pease, Theodore C. "The Ordinance of 1787." *Mississippi Valley Historical Review* 25, no. 2 (September 1938): 167–180.

Peckham, Howard H. *The Colonial Wars, 1689–1762*. Chicago: University of Chicago Press, 1964.

Pennsylvania Archives. Series 1. 12 vols. Philadelphia, 1852–1856.

Peters, Richard, ed. *The Public Statutes at Large of the United States of America*. Vol. 1. Boston, 1845.

Peters, William E. *Ohio Lands and Their Subdivision*, 2nd ed. Athens, OH, 1918.

Philbrick, Francis S. *The Rise of the West, 1754–1830*. New York: Harper & Row, 1965.

Poole, William Frederick. "Dr. Cutler and the Ordinance of 1787." *North American Review* 122, no. 251 (April 1876): 229–265.

Potts, Louis W. "'A Lucky Moment': The Relationship of the Ordinance of 1787 and the Constitution of 1787." *Mid-America* 68 (October 1986): 141–151.

Puls, Mark. *Henry Knox: Visionary General of the American Revolution*. New York: Palgrave Macmillan, 2008.

Putnam, Rufus. *The Memoirs of Rufus Putnam*. Edited by Rowena Buell. Boston, 1903.

Quaife, Milo Milton. *Chicago and the Old Northwest, 1673–1835*. Chicago, 1913.

_____, ed. "A Narrative of Life on the Old Frontier: Henry Hay's Journal from Detroit to the Miami River." In *Proceedings of the State Historical Society of Wisconsin at its Sixty-Second Annual Meeting*. Madison, 1915, 208–261.

Rakove, Jack N. *The Beginnings of National Politics: An Interpretive History of the Continental Congress*. Baltimore: Johns Hopkins University Press, 1979.

Rappleye, Charles. *Robert Morris: Financier of the American Revolution*. New York: Simon & Schuster, 2010.

Richards, Leonard L. *Shays's Rebellion: The American Revolution's Final Battle*. Philadelphia: University of Pennsylvania Press, 2002.

_____. *The Slave Power: The Free North and Southern Domination, 1780–1860*. Baton Rouge: Louisiana State University Press, 2000.

Robert, Jorge M. "James Monroe and the Three-To-Five Clause of the Northwest Ordinance." http://www.earlyamerica.com/early-america-review/volume-5/northwest-ordinance.

Robertson, Lindsay G. *Conquest by Law: How the Discovery of America Dispossessed Indigenous Peoples of Their Lands*. New York: Oxford University Press, 2005.

Rohrbough, Malcolm J. *The Trans-Appalachian Frontier: People, Societies, and Institutions, 1775–1850*. New York: Oxford University Press, 1978.

Rowland, Kate Mason. *The Life of George Mason, 1725–1792*. 2 vols. New York, 1892.

Rutland, Robert Allen. *George Mason: Reluctant Statesman*. Foreword by Dumas Malone. Baton Rouge: Louisiana State University Press, 1969.

Ryan, Daniel J. "The Scioto Company and Its Purchase." *Publications of the Ohio Archaeological and Historical Society* 3 (1891): 107–136.

Saunders, William Laurence, ed. *The Colonial Records of North Carolina*. Vol. 7. Raleigh, 1890, 851–855.

Savelle, Max. *George Morgan: Colony Builder*. New York: Columbia University Press, 1932.

Schaaf, Gregory. *Wampum Belts and Peace Trees: George Morgan, Native Americans, and Revolutionary Diplomacy*. Golden, CO: Fulcrum Publishing, 1990.

Schlenther, Boyd Stanley. *Charles Thomson: A Patriot's Pursuit.* Newark: University of Delaware Press, 1990.

Shoemaker, Nancy. *A Strange Likeness: Becoming Red and White in Eighteenth-Century North America.* New York: Oxford University Press, 2004.

Seed, Geoffrey. *James Wilson.* Millwood, NY: KTO Press, 1978.

Sheridan, Eugene R., and John M. Murrin, eds. *Congress at Princeton: Being the Letters of Charles Thomson to Hannah Thomson, June–October 1783.* Princeton: Princeton University Library, 1985.

Simpson-Poffenbarger, Livia. "Battle of Point Pleasant: First Battle of the American Revolution, October 10, 1774." Reproduced from the Report made to the West Virginia State Board of Control for its Report of 1927. http://www.pointpleasantwv.org/Parks&Campgrounds/StateParks/TuEndiWei/BattleStory.htm.

Skaggs, David Curtis, ed. *The Old Northwest in the American Revolution: An Anthology.* Madison: Wisconsin Historical Society, 1977.

Skaggs, David Curtis, and Larry Lee Nelson, eds. *The Sixty Years' War for the Great Lakes.* East Lansing: Michigan State University Press, 2010.

Skinner, Claiborne A. *The Upper Country: French Enterprise in the Colonial Great Lakes.* Baltimore: Johns Hopkins University Press, 2008.

Slocum, Charles Elihu. *The Ohio Valley Between the Years 1783 and 1815.* New York, 1910.

Smith, G. Hubert. "A Letter from Kentucky." *Mississippi Valley Historical Review* 19, no. 1 (June 1932): 90–95.

Smith, James. *An Account of the Remarkable Occurrences in the Life and Travels of Col. James Smith.* 1799. Reprint, Cincinnati, 1907.

Smith, Charles Page. *James Wilson, Founding Father, 1742–1796.* Westport, CT: Greenwood, 1973.

Smith, Paul H., et al., eds. *Letters of Delegates to Congress, 1774–1789.* 25 vols. Washington, D.C.: Library of Congress, 1976–2000.

Smith, William Henry, ed. *The St. Clair Papers: The Life and Public Services of Arthur St. Clair.* 2 vols. Cincinnati, 1882.

Sparks, Edwin Erie. "The Influence of the Ohio River in Western Expansion." *Ohio Archaeological and Historical Quarterly* 22, no. 1 (Jan. 1913): 7–10.

Sparks, Jared, ed. *The Writings of George Washington.* 12 vols. New York, 1847.

Speed, Thomas. *The Wilderness Road: A Description of the Routes of Travel by Which the Pioneers and Early Settlers First Came to Kentucky.* Louisville, 1886.

Stewart, David O. *The Summer of 1787: The Men Who Invented the Constitution.* New York: Simon & Schuster, 2007.

Stewart, Richard, ed. "The Formative Years: 1783–1812." Chapter 5 of *American Military History.* 2 vols. Washington, D.C.: Center of Military History, United States Army, 2004–2005. http://www.history.army.mil/books/amh/AMH-05.htm.

Stone, Frederick D. *The Ordinance of 1787.* Philadelphia, 1889.

Stone, William L. *Life of Joseph Brant (Thayendanegea).* 2 vols. Albany, NY, 1865.

Sword, Wiley. *President Washington's Indian War: The Struggle for the Old Northwest, 1790–1795.* Norman: University of Oklahoma Press, 1985.

Tanner, Helen Hornbeck. *Atlas of Great Lakes Indian History.* Norman: University of Oklahoma Press, 1987.

Tanner, Helen Hornbeck, and Erminie Wheeler-Voegelin. *Indians of Ohio and Indiana Prior to 1795; The Greenville Treaty, 1795; Ethnohistory of Indian Use and Occupancy in Ohio and Indiana Prior to 1795.* Reports to the Indian Claims Commission. 2 vols. New York, 1975.

Tanner, John. *The Falcon: A Narrative of the Captivity and Adventures of John Tanner.* 1830. New York: Penguin, 1994.

Taylor, Alan. *American Colonies*. New York: Viking, 2002.

Taylor, Robert J. *Western Massachusetts in the Revolution*. Providence, RI: Brown University Press, 1954.

Taylor, Robert M., ed. *The Northwest Ordinance: A Bicentennial Handbook*. Indianapolis: Indiana Historical Society, 1987.

Thompson, David. *David Thompson's Narrative of His Explorations in Western America, 1784–1812*. Edited by J. B. Tyrell. Toronto, 1916.

Thomson, Charles. Appendix 1 in *Notes on the State of* Virginia, by Thomas Jefferson, 205–216. 1785. Edited with an introduction and notes by Frank Shuffelton. New York: Penguin, 1999.

_____. *An Enquiry into the Causes of Alienation of the Delaware and Shawanese Indians from the British Interest*. London, 1759.

_____. "An Essay upon Indian Affairs." *Collections of the Historical Society of Pennsylvania* 1 (Philadelphia, 1853): 81–84.

_____. *The Papers of Charles Thomson, Secretary of the Continental Congress*. In *Collections of the New York Historical Society for the Year 1878*. New York, 1879, 1–286.

Todd, Charles Burr. *Life and Letters of Joel Barlow*. New York, 1886.

Townsend, Camilla. *Pocahontas and the Powhatan Dilemma*. New York: Hill and Wang, 2004.

Treat, Payson Jackson. *The National Land System, 1785–1820*. New York, 1910.

"The Treaty of Logg's Town, 1752." *Virginia Magazine of History and Biography* 13 (1906): 154–174.

Trist, Elizabeth. "The Travel Diary of Elizabeth House Trist: Philadelphia to Natchez, 1783–84." In *Journeys in New Worlds: Early American Women's Narratives*, edited by William L. Andrews. Madison: University of Wisconsin Press, 1990, 181–232.

Turner, Frederick Jackson, *The Frontier in American History*. New York: Henry Holt, 1920.

United Nations General Assembly. *United Nations Declaration on the Rights of Indigenous Persons*. September 13, 2007. http://www.un.org/esa/socdev/unpfii/documents/DRIPS_en.pdf.

United States Bureau of the Census. *A Century of Population Growth: From the First Census of the United States to the Twelfth, 1790–1900*. Washington, D.C.: Government Printing Office, 1909.

United States Department of State. *The Diplomatic Correspondence of the United States, from the Signing of the Definitive Treaty of Peace ... to the Adoption of the Constitution*. 7 vols. Washington, D.C., 1833–1834.

Van Cleve, George William. *A Slaveholder's Union: Slavery, Politics, and the Constitution in the Early American Republic*. Chicago: University of Chicago Press, 2010.

Volney, Constantin F. *View of the Climate and Soil of the United States*. Translated from the French. London, 1804.

Volwiler, Albert T. *George Croghan and the Westward Movement, 1741–1782*. Cleveland: Arthur H. Clark, 1926.

Waldstreicher, David. *Slavery's Constitution: From Revolution to Ratification*. New York: Hill and Wang, 2009.

Walker, Felix. "The First Settlement of Kentucky: Narrative of an Adventure in Kentucky in the Year 1775." *De Bow's Review* 16, no. 2 (Feb. 1854): 150–155.

Wallace, Anthony F. C. *Jefferson and the Indians: The Tragic Fate of the First Americans*. Cambridge, MA: Belknap Press of Harvard University Press, 1999.

Washington, George. The George Washington Papers at the Library of Congress, 1741–1799. http://memory.loc.gov/ammem/gwhtml/gwhome.html.

Weidensaul, Scott. *The First Frontier: The Forgotten History of Struggle, Savagery, and Endurance in Early America*. Boston: Houghton Mifflin, 2012.

White, Richard. *The Middle Ground: Indians, Empires, and Republics in the Great Lakes Region, 1650–1815.* Cambridge: Cambridge University Press, 1991.

Williams, Frederick L., ed. *The Northwest Ordinance: Essays on Its Formulation, Provisions, and Legacy.* East Lansing: Michigan State University Press, 1989.

Willig, Timothy D. *Restoring the Chain of Friendship: British Policy and the Indians of the Great Lakes, 1783–1815.* Lincoln: University of Nebraska Press, 2008.

Wilson, James. *On the Improvement and Settlement of Lands in the United States.* 1795. Philadelphia: Free Library of Philadelphia, 1946.

Winsor, Justin. *The Westward Movement: The Colonies and the Republic West of the Alleghanies, 1763–1798.* Boston, 1897.

Withers, Alexander Scott. *Chronicles of Border Warfare.* 1831. New ed. Edited by Reuben Gold Thwaites. Cincinnati, 1895.

Wood, Gordon S. *The Creation of the American Republic, 1776–1787.* Chapel Hill: University of North Carolina Press, 1969.

Zeisberger, David. *David Zeisberger's History of the North American* Indians. 1779–1780. Edited by Archer Butler Hulbert and William Nathaniel Schwarze. Lewisburg, PA: Wennawoods, 1999. First published 1910 by the Ohio State Archeological and Historical Society.

Newspapers

American Mercury (Hartford)
Federal Gazette (Philadelphia)
Independent Gazetteer (Philadelphia)
Maryland Journal (Baltimore)

New-York Packet (New York, NY)
Pennsylvania Packet (Philadelphia)
Worcester Magazine (Massachusetts)

Index

Numbers in **bold italics** indicate photographs.

www.ingramcontent.com/pod-product-compliance
Lightning Source LLC
Chambersburg PA
CBHW031131270326
41929CB00011B/1577